Praise for *Imp*

"With insight, wisdom, affection, and concern, Sunstein has written the story of impeachment every citizen needs to know. This is a remarkable, essential book."
—Doris Kearns Goodwin, Pulitzer Prize–winning author of
Team of Rivals: The Political Genius of Abraham Lincoln

"Thoroughly grounded in constitutional history and past practice . . . Excellent."　　　　　　　　　—Noah Feldman and Jacob Weisberg,
The New York Review of Books

"Sunstein's goal was to lay out a legal and historical framework for thinking about impeachment, independent of any specific president. I've been thinking about the topic a lot since finishing the book, and I want to recommend [it]. . . . [It's a] careful history of impeachment— of when the founders believed it was appropriate and necessary."
—David Leonhardt, *The New York Times*

"Considering that the only executive branch event more unnerving for voters than impeachment is assassination, Sunstein's book . . . is a surprisingly cheerful read."　　　—Sarah Vowell, *The New York Times*

"Sunstein has written a concise, enlightening, and argumentative history and guide to getting rid of presidents. . . . It's more of a why-to and when-to, and a what-were-they-thinking-when-they-decided-to kind of book. Sunstein delves into the writings, speeches, and deliberations of America's revolutionary generation."
—Carlos Lozada, *The Washington Post*

"An elegant new monograph."
—Andrew Sullivan, *The New York Times Book Review*

"A lively, compact, and authoritative account . . . [Sunstein] addresses the most intriguing questions posed by this little used but pivotal constitutional provision. . . . Truly lives up to its promise of being 'A Citizen's Guide' . . . Excellent."
—Stephen Rohde, *Los Angeles Review of Books*

"Explains the historical origins of the impeachment concept, and offers a checklist as to when the principle might be applied . . . Now, more than ever, cool heads are needed to safeguard the U.S. Republic: thank goodness for this book—and its handy impeachment checklist." —Gillian Tett, *Financial Times*

"*Impeachment: A Citizen's Guide* offers edifying background for an argument that might soon be in need of eloquent, as well as passionate, delivery." —Richard Blaustein, *Los Angeles Review of Books*

"A compact, concise, and highly relevant civics lesson. There have been a number of books published about impeachment, many of them partisan manifestos. What makes Sunstein's book of such great interest is its lack of fanfare and knife-sharpening. The author is a learned and accessible guide as he maneuvers his way through the history of democracy's nuclear option. . . . A welcome, timely, ideal primer."
—*Kirkus Reviews*

"The book is a tribute to the Founding Fathers' wisdom in providing for a remedy in case someone who is vicious, lawless, and unfit should somehow end up in power." —Scott McLemee, *Inside Higher Ed*

"Sunstein is well positioned to provide this balanced and timely overview of the role of impeachment in American democracy . . . An essential guide to understanding impeachment's function within the 'constitutional system as a whole' and a persuasive argument that the impeachment clause places 'the fate of the republic' in the hands of its citizenry." —*Publishers Weekly*

"This slim book is thoroughly researched, easy to read, and for some perhaps a real eye-opener." —Owen Dawson, *The Irish Times*

"Offers a highly accessible, brilliantly thoughtful, and politically neutral analysis of what the Constitution means for our present moment and for generations that follow." —Ryan Goodman, *Just Security*

"With speculation rife about the possibility of impeaching President Trump, this little book is indeed timely."
—Felix M. Larkin, *The Irish Catholic*

"Sunstein provides a brief, readable survey of the issue, beginning with early English history and continuing to the present. . . . Sunstein concludes with key questions that every American should consider together with the constitutional standards that would govern it."
—W. C. Johnson, *Choice*

PENGUIN BOOKS

IMPEACHMENT

Cass R. Sunstein is the Robert Walmsley University Professor at Harvard University, where he is founder and director of the Program on Behavioral Economics and Public Policy. He is the most cited law professor in the United States and probably the world. He has served as administrator of the White House Office of Information and Regulatory Affairs and as a member of the President's Review Group on Intelligence and Communications Technologies. Winner of the 2018 Holberg Prize, Sunstein is a columnist for Bloomberg Opinion and a frequent adviser to governments all over the world. His many books include the bestsellers *Nudge: Improving Decisions About Health, Wealth, and Happiness* (with Richard H. Thaler) and *The World According to Star Wars*.

IMPEACHMENT
A Citizen's Guide

Cass R. Sunstein

PENGUIN BOOKS

PENGUIN BOOKS
An imprint of Penguin Random House LLC
penguinrandomhouse.com

First published in the United States of America by Harvard University Press 2017
Published, in slightly different form, in Penguin Books 2019

Published by arrangement with Harvard University Press.

ISBN 9780143135173 (paperback)
ISBN 9780525506843 (ebook)

Printed in the United States of America
1   3   5   7   9   10   8   6   4   2

Set in Garamond Premier Pro

To all those who fought, and fight, for our beloved country,
from 1775 to the present

I go on this great republican principle, that the people will have virtue and intelligence to select men of virtue and wisdom. Is there no virtue among us? If there be not, we are in a wretched situation. No theoretical checks—no form of government can render us secure. To suppose that any form of government will secure liberty or happiness without any virtue in the people, is a chimerical idea. If there be sufficient virtue and intelligence in the community, it will be exercised in the selection of these men. So that we do not depend on their virtue, or put confidence in our rulers, but in the people who are to choose them.

JAMES MADISON

But even the president of the United States
Sometimes must have to stand naked

BOB DYLAN

CONTENTS

Preface   xiii

PREFACE

Should President Donald Trump be impeached?

Of course he should be. He and his campaign cooperated with Russia to obtain the presidency. When his own Department of Justice decided to investigate Russia's horrifying role, he tried desperately to derail the investigation. He obstructed justice not once but ten times. He committed egregious crimes in an effort to fend off an inquiry into an unfriendly nation's successful attack on our democracy—and into his own criminal behavior.

Alternatively: Of course he shouldn't be. The very question is ridiculous. President Trump didn't work with Russia at all. There was no collusion or conspiracy of any kind. Nor did he commit any crime. On the contrary, he exercised his constitutional authority. He expressed perfectly reasonable objections to a pointless, baseless, politically motivated investigation, designed to undo a legitimate presidential election. He defended himself vigorously. That's hardly impeachable.

This book does not choose between these two views. It does not say whether President Donald Trump should be impeached. It is designed to answer more enduring questions, including: *Why does the U.S. Constitution include an impeachment mechanism? What's a "high crime or misdemeanor"? How does impeachment work? Is impeachment a question of law or politics? What was the American Revolution all about? Why were people willing to give their lives for it? What was the "shot heard round the world"? What is American exceptionalism, anyway?*

For those who are focused on President Trump or on any particular president, answers to these questions are essential. It is alarming—maybe inevitable, but still alarming—that many people use a simple rule of thumb to answer questions about impeachment: *Do I like the president in question?* If the answer is "yes" or "mostly," or even "kind of," they tend to think that impeachment is a terrible idea—whatever the law and whatever the facts. If the answer is "definitely not," they will be open to the idea of impeachment. They might even welcome it.

One of my main goals here is to show that once we move beyond that unhelpful rule of thumb and get clarity on impeachment, we will find something much better and even inspiring. Impeachment is a window onto the whole enterprise of self-government and the American commitment to the fundamental equality of human beings. There is an intimate relationship between the impeachment mechanism and the Declaration of Independence, the system of checks and balances, the right to freedom of speech, the right to a jury trial, the right to private property, and the right to free exercise of religion. There is an even more intimate relationship between the impeachment mechanism and the most important words of the U.S. Constitution, which launch the document: "We the People."

Oh, and I'm going to have a few words to say about President Trump. But you're going to have to wait.

Impeachment: A Citizen's Guide

chapter 1

Majesty and Mystery

It's an old story, and it's probably even true. When the authors of the new American Constitution declared, after their months of work in Philadelphia, that they had finally reached consensus, one Mrs. Powel shouted a question to the revered Benjamin Franklin, then eighty-one years old: "Dr. Franklin, what have you given us—a monarchy or a republic?" He gave this answer: "A republic, if you can keep it."[1]

With those words, Franklin deflected the thrust of the question. True, he didn't refuse to answer: "a republic," he said, and not a monarchy. But in his view, the question wasn't what the framers, a band of good and great men, had given to the American people. The Constitution is not a gift. The question was what We the People would *do* with the framework that the framers had produced.

The real agents, the most important actors in the nation's history, were, and are, the "you." You have a task, which is to keep it. And what you are to keep is a republic, which is what the American Revolution was fought to establish, and which is opposed to what the colonies fought against: a monarchy, headed by a king, who could not be removed from office, and who could rule as a tyrant. From the Declaration of Independence: "The history of the present King of Great Britain is a history of repeated injuries and usurpations, all having in direct object the establishment of an absolute Tyranny over these States."

Just a few decades before he spoke, Franklin's words would have been unfathomably radical. But he captured the spirit of his age. Here's Alexander Hamilton, writing in the very first of the *Federalist* papers, which defended the American Constitution to a nation that was sharply divided on whether to ratify it. Hamilton sounded a lot like Franklin, though much more grave:

> It has been frequently remarked that it seems to have been reserved to the people of this country, by their conduct and example, to decide the important question, whether societies of men are really capable or not of establishing good government from reflection and choice, or whether they are forever destined to depend for their political constitutions on accident and force. If there be any truth in the remark, the crisis at which we are arrived may with propriety be regarded as the era in which that decision is to be made; and a wrong election of the part we shall act may, in this view, deserve to be considered as the general misfortune of mankind.[2]

Franklin, Hamilton, and their colleagues thought a lot about impeachment. In their view, the power to impeach was central to the establishment of "good government from reflection and choice." Without the power to impeach, We the People would probably have refused to ratify the Constitution in the first place. Impeachment lay at the core of the founders' intricate and majestic effort to balance the defining republican commitments to liberty, equality, and self-rule with the belief in a strong, energetic national government. They achieved that balance with diverse features of the Constitution, including a four-year term for the president, electoral control, the separation of powers, and a system of individual rights. It is ironic that impeachment, regarded in 1787 as an essential component of the balance, is now little understood by "the people of this country."

As Exhibit 1, consider the 1970 pronouncement by Gerald Ford, then a member of Congress and later President of the United States, that an impeachable offense "is whatever a majority of the House" believes it "to be at a given moment in history."[3] As Exhibit 2, consider the 2017 claim by Nancy Pelosi, then the House minority leader and former Speaker of the House, that a president cannot be impeached unless he has broken the law.[4] As we will see, both Ford and Pelosi got it fundamentally wrong. Their views make a mockery of the constitutional design. They are also anti-republican.

In American history, three presidents have been subject to serious impeachment proceedings: Andrew Johnson, Richard Nixon, and Bill Clinton. During the impeachment process against Nixon, I was in my late teens. In a way, the controversy was inspiring. We the People were rising up against a president who had apparently done awful things. But I liked Nixon, and I didn't much like the Democrats, and I was torn. Riveted by the national debates, I wondered: Are people trying to impeach Nixon because they hate him and his policies, or because he actually did something terribly wrong?

Like many millions of Americans, I also wondered: What is impeachment all about, anyway? The very word was unfamiliar and seemed like a kind of relic, something from a bygone age. The nation (and Nixon himself) received an un-forgettable civics lesson back then in the 1970s, but I'm not sure that we got a full answer to either question.

When I decided to go to law school a few years later, I can't say that I was motivated by the Nixon proceedings, but they certainly helped to inspire my interest in our constitu-tional system. Like many others in my law school class, I was certain that some courses would be focused on the intrigu-ing questions raised by Nixon's resignation. Above all: What were the framers doing with the impeachment provision? What are high crimes and misdemeanors? But no class spent as much as a single minute on impeachment. It was as if the whole topic was irrelevant—part of history's dustbin, a tiny footnote to the real issues in constitutional law. Sure, we talked about the power of the president, about when he could make war, about what he could do on his own, about when he needed Congress, about how courts control him.

But how can you get rid of him, if he screws up, or worse?

As a young law professor in the 1980s, I became a coau-thor of a constitutional law casebook, one of those massive, supposedly comprehensive tomes. It consisted of more than 1,500 densely packed pages. In the early drafts of the first edi-tion, our book had nothing on impeachment—not a page, not even a paragraph. I was personally responsible for that section of the book, so the negligence was all mine. As a kind of formality, I added a short discussion, about two pages, just to cover the bases. In my courses, I spent no time on impeachment; it seemed too remote from what law stu-dents would be doing in their careers.

When the Clinton impeachment proceedings heated up in the 1990s, there was a sudden demand for the views of law

professors. For many of us, phone calls came from news-
papers, radio and television stations, Congress, even the
White House itself. The Nixon controversy had become an-
cient history, and to those who remembered what Nixon
had done, Clinton's behavior seemed a lot less horrible. But
Clinton might have lied under oath and obstructed justice,
and thus committed real crimes. Above all, people wanted
to know whether the constitutional standards for impeachment were met.

I was no expert on the legal intricacies, and I decided
to get up to speed in a hurry. I read everything I could on
the subject—old books and new books, and primary sources
too, including the debates at the Constitutional Convention. Because there was so much to learn, and because the
topic turned out to be so fascinating, a kind of unused key
that might unlock the whole republic, I studied it obsessively.

To my amazement, and through some twists of fate, I
ended up as an active participant in the Clinton proceedings. I testified before Congress on the meaning of "high
crimes and misdemeanors." I met privately with numerous
members of Congress (dozens, I think). I made appearances
on radio and television. I spent a little time at the White
House, working on my own but also consulting with the
president's legal team, with whom I was broadly in accord. I
nearly broke off the conversations when one of the president's advisers essentially ordered me to write a newspaper
column with a specific theme; the idea of taking direction
from the White House struck me as corrupt.

No less than the Nixon controversy, Clinton's impeachment captured the nation's attention. There was plenty of

talk about the meaning of constitutional standard and that opaque phrase, "high crimes and misdemeanors." At the same time, most of the national discussion was focused elsewhere, above all on the question whether the president was a terrible person, and how he could have done what he apparently did. There is no question that the effort to impeach Clinton was politically motivated; for his opponents, the whole process seemed exhilarating, a kind of thrill, a highlight of their lives. (The same was true for the Nixon impeachment.) The smallness of the national debates over Clinton's relationship with Monica Lewinsky, and over whether he had lied about it, could not have been in sharper contrast with the largeness of Benjamin Franklin's words, and of what he and his colleagues had managed to produce back in Philadelphia. And just a few years after the Clinton impeachment, the real issues, small and large, became shrouded in some kind of mist.

That's a shame. My principal goal in this book is to try to dissolve the mist, and in the process recover something about our nation's origins and aspirations. But what ultimately inspired me to pursue this topic was something far more personal.

Embattled Farmers

A few months ago, I moved from New York to Massachusetts. My wife and I chose to live in Concord, even though we are not working there. That wasn't the most practical decision, but still, it made some sense. Concord is breathtakingly beautiful. It is also historic. It's where the Revolutionary

War started on April 19, 1775, when about seven hundred British soldiers were given what they thought were secret orders—to destroy colonial military supplies being held in Concord. That's where Paul Revere rode, where dozens of people died and dozens were badly hurt, and where our nation started to be born.

Know the phrase "the shot heard 'round the world"? If you'd asked me a year ago, I would have said, with complete confidence, that it referred to Bobby Thomson's game-winning home run in 1951, which won the pennant for the New York Giants. Wrong answer.

The phrase is a lot older than that. Here's "Concord Hymn," written in 1836 by Concord's Ralph Waldo Emerson for the dedication of the Obelisk, a monument commemorating the Battle of Concord. You might focus on the fourth line (though I confess it is the third that really gets to me):

> By the rude bridge that arched the flood,
> Their flag to April's breeze unfurled,
> Here once the embattled farmers stood,
> And fired the shot heard round the world.
>
> The foe long since in silence slept;
> Alike the conqueror silent sleeps;
> And Time the ruined bridge has swept
> Down the dark stream which seaward creeps.
>
> On this green bank, by this soft stream,
> We set to-day a votive stone;
> That memory may their deed redeem,
> When, like our sires, our sons are gone.

Spirit, that made those heroes dare
To die, and leave their children free,
Bid Time and Nature gently spare
The shaft we raise to them and thee.[5]

Emerson wrote that sixty-one years after the event. No single shot is known to have started the Revolutionary War, but it was in Concord that British soldiers confronted the American militia on North Bridge. The Americans were under strict orders not to shoot unless the British shot first. The British began by firing two or three shots into the Concord River; the Americans interpreted those shots as mere warnings. Consistent with their orders, they did not respond. But the British soon followed with a volley, killing two Americans, including one of their leaders, Captain Isaac Davis, who was shot in the heart—the first American officer to lose his life in the Revolution. He left a widow and four children.

Seeing this, Major John Buttrick, a leader of the Concord militia, immediately leaped up from the ground and exclaimed, "Fire, fellow soldiers, for God's sake, *fire*." According to those who were actually there, "the word *fire* ran like electricity through the whole line of Americans . . . and for a few seconds, the word, *fire, fire* was heard from hundreds of mouths."[6] Acting as one, Concord's embattled farmers followed Buttrick's order. (That, I like to think, was the famous shot—the first battle in which the Americans defended themselves.) Two British soldiers were killed. The rest immediately retreated. To their own surprise, the Americans won the initial engagement. The war was on.

Today, schoolchildren read Emerson's words when they visit the Minute Man National Historical Park. But to

Benjamin Franklin, Alexander Hamilton, James Madison, and their peers, revolutionary Concord was hardly history. It was fresh. It was where their friends and colleagues fought, and where some of them died. It was where the national project began. With such a background, Mrs. Powel's insistent question—"What have you given us?"—produced Franklin's inevitable answer.

Having settled on Concord, my wife and I had to decide among possible houses, for us and our two young children (and the puppy we knew we would soon get—as it turned out, a yellow Labrador retriever named Snow). There were two finalists. The first had been completed just a few months before we visited. It was perfect—gorgeous, sunlit, shining, functional, clean, with a new air-conditioning system, a kitchen to die for, and all the modern amenities. You had to love it. I certainly did.

The second finalist was built in 1763, by an active participant in the American Revolution named Ephraim Wood, Jr. In 1771, Wood was chosen as one of Concord's selectmen, town clerk, and assessor and overseer of the poor. (He was reelected to those offices—seventeen times.) In 1773, he served on the committee that decided to protest the tax on tea. According to the Massachusetts Historical Commission, the Wood house, as it is called, is "one of the most important of Concord's early farmhouses."[7] The house played a role in the Revolutionary War. It stood proud at the inception. Actually, it helped precipitate the fighting. It was one of the places where munitions were being held, which is what prompted the initial British expedition.

As the Commission explains, "In the weeks before April 19, 1775, when military stores were being sent inland to

Concord for hiding, six of 35 barrels of powder and some bullets were hidden on Ephraim Wood's farm." Some time before shots were fired, the British forces went to that farm, look-ing for the munitions and also for Wood. They didn't find either. Walking home, Wood spotted British soldiers, and he managed to escape, carrying munitions on his back. Wood was one of Emerson's embattled farmers.

On that fateful day, British soldiers destroyed a lot of property, including every public store they could find. But they didn't burn down or even damage the houses. Wood returned. As the fighting moved on, got terrible, and then worse, the house remained intact. It was there before the United States turned into a country, and it was there when Jefferson wrote the Declaration of Independence. Just a few months after Jefferson did that, Wood himself, a short distance from his house, was a member of a small group that wrote a document calling for a Constitutional Convention in Concord, resolving:

> that the supreme Legislative, Either in their proper capacity or in Joint Committee are by no means a Body Proper to form & Establish a Constitution or form of Government for Reasones following, viz—first Because we conceive that Constitution, in its proper Idea intends a system of principals established to secure the subject in the Possession of and enjoyment of their Rights & Privileges against any encrouchment of the Governing Part. . . . [8]

Wood's group, which included Major Buttrick ("Fire, fellow soldiers, for God's sake, *fire!*"), has been credited with inventing the whole idea of a convention for constitution-making. His house was there when the Articles of Confederation ruled the land, and it was there when the *Federalist* papers were written and when the Constitution was ratified. Wood himself was a shoemaker and he set up shop there, as did one of his sons. In the late nineteenth century, it became the site of the Concord Home School.

But in the twenty-first century, the Wood house had been on the market for a long time. Nobody wanted to buy it. It isn't close to perfect. Its eighteenth-century origins show. Upstairs, some of the old floors tilt; you feel as if you're dizzy, or in some kind of fun house. People used to be a lot shorter, and as you enter the front door, you have to bend down. For the same reason, the original ceilings are uncomfortably low.

The master bedroom seemed built for people under five feet tall. On the property you could find a small "pony barn," but it was dilapidated. No pony would want to live there. The house and the barn needed a lot of work.

Of course the Wood house didn't have air-conditioning. The basement was a mess, full of crazy wires from various decades. We asked a friend of ours, an architect, to have a close look and to give us an evaluation. When he did so, his face was grim. He didn't have a nice word to say about the house.

But still: whenever you enter the front door, and bend down, you know that you are where the Revolution started, and where Americans hid arms, ready to fight for their liberty, and where they felt a spirit "that made those heroes dare / To die, and leave their children free."

I am one of those children. Reader, I bought it.

Something Different

Because impeachment has been so rare, the American people rarely focus on it. That's good. In a way, it's great. Impeachment is a remedy of last resort. If We the People don't discuss impeachment for a decade or two, or three, that's not the worst news. The likely reason is that our presidents are performing well, or at least well enough. We don't have to worry over how and whether to get rid of them.

But in a way, the citizenry's failure to discuss impeachment is a big problem, above all on republican grounds. Thanks to the fighters and the founders, we are a self-governing people. In the view of some of the authors of our founding document, the impeachment clause was among the most important parts of the entire Constitution.

Pause over that. With the monarchical history looming in the background, they greatly feared a king. Sure, most of them wanted a powerful executive, with Alexander Hamilton helping to lead the charge. But they were ambivalent. They were gravely concerned about the possibility of abuse. They insisted on safeguards in the event that things went badly wrong (and they had a concrete sense of what that might mean). The impeachment mechanism was the most important of these safeguards. If the nation's leader proved corrupt, invaded their rights, neglected his duty, or otherwise abused his authority, that mechanism gave We the People a way to say: NO MORE.

To ordinary citizens, constitutional law has become abstruse, sometimes even unintelligible. The framers could not have anticipated this, and many of them would be surprised and disappointed, even appalled. But it's true. For example, the First Amendment's protection of free speech seems straightforward. It may be the most fundamental right of all, and it helps to define our nation's self-understanding. But the text's apparently simple words—"Congress shall make no law abridging the freedom of speech"—have given rise to legal doctrines, tests, and subtests applied to such problems as obscenity, commercial speech, and campaign finance regulation. Those doctrines, tests, and subtests aren't exactly dinner table fare. To understand freedom of speech, law students study casebooks, and the free-speech sections cover hundreds of pages.

Maybe that's not ideal, but much of constitutional law is now for specialists, and above all, lawyers and federal judges. Our courts, consisting of unelected judges, devise and apply the tests and subtests.

But impeachment is something altogether different. It really is designed for We the People, not the judges at all. It's not just for specialists. It can't be. As much as any part of the Constitution, the impeachment clause puts the fate of the republic squarely in our hands. And as we'll see, an understanding of that clause tells us a great deal about our constitutional system as a whole. It's impossible to understand impeachment without appreciating its intimate connections with other features of that system, and without seeing its origins in the Revolution itself.

The Constitution is not a seamless web. But it's definitely a web.

Neutrality

Suppose that a president engages in certain actions that seem to you very, very bad. Suppose that you are tempted to think that he should be impeached. You should immediately ask yourself: *Would I think the same thing if I loved the president's policies, and thought that he was otherwise doing a splendid job?*

That's a good way of ensuring the requisite neutrality. The impeachment mechanism isn't a way for political losers to overturn the outcome of a legitimate election. Nor is it a way for the public to say: Our leader is doing a rotten job. Put differently, loathing a president is not sufficient grounds for impeaching him, and the risk is that if you loathe him, you might find certain actions a legitimate basis for impeachment even if you would find those grounds patently inadequate if you loved him.

Here's a second test. Suppose that you do *not* think that the president should be impeached. You should ask yourself: *Would I think the same thing if I abhorred the president's policies, and thought that he was otherwise doing a horrific job?* That's an important question as well. If the president's supporters do not think that he has committed an impeachable offense, they should test their neutrality by asking whether their judgment is being distorted by their political convictions.

Here's a third test, and the best of all. Try to put yourself behind a veil of ignorance, in which you know nothing about the president and his policies. You have no idea whether he would win your vote or your support. All you know about are the actions that are said to be a basis for impeachment. *If that is all you know, would you think that he should be impeached?*

With the goal of neutrality in mind, I am not going to speak of any current political figure. I am going to focus on the majesty, and the mystery, of impeachment under the U.S. Constitution.

chapter 2

From King to President

With respect to impeachment, the text of the Constitution seems pretty straightforward. There are three principal provisions.

Article 1, section 2, clause 5, states: "The House of Representatives . . . shall have the sole Power of Impeachment." Clear enough.

Section 3, clause 6 of the same article adds, "The Senate shall have the sole Power to try all Impeachments. . . . When the President of the United States is tried, the Chief Justice shall preside: And no Person shall be convicted without the Concurrence of two thirds of the Members present."

That's also clear. The House of Representatives has the power of impeachment, which is akin to an indictment, to be followed by a trial. No official can be removed until he is tried and convicted in the Senate, which operates like a court.

Clause 7 goes on to say, "Judgment in Cases of Impeachment shall not extend further than to removal from Office, and disqualification to hold and enjoy any Office of honor, Trust or Profit under the United States: but the Party convicted shall nevertheless be liable and subject to Indictment, Trial, Judgment and Punishment, according to Law."

Okay. If an official is convicted, he's out of office (forever). He is removed, but not punished. Still, he can be indicted, tried, and punished separately. We'll find some puzzles there, but we're hardly at sea.

Article 2, section 4, states: "The President, Vice President and all civil Officers of the United States, shall be removed from Office on Impeachment for, and Conviction of, Treason, Bribery, or other high Crimes and Misdemeanors."

That's where things get trickiest. The more you stare at the critical words "high Crimes and Misdemeanors," the more obscure they seem. Note, by the way, that all civil officers, including members of the cabinet and federal judges, can be impeached, though my principal focus here is on the president.

The good news is that if we spend a little time in the last decades of the eighteenth century, we can find a framework. The framework turns out to answer most questions (not all of them, but most). In the process, it offers some clues to the deepest aspirations of the Constitution's founders, and helps tell us what the American Revolution, and American exceptionalism, are all about.

"Would You Like to Hear My Opinion of Princes?"

Here's a part of the Constitution that you might not know, but that provides indispensable context for the impeachment clause:

> No Title of Nobility shall be granted by the United States: And no Person holding any Office of Profit or Trust under

them, shall, without the Consent of the Congress, accept of any present, Emolument, Office, or Title, of any kind whatever, from any King, Prince or foreign State.

The most revealing words are those prohibiting titles of nobility. No kings, no queens, and no princes or princesses. The clause goes back to the Declaration of Independence, which announced that "all men are created equal."

In the early 1980s, I was privileged to serve as law clerk for Justice Thurgood Marshall, one of the greatest lawyers and judges in American history, and an architect of the legal strategy that struck down "separate but equal" in public schools. Marshall was also irreverent, and he had a twinkle in his eye, and he was tough. He told me a story about meeting a member of British royalty, Prince Philip, who asked him, immediately after shaking hands, "Would you like to hear my opinion of lawyers?" Marshall shot back, "Would you like to hear my opinion of princes?"

After that was established, the two got along famously. But Marshall knew all about the prohibition on titles of nobility, and his edgy response to the prince runs in the American bloodstream. It is traceable to the founding document and those events in Concord, back on April 19, 1775.

The impeachment clause is a sibling to the titles of nobility clause. In the colonies, impeachment was used to fight royal prerogatives. It was itself a kind of shot—a mechanism by which colonial legislatures struck a blow against what they saw as illegitimate governance. After independence was won, impeachment became a republican mechanism for controlling officials who abused their authority. As the founding generation saw it, the power to get rid of the president was indispensable to avoiding a return to the monarchical heritage. But on what grounds? People strongly disagreed. The question provoked an intense and terrific debate, which produced the defining principles.

But the tale starts well before the American colonists started to resent the idea of being ruled by a king. With respect to impeachment, we're going to take a very brisk tour, starting with English practice, turning to the experience in the colonies, shifting to the Revolution, exploring the post-revolutionary experience, moving to the drafting of the Constitution, and concluding with the ratification debates.

All the while, let's think of the participants not as formal, white-haired, elderly men from history books, but as passionate, active, full of life but willing to die, and very much focused on what they were handing over to posterity. To appreciate the spirit of what we're about to see, and the period in which the impeachment clause was drafted, remember these words spoken by Patrick Henry, on March 23, 1775:

> They tell us, sir, that we are weak; unable to cope with so formidable an adversary. But when shall we be stronger? Will it be the next week, or the next year? Will it be when we are totally disarmed, and when a British guard shall be stationed in every house? Shall we gather strength by irresolution and inaction? Shall we acquire the means of effectual resistance, by lying supinely on our backs, and hugging the delusive phantom of hope, until our enemies shall have bound us hand and foot? . . .

The war is actually begun! The next gale that sweeps from the north will bring to our ears the clash of resounding arms! Our brethren are already in the field! Why stand we here idle? What is it that gentlemen wish? What would they have? Is life so dear, or peace so sweet, as to be purchased at the price of chains and slavery? Forbid it, Almighty God! I know not what course others may take; but as for me, give me liberty or give me death![1]

Our Radical Revolution

We often think of the American Revolution as pretty conservative, certainly as revolutions go. The French Revolution shook the world, and so did the Russian Revolution. The American Revolution seems much milder.

Maybe it was a matter of escaping British rule, but without fundamental changes in people's understandings of society and politics. After all, much of American law and culture reflects our British heritage, and in many respects, our constitution draws directly on that heritage. Americans refer proudly to Anglo-American traditions. They love Shakespeare, Wordsworth, and the Beatles. Long before the Constitution, there was the Magna Carta. Were the British really so bad? Sure, the Americans didn't want to be ruled by a king, and no taxation without representation and all that, and we had some kind of tea party in Boston—but was there such a big break?

Yes, there was. If you study the decades that preceded the revolution, you can see the rise of republicanism everywhere, and it was a radical creed. As the American colonists understood it, republicanism entailed self-government; their objection to British rule was founded on that principle. Republicanism takes many forms, and it can be traced all the way back to Rome. But the colonists were particularly influenced by the French theorist Montesquieu, who famously divided governments into three kinds, with associated definitions, over which it is worth lingering:

> a republican government is that in which the body, or only a part of the people, is possessed of the supreme power; monarchy, that in which a single person governs by fixed and established laws; a despotic government, that in which a single person directs everything by his own will and caprice.[2]

The colonies came to despise both monarchy and despotism. They thought that the former often led to the latter. If you have any doubt on that count, consider the Declaration of Independence, which objects that "a long train of abuses and usurpations" from the monarchy "evinces a design to reduce" the colonies "under absolute Despotism"—which is what led to the conclusion that "it is their right, it is their duty, to throw off such Government, and to provide new Guards for their future security."

In the colonies, republican thinking, focused on the supreme power of the body of the people, led to fresh ideas about what governments can legitimately do. It also fueled novel uses of impeachment. More broadly, it spurred new understandings of how human beings should relate to one another, and in the process it undid established hierarchies of multiple kinds. Thurgood Marshall's quip to Prince Philip was an outgrowth of distinctly American thinking in the last four decades of the eighteenth century.

The best and most vivid account comes from the historian Gordon Wood, who shows that the American Revolution was social as well as political, and that it involved an explosive principle: the equal dignity of human beings.[3] Wood does not say a word about impeachment, but his account is indispensable to an understanding of how that issue was resolved at the Constitutional Convention.

In the early decades of the eighteenth century, Americans lived in a traditional society, defined by established hierarchies, which permeated people's daily lives, even their beliefs and their self-understandings. Wood writes that "common people" were "made to recognize and feel their subordination to gentlemen," so that those "in lowly stations . . . developed what was called a 'down look,'" and "knew their place and willingly walked while gentlefolk rode; and as yet they seldom expressed any burning desire to change places with their betters."[4] In Wood's account, it is impossible to "comprehend the distinctiveness of that premodern world until we appreciate the extent to which many ordinary people *still accepted their own lowliness.*"[5] That acceptance had a political incarnation. In England, of course, national sovereignty was found in the king, and for a long time, the American subjects of the king humbly accepted that understanding.

As late as 1760, the colonies consisted of fewer than two million people, subjects of the monarchy, living in economically underdeveloped communities, isolated from the rest of the world. They "still took for granted that society was and ought to be a hierarchy of ranks and degrees of dependency."[6]

Over the next twenty years, their whole world was turned upside down, as the monarchical view of the world crumbled. This was a revolution of everyday values as well as politics. In Wood's words, the American Revolution was "as radical and social as any revolution in history," producing "a new society unlike any that had ever existed anywhere in the world."[7]

It was republicanism, with its proud commitment to liberty and equality, that obliterated the premodern world. To be sure, the transformative power of republicanism could be felt everywhere, including in England itself. As David Hume put it, "to talk of a king as God's vice-regent on earth, or to give him any of those magnificent titles which formerly dazzled mankind, would but excite laughter in everyone."[8] But in the American colonies, the authority of republican thinking was distinctive and especially pronounced. As the Revolution gathered steam, people were not laughing. Rule by the king wasn't funny. In 1776, Thomas Paine described the king as "the Royal Brute" and a "wretch," who had "the pretended title of FATHER OF HIS PEOPLE."[9] With amazement, John Adams wrote that "Idolatry to Monarchs, and servility to Aristocratical Pride, was never so totally eradicated, from so many Minds in so short a Time."[10]

David Ramsay, one of the nation's first historians (himself captured by the British during the Revolution), marveled that Americans were transformed "from subjects to citizens," and that was an "immense" difference, because citizens "possess sovereignty. Subjects look up to a master, but citizens are so far equal, that none have hereditary rights superior to others."[11] Paine put it this way: "Our style and manner of thinking have undergone a revolution more extraordinary than the political revolution of a country. We see with other eyes; we hear with other ears; and think with other thoughts, than those we formerly used."[12] As the transformation started to occur, the idea of impeachment, which originated in England but had fallen into disuse there, began to take on a whole new meaning. It became thoroughly Americanized. It turned into an instrument of popular sovereignty, an emphatically republican weapon, a mechanism by which the people might rule.

The thinking behind the Revolution led to an attack on royalty and aristocracy, to be sure. If republicanism was about anything, it was about that. But the same thinking placed a new focus on the aspirations, the needs, and the authority of ordinary people. Hierarchies of all kinds were bound to disintegrate—not through anything like envy, but through the simple assertion, immortalized in the Declaration of Independence, that all men are created equal. As Wood puts it, "To focus, as we are today apt to do, on what the Revolution did not accomplish—highlighting and lamenting its failure to abolish slavery and change fundamentally the lot of women—is to miss the great significance of what it did accomplish: indeed, the Revolution made possible the anti-slavery and women's rights movements of the nineteenth century and in fact all our current egalitarian thinking."[13]

In the nineteenth century, Walt Whitman, America's poet laureate, spoke for the Revolution when he wrote, "Of Equality—as if it harm'd me, giving others the same chances and rights as myself—as if it were not indispensable to my own rights that others possess the same."[14] Bob Dylan, Whitman's successor, put it more simply: "While preachers preach of evil fates / Teachers teach that knowledge waits / Can lead to hundred-dollar plates / Goodness hides behind its gates / But even the president of the United States / Sometimes must have to stand naked."[15]

The Failed Confederacy

The Declaration of Independence was signed in 1776. Hostilities with England substantially ceased in 1781 after the Yorktown campaign, which trapped the British Army and forced the surrender of General Cornwallis. The American Revolution was formally completed in 1783 with the signing of a peace treaty with England.

As early as the summer of 1776, the Americans started to draft a kind of constitution, which they submitted to the states in 1777. It was ratified in 1781. Only it wasn't called a constitution at all. Its name: Articles of Confederation. That's not an uplifting title, but it's revealing. The nation operated as a confederation of states, each of which enjoyed a lot of independence. The Articles begin without any poetry:

> To all to whom these Presents shall come, we the under-signed Delegates of the States affixed to our Names send greeting. . . .
>
> Articles of Confederation and Perpetual Union be-tween the states of New-Hampshire, Massachusetts-Bay, Rhode-Island and Providence Plantations, Connecticut, New-York, New-Jersey, Pennsylvania, Delaware, Mary-land, Virginia, North-Carolina, South-Carolina, and Georgia.

Notice that the Articles are formed by the states and their delegates—not by We the People. Compare, if you would, the soaring start of the Constitution that followed the Articles, produced just sixteen years later:

> We the People of the United States, in Order to form a more perfect Union, establish Justice, insure domestic Tranquility, provide for the common defense, promote the general Welfare, and secure the Blessings of Liberty to our-selves and our Posterity, do ordain and establish this Con-stitution for the United States of America.

There's poetry there, and plenty of substance, too. With the first seven words, you know who is in charge. A lot hap-pened during the years that separated the two documents.

The very first article of the Articles did give a good name to the confederacy: "the United States of America." But the second kind of took it back: "Each state retains its sover-eignty, freedom, and independence, and every power, ju-risdiction and right, which is not by this confederation expressly delegated to the United States in Congress assem-bled."

The Articles of Confederation were written when the colonies were fighting against King George III. The colonists were not eager to have a king of their own. But they didn't merely dispense with monarchy. More than that, they refused to create an executive at all—which meant that there would be no one to impeach.[16] The Articles did create a legislature, but a weak one. For example, it had no power to tax or to regulate commerce. There were no national courts of general jurisdiction.

Under the Articles, the young nation, if you could call it that, was riven by discord and instability. States were at odds with one another. They failed to cooperate; protectionism was rampant. Local economies were failing. The nation could not raise revenue. To many people, the United States seemed on the verge of disintegration. A mere decade after the American Revolution, the nation's high ideals and aspirations appeared doomed. James Madison wrote to one friend that people "unanimously agree that the existing Confederacy is tottering to its foundation," and to another, "It is not possible that a government can last long under these circumstances."[17]

In 1786, state representatives met in Annapolis to consider commercial problems arising under the Confederation. Because so few delegates showed up (only twelve from five states), they adopted a resolution to hold a convention in Philadelphia to address the deteriorating situation. But the charge to the delegates was narrower and more modest than the ultimate product would suggest. The delegates, chosen by state legislatures (except in South Carolina, where they were chosen by the governor), were instructed "to meet at

Philadelphia . . . to take into consideration the situation of the United States, to devise such further provisions as shall appear to them necessary to render the constitution of the Federal Government adequate to the exigencies of the Union."[18]

The limited character of this charge raised some problems for the delegates, whose product reflected their view that it was necessary to provide not "further provisions" but an altogether novel document. Among the most important changes were the creation of an executive branch; the grant to Congress of the powers to tax and to regulate commerce; and the creation of a federal judiciary, including the Supreme Court and, if Congress chose, lower federal courts. To its defenders and to its critics, the most noteworthy feature of the new Constitution was its dramatic expansion of the national government, giving it fresh powers and authorizing both the executive and the judiciary to exercise considerable authority over the citizenry.

For present purposes, the most important point is that when the delegates originally came to Philadelphia, the absence of an executive seemed, to essentially all of them, to be among the most glaring defects of the Articles. The United States needed someone who could speak for the nation with respect to foreign affairs. It needed someone who could execute the laws. The chief executive would need a staff, consisting of departments and agencies. By and large, it would work for him. And to help make the new nation work, he needed to be powerful.

Just how powerful? Excellent question.

The Unitary Executive

For the framers, an initial issue was structural. Should the executive branch consist of one person, or of several? Should it be unitary, or plural, with powers shared or divided among a group of people? The answers to these questions were closely connected to the debates over impeachment.

At the Convention, James Wilson, a leading thinker who had signed the Declaration of Independence and was later appointed to the Supreme Court, argued for a unitary executive on the grounds that it would give the "most energy, dispatch and responsibility to the office."[19] With recent history firmly in mind, some of the delegates vigorously disagreed. Edmund Randolph contended that a unitary executive would be "the fetus of monarchy."[20] Hugh Williamson said it would mean that the nation would have "an elective king."[21] John Dickinson, also a leading thinker, objected that Wilson's approach would produce an executive "not consistent with a republic" and more akin to that in Great Britain.[22] The great Dickinson knew how to go for the jugular.

Nonetheless, the delegates opted, by a vote of seven to three, for a unitary executive, as captured in these words, which have resonated through the centuries:

> The executive power shall be vested in a President of the United States of America.

Even more than Wilson, Alexander Hamilton was a major force behind that sentence. In *The Federalist,* he wrote with a kind of pride: "The first thing which strikes our attention is, that the executive authority, with few exceptions, is to be vested in a single magistrate."[23] But doesn't that sound like a kind of king? Explaining why a single magistrate would be tolerable, Hamilton immediately added: "That magistrate is to be elected for FOUR years; and is to be re-eligible as often as the people of the United States shall think him worthy of their confidence. In these circumstances there is a total dissimilitude between HIM and a king of Great Britain, who is an HEREDITARY monarch, possessing the crown as a patrimony descendible to his heirs forever."

And then Hamilton emphasized:

> The President of the United States would be liable to be impeached, tried, and, upon conviction of treason, bribery, or other high crimes or misdemeanors, removed from office; and would afterwards be liable to prosecution and punishment in the ordinary course of law. The person of the king of Great Britain is sacred and inviolable; there is no constitutional tribunal to which he is amenable; no punishment to which he can be subjected without involving the crisis of a national revolution.

We can see here a chain with three links: a single magistrate; election every four years; and impeachment. The first two links are familiar to every American. The third is, of course, much more obscure.

The decision to have a unitary president had three distinct motivations, all relevant to the question of impeachment. First, it would allow the executive to be energetic and actually capable of getting things done. If the executive were plural, it would get bogged down in internal debate. As Hamilton put it: "That unity is conducive to energy will not be disputed. Decision, activity, secrecy, and dispatch will generally characterize the proceedings of one man in a much more eminent degree than the proceedings of any greater number; and in proportion as the number is increased, these qualities will be diminished."[24]

It is true that in government, paralysis has its charms. It can be favorable to liberty. But from Hamilton's standpoint, a paralyzed executive might turn out to be incapable of action, and so no executive at all.

Second, a unitary president is more accountable. With a single magistrate, you know exactly whom to blame if things go wrong. Here again, Hamilton nailed the point:

> [O]ne of the weightiest objections to a plurality in the Executive, and which lies as much against the last as the first plan, is, that it tends to conceal faults and destroy responsibility. . . . But the multiplication of the Executive adds to the difficulty of detection. . . . It often becomes impossible, amidst mutual accusations, to determine on whom the blame or the punishment of a pernicious measure, or series of pernicious measures, ought really to fall. It is shifted from one to another with so much dexterity, and under such plausible appearances, that the public opinion is left in suspense about the real author.[25]

When the president is unitary, there is no such suspense. The third and final point is that a unitary executive is more likely to be centralized and coordinated. If one person is in charge, he can better ensure that the executive branch is properly managed and that those who work for him are working together.

The unitary executive must be contrasted with the legislature, which was, and remains, at an opposite pole. Hamilton was onto this point as well, and so let's hear him one more time: "In the legislature, promptitude of decision is oftener an evil than a benefit. The differences of opinion, and the jarrings of parties in that department of the government, though they may sometimes obstruct salutary plans, yet often promote deliberation and circumspection, and serve to check excesses in the majority."[26]

There's a lot in those two sentences. Hamilton was fine with a degree of paralysis in Congress. Obstruction of "salutary plans" would be unfortunate, but it was a price worth paying if it served "to check excesses in the majority." Congress consists of two houses, with different kinds of accountability: members of the House of Representatives (the more populist branch) are elected every two years, and members of the Senate (the more insulated branch) every six. The American constitutional order is meant to create a *deliberative democracy,* in which debate and discussion accompany accountability. This is not merely a system of majority rule, through which majorities get to do as they like simply because they are majorities. Reason-giving is central, and a deliberative democracy gives reasons.

In Congress, the sheer number of representatives, combined with bicameralism, would promote deliberation, which would occur among people who were very different from one another. The framers viewed the system of bicameralism as a way of ensuring increased "deliberation and circumspection," in large part because it enlists diversity both as a safeguard and as a way of enlarging the sheer range of arguments. The bicameral system, along with the concern for deliberation and circumspection, played a key role in debates over impeachment.

chapter 3

"Shall Any Man Be Above Justice?"

While most of the delegates supported the idea of a unitary executive, they were alert to the counterarguments, and their desire to avoid a king was undiminished. So the question was: How do you get rid of a president who turns out to be a miscreant?

That question in turn raised four further questions: (1) Should impeachment be available? (2) If so, on what grounds? (3) Who, exactly, gets to undertake impeachment? (4) What are the consequences of impeachment, or in other words, is a further step necessary to remove a president (or other officials) from office? In Philadelphia, the delegates had an extensive background with which to approach these questions.

British Antecedents

At least since 1635, impeachment had been discussed intensely in the colonies.[1] Before and after independence, Americans adopted concrete, and quite novel, understandings of what the impeachment weapon was all about. Something remarkable happened here, because in England, impeachment had fallen into near-disuse in the seventy years before the Constitutional Convention. Despite that fact, John Adams went so far as to count impeachment among the fundamental "Rights and Privileges of Englishmen."[2]

Adams had a point. In 1679, nearly a hundred years before the American founding, it was proclaimed in the House of Commons that impeachment was "the chief institution for the preservation of the government."[3] Edmund Burke described impeachment as the "great guardian of the purity of the Constitution."[4]

Those are strong words, and they have a specific background. The question was this: Were the King's ministers, who had immense power, accountable to the English parliament, or were they accountable only to the King? You can think of impeachment as an unambiguous answer to that question: the English parliament. Impeachment was a movement in the direction of replacing monarchical absolutism with something closer to parliamentary supremacy. In that way, impeachment was, in England, a major step in the direction of republican self-government. Adams, Madison, and Hamilton were aware of that.

More specifically, the English idea of impeachment arose largely because its objects were free from the reach of conventional criminal law. Parliament made the ministers and functionaries of the King subject to impeachment for public offenses. The phrase "certain high treasons and offenses and misprisions" appeared as early as 1386, in an impeachment proceeding, but on one account, the precise term "high crimes and misdemeanors" did not appear until 1642, after which it was regularly used.[5] Under English law, the House of Commons took the term "misdemeanor" to refer to distinctly public misconduct, including but not limited to actual crimes.[6] Thus "high Crimes and Misdemeanors," the standard basis for impeachment, represented "a category of *political* crimes against the state."[7] Impeachment was a political weapon, used to challenge official wrongdoing. The House of Commons would make the decision whether to impeach, and if it chose to do so, a trial would be held in the House of Lords. The penalty for conviction could be severe; it could even include execution.

In English law, there was some ambiguity in the use of the word "high." Did the term refer to the seriousness of the offense, or to the nature of the office against which the proceeding was aimed? Some of the actual practice suggests the term referred to both: for impeachment to be appropriate, a holder of high office had to do something terrible. As practice unfolded, "high Crimes and Misdemeanors" could mean serious crimes, but it could also mean serious offenses that were not in technical violation of criminal law. Egregious misconduct, as in the form of committing the nation to "an ignominious treaty," could count as a legitimate basis for impeachment in England.[8]

For present purposes, the more important point is that the great cases involving charges of impeachable conduct in England usually involved serious abuses of the authority granted by public office, or, in other terms, the kind of misconduct in which someone could engage only by virtue of holding such an office. Consider the following charges, drawing on a list compiled by Raoul Berger from actual impeachment cases, and invoking the term "high crimes and misdemeanors":

:: applying appropriated funds to purposes other than those specified
:: procuring offices for people who were unfit and unworthy of them
:: commencing but not prosecuting suits
:: allowing contracts for greatly needed powder to lapse for want of payment
:: thwarting Parliament's order to store arms and ammunition in storehouses
:: preventing a political enemy from standing for election and causing his illegal arrest and detention
:: losing a ship through neglect to bring it to mooring
:: assisting the Attorney General in drawing a proclamation to suppress petitions to the King to call a parliament
:: accepting 5,500 guineas from the East India Company to procure a charter of confirmation[9]

It is clear that in cases of this kind, impeachment proceedings were brought for the abuse of the distinctive authority vested in public officers. The most highly publicized and well-known cases fell within the category of the egregious misuse of official powers. But the actual English practice was somewhat more wide-ranging.

The American Reformulation

When the framers met in Philadelphia, many of them knew about the English practice, but they had a long history of their own, going back to the early seventeenth century. From that period until the founding, the idea of impeachment was adapted to an increasingly different culture, and reformulated as a result of the rise of republican thinking. If you are curious about the origins of American exceptionalism, that reformulation is a pretty good place to start.

As the American tradition developed, the concern was abuse of official power, just as in England—but it was understood in distinctly republican terms. In the colonies, impeachment was a mechanism by which representative institutions could start the pro cess for removing executive and judicial officers for intolerable wrongdoing. There were early efforts to impeach people for purely political reasons, as captured in the idea that officials could be impeached for violations of "popular will" or for showing a "dangerous tendency." But before the Revolution, the dominant idea was that impeachment would be limited to serious criminality or the abuse or misuse of the responsibilities of high office.

In the crucial years between 1755 and the signing of the Declaration of Independence, impeachment was used as a weapon against abuses of authority that came from imperial policy. In this way, impeachment was a tool for the exercise of popular sovereignty, ensuring a close link between impeachment and republicanism in the colonies.

In Massachusetts, for example, Chief Justice Peter Oliver was impeached for obeying an order from the crown.[10] In Pennsylvania, the assembly asserted that its principal powers were "those of making laws, granting aids to the Crown, and redressing the grievances and oppressions of the People." Impeachment was an important mechanism for that republican redress. While many of the colonists were acquainted with English practice, "its American unfolding had led to a new meaning for impeachment," write Peter Hoffer and Natalie Hull in their authoritative treatment. "The people, through their own representatives, not virtually through the Commons in England, had the right and power to oust wrongdoers in office."[11] There is no question that in the colonies, violations of criminal law were not the only basis for impeachment. The focus was on "palpable misconduct and willful misuse of power."[12] In this qualitatively distinctive category, criminality was neither necessary nor sufficient.

By the 1770s, colonial Americans came to see impeachment as the mechanism by which the people could begin the process for ousting official wrongdoers, understood as those who betrayed republican principles, above all by abusing their authority through corruption or misuse of power. In that sense, it was a legal instrument for carrying out the aims of the coming Revolution.

Immediately after independence was won, several state constitutions included a mechanism for impeachment. Such a mechanism could be found in the very first constitutions of Delaware, Massachusetts, New York, North Carolina, and Pennsylvania (and also Vermont, which had a constitution but did not become a state until 1791). During the 1780s, impeachment was embraced as well by Georgia, New Hampshire, and South Carolina.[13] Delaware was the first state to specify categories of impeachable offenses, referring to "offending against the state by maladministration, corruption, or other means, by which the safety of the commonwealth might be endangered."[14] In Massachusetts and New Hampshire, officers could be impeached for misconduct or maladminis-tration.[15] In New York, impeachment was available against all officers for "mal and corrupt conduct" while in office, with a two-thirds vote required; it was followed by a trial in a spe-cial court created for the purpose.[16]

The central conclusion is that impeachment was estab-lished as "an appropriate instrument of republican rule."[17] But there was division and controversy about who, exactly, would be trying the impeachment. Following the British practice, states tended to adopt a two-step process. A repre-sentative institution was authorized to undertake impeach-ment proceedings. If an official were impeached, he would not be removed; impeachment itself was akin to an indict-ment. An impeached official would then face a trial in some separate institution. In 1783, Thomas Jefferson built on this model in suggesting the need for a court of impeachments in Virginia, consisting of a mix of judges and legislators.[18] Madison vigorously objected to Jefferson's proposal and ar-gued that any trial should be undertaken within a more un-ambiguously judicial process.[19]

After national independence, there was a great deal of activity under the new provisions. Impeachment was used against officials who had engaged in fraud, extortion, brib-ery, mismanagement of funds, and even bullying of ordi-nary citizens.[20] Neglect of duty and incompetence were also taken to be sufficient grounds for impeachment—but only if they rose to a level that was thought to endanger the state. Many people believed that one of the virtues of the im-peachment mechanism was that, in view of its availability, "people did not have to take their complaints against of-ficeholders into the streets."[21]

None of this was foreign to the delegates at the Convention. Indeed, Hamilton, Madison, George Mason, Edmund Randolph, Gouverneur Morris, James Wilson, William Paterson, Rufus King, Elbridge Gerry, Hugh Williamson, and Charles Pinckney were experts on impeachment. It is no accident that they were the most influential participants in the debates.

Impeachment at All?

While the impeachment question didn't get a ton of attention, the attention it got tells us a ton. Essentially all of the discussion focused on impeachment of the president, though as noted, the constitutional provision extends to all civil officers.

The early plans submitted for the delegates' consideration pointed in different directions. The Virginia plan, drafted by Madison, offered not a word about presidential impeachments, but generally allowed the nation's judiciary to oversee "impeachments of any national officers."[22] Puzzlingly, it did not specify what national officers could be impeached *for*. Under the New Jersey plan, the chief executive could be removed by Congress, after a majority of state executives (governors) applied for removal.[23]

Hamilton offered his own plan, which included a "Governor" who would have "supreme Executive authority" and "serve during good behaviour." Hamilton's plan would allow the Governor (along with Senators and all officers of the United States) to be impeached for "mal and corrupt conduct." Impeachments would be "tried by a Court to consist of the judges of the Supreme Court chief or Senior Judge of the superior Court of law of each state."[24] (What a mess—probably not Hamilton's best idea.) Building on the Virginia plan, Edmund Randolph offered an early reference to impeachment, supporting the creation of a special judiciary to hear "impeachments of any National officers."[25]

In early June, the question was vigorously debated. The widely admired Roger Sherman, who had signed both the Declaration of Independence and the Articles of Confederation, took an extreme position. He claimed that Congress should be authorized to remove the president whenever it wanted to do so.[26] Thomas Jefferson described Sherman as "a man who never said a foolish thing in his life," but almost all the delegates agreed that this approach would be crazy.[27] Sherman had fifteen children. Maybe he was tired.

The problem was that if Sherman's approach were adopted, the whole system of separation of powers would be at risk. The president needed a degree of insulation and independence. George Mason made the decisive objection, contending that Sherman's approach would turn the executive into "the mere creature of the legislature."[28]

In a variation on the New Jersey plan, John Dickinson offered an institutional fix, suggesting that Congress should be able to remove the president, but only if a majority of state legislatures requested it.[29] (Dickinson was apparently thinking of something akin to a vote of no confidence.) The delegates rejected that suggestion too, in favor of an approach supported by North Carolina's Hugh Williamson, which would allow removal by "impeachment & conviction" on the basis of "mal-practice or neglect of duty."[30] That language is pretty broad; it seems to suggest that impeachment could occur for either bad actions (malpractice) or bad omissions (neglect). And indeed, Williamson drew directly from his home state, where impeachment was available for "offenses against the public interest which need not be indictable under the criminal law."[31]

The issue was taken up on several occasions in June. On June 2, Williamson offered his phrase "mal-practice or neglect of duty" and moved that impeachment be available on those grounds.[32] The motion passed.[33] On June 13, one of the early resolutions contained that formulation.[34] On June 18, Hamilton offered his own proposal, with its reference to "impeachment for mal and corrupt conduct."[35] The proposal did not go anywhere. The impeachment provision stood with the words "mal-practice or neglect of duty." How different American history would be if things had been left there!

In late July, this provision provoked the most extended debate it would ever receive. On July 19, Gouverneur Morris worried that if the president could be impeached at all, he would be "dependent on those who are to impeach," thus undermining the separation of powers.[36] (Note that for most of the Convention, the delegates were operating on the assumption that Congress would be picking the president, which bolsters the concern about dependence.) The next day, Charles Pinckney took up Morris's point, arguing that in the new republic, the president "ought not to be impeachable whilst in office."[37] In defense of this position, Pinckney argued that impeachment would allow the legislature to have "a rod over the Executive and by that means effectually destroy his independence."[38]

Pinckney's view received a fair bit of support, and it played a big role in the day's debate. Along with Morris, some people emphasized the system of separation of powers, which, in their view, would be badly compromised by allowing for any kind of impeachment. Others referred to the fact that the president, unlike a monarch, would be subject to periodic elections, a point that seemed to make impeachment unnecessary. With a limited term, was it really necessary to have any kind of impeachment mechanism? Wasn't accountability enough?

But Pinckney's view never came close to prevailing. On the contrary, it seemed to terrify some of the founders. George Mason was the most eloquent:

> No point is of more importance than that the right of impeachment should be continued. Shall any man be above Justice? Above all shall that man be above it, who can commit the most extensive injustice? . . . Shall the man who has practiced corruption & by that means procured his appointment in the first instance, be suffered to escape punishment, by repeating his guilt?[39]

In the same vein, Edmund Randolph urged, "The Executive will have great opportunitys of abusing his power; particularly in time of war when the military force, and in some respects the public money will be in his hands."[40] In his inimitable way, the pragmatic Franklin recalled past history: "What was the practice before this in cases where the chief Magistrate rendered himself obnoxious? Why, recourse was had to assassination in [which] he was not only deprived of his life but of the opportunity of vindicating his character."[41]

Madison pleaded that it was "indispensable that some

provision should be made for defending the Community [against] the incapacity, negligence or perfidy of the chief Magistrate. The limitation of the period of his service, was not a sufficient safeguard."[42] (There's a lot there: incapacity, negligence, or perfidy.) He feared that the president "might lose his capacity after his appointment." Madison was especially concerned that the president "might pervert his administration into a scheme of peculation or oppression. He might betray his trust to foreign powers."[43] And if the president were either corrupt or incapacitated, the situation might be "fatal to the republic" unless impeachment were available.[44]

More concisely, Elbridge Gerry, who had signed the Declaration of Independence, recalled the Revolution itself; he "hoped the maxim will never be adopted here that the chief Magistrate could do no wrong."[45] The circumspect Gouverneur Morris, who had previously been concerned that impeachment would make the president too weak and dependent, offered a constructive suggestion, to the effect that "corruption & some few other offenses" should be impeachable, but "the cases ought to be enumerated and defined."[46] As he put it, "The people are the king."[47]

Informed by the reasonable and clear arguments made by Madison and Morris, the discussion seemed to be moving toward a distinctive view: the president should be impeachable, but only for a narrow and specified category of abuses of the public trust. This would be a compromise position— one that would retain the sharp separation between the president and Congress, but still permit impeachment and removal of the president in extreme cases.

But the discussion ended without agreement on any particular set of terms. The only vote was on the fundamental question: Shall the executive be removable by impeachment? The Ayes had it, 8 to 2. South Carolina and Massachusetts were alone in opposition.[48]

That settled the question. The president was no king. We the People would have a way to remove him from office.

Impeachment for What? The Cavalry

A big question remained: On what grounds?

During the early debates, the answer lay in an assortment of broad and vague terms: misconduct, neglect of duty, corruption, perfidy. But what about the concern, expressed by Madison and Gouverneur Morris, that the bases for impeachment should be specified?

The Committee on Detail, chosen by the Convention to turn the various proposals and recommendations into a draft of the Constitution, produced a new text of the impeachment clause on August 6. Evidently informed by Morris, this version would permit impeachment of the president, but only for treason, bribery, and corruption (exemplified by the president's securing his office by unlawful means).[49] But two weeks after that, on August 20, a radically different draft emerged, allowing impeachment and removal of multiple officers "for neglect of duty, malversation, or corruption."[50] That's something new (what's "malversation"?), and it sounds quite broad as well as vague.

On September 4, the Committee of Eleven, appointed to address unresolved issues, offered a much narrower provision, which proposed just two grounds for impeachment:

"treason, or bribery."[51] Whatever happened to neglect of duty, malversation, and corruption? On September 8, the delegates took up the impeachment clause anew. Here they broadened the grounds for removing the president, but in a way that stayed close to the compromise position that appeared to attract support in July.

What we have of the full debate, from Madison's notes, is astoundingly brief. It is essential reading. Here it is:

> Col. Mason. Why is the provision restrained to Treason & bribery only? Treason as defined in the Constitution will not reach many great and dangerous offenses. Hastings is not guilty of Treason. Attempts to subvert the Constitution may not be Treason as above defined—as bills of attainder which have saved the British Constitution are forbidden, it is the more necessary to extend the power of impeachments.
>
> He moved to add after "bribery" "or maladministration." Mr. Gerry seconded him—
>
> Mr. Madison. So vague a term will be equivalent to a tenure during pleasure of the Senate.
>
> Mr. Govr Morris., it will not be put in force & can do no harm—An election of every four years will prevent maladministration.
>
> Col. Mason withdrew "maladministration" & substitutes "other high crimes & misdemeanors" agst. the State.[52]

That's it.

Remarkably, there was apparently no discussion of just what "other high crimes and misdemeanors" meant. Those words seem to be a bit like the cavalry, coming at the end to save the day. By the way, Mason did not just make up the word "maladministration." It was used in the Pennsylvania constitution, where it was, in fact, the only impeachable offense. Vermont had mimicked that approach, and as noted, Massachusetts and New Hampshire also used the term, which referred to endangerment of the public good.[53] To contemporary ears, however, Madison's objection seems convincing, and apparently it was to eighteenth-century ears as well.

After Mason offered his seemingly narrower phrase, the text passed by a vote of 8 to 3. Just for clarity, there was an additional change in the text. To remove ambiguity, the words "against the State" were changed to "against the United States."[54] In either case, the clear goal was to ensure that impeachment would be designed for offenses against the public as such, suggesting that we are speaking of abuses of official power (consistent with the American understanding of impeachment as it had evolved over time).

With respect to the grounds for impeachment, there was a final wrinkle. The draft was submitted to the Committee on Arrangement and Style, which deleted those clarifying words "against the United States."[55] Was the deletion designed to broaden the legitimate grounds for impeachment? That is extremely unlikely. As its name suggests, the Committee on Style and Arrangement lacked substantive authority (which is not to deny that it made some substantive changes), and it is far more likely that this particular change was made on grounds of redundancy. Hence the impeachment clause, in its final incarnation, was targeted at "high Crimes and Misdemeanors"—period.

Who Impeaches? Who Convicts?

All the while, the delegates were exploring the institutional question: Who's going to be in charge of impeachment, anyway? And who's going to convict, and thus ensure removal from office? These were tough questions. Madison said that establishing where to try impeachment ranked "among the most puzzling articles of a republican Constitution."[56]

The major role might be played by federal courts, which would of course be accustomed to conducting trials. Alternatively, the House of Representatives might be authorized to impeach, while the Supreme Court might conduct the trial of impeachments. James Madison preferred that solution, and it stayed in a draft of the Constitution into August. In September, some delegates thought that the Convention should give the Senate the power to try impeachments. On September 8, Madison strenuously objected that, under such an approach, the president would be "improperly dependent" on the Senate in the event of "any act which might be called a misdemeanor."[57] He continued to favor the Supreme Court.

For his part, Gouverneur Morris argued that the Senate would be best, for "there could be no danger that the Senate would say untruly on their oaths that the President was guilty of crimes."[58] He feared that in light of the fact that the president appointed members of the Supreme Court, its members "might be warped or corrupted" if they tried impeachments.[59] Morris's position prevailed before the Convention, evidently on the theory that it was the least bad of the various imperfect solutions. An important wrinkle was the requirement, for conviction, of a two-thirds majority in the Senate—to ensure that conviction would occur only if there were something close to a consensus that it should.

As you might have noticed, the institutional arrangement can do the work of the legal standard, and vice versa. If you wanted to protect the president from unjustified impeachments, you could choose a pretty low standard (say, "neglect of duty"), but accompany it with a system of institutional constraints, ensuring that the system would never find that the standard had been met.

Revealingly, the Constitution chooses both a high standard (high crimes and misdemeanors) and institutional constraints (participation of two branches, and the two-thirds requirement for conviction in the Senate). At the Convention, the delegates apparently did not discuss that fact, but it is unmistakable. After the fact, Hamilton made it clear that he knew exactly what had been done:

> assigning to one the right of accusing, to the other the right of judging, avoids the inconvenience of making the same persons both accusers and judges; and guards against the danger of persecution from the prevalency of a factious spirit in either of those branches. As the concurrence of two-thirds of the Senate will be requisite to a condemnation, the security to innocence, from this additional circumstance, will be as complete as itself can desire.[60]

Let's underline his point. We the People can oust a president, if we insist, but we have to run the gauntlet. By the way, the great French theorist Alexis de Tocqueville disagreed with Hamilton on this point. He thought that because the penalties for impeachment and conviction were so weak (consisting only of removal from office), the device would be used often. Score one for Hamilton.

Questions Answered

Because of the absence of discussion of the meaning of "high crimes and misdemeanors," the debates leave important questions unanswered. But they do rule out two positions.

The first would allow the House and Senate to tell the president whenever they liked: "You're fired." Sherman embraced that idea, but Madison did not. Nor did Morris or Mason.[61] The second would restrict the grounds for impeachment to treason, bribery, and corruption, and thus allow the president to commit "many great and dangerous offenses." Mason did not want that, and Madison agreed.[62]

To see what they agreed about, we need to understand Mason's brilliant, compressed argument. He referred to the narrow scope of treason as defined in the Constitution, and he had a point. The Constitution says, "Treason against the United States shall consist only in levying War against them, or in adhering to their Enemies, giving them Aid and Comfort." That sentence leaves real ambiguity, but you could imagine forms of disloyalty and corruption that would fall well short of "levying War" against the United States, or "adhering to their Enemies, giving them Aid and Comfort."

Mason's concern about the definition of treason helps to explain his reference to Hastings—Warren Hastings, that is, Britain's Governor General of India, who had been subject to a widely publicized, seven-year-long impeachment trial.

The great Edmund Burke, who conducted the prosecution, charged Hastings with exercising arbitrary power, disregarding treaty obligations, selling favors, and engaging in fraud and corruption in making contracts. Hastings was acquitted, but Mason's point was apparently convincing to the delegates: if a president did the kinds of things that Hastings did, he should not be able to retain office, even if neither treason nor bribery was involved.

Mason also emphasized that the U.S. Constitution forbids "bills of attainder," which are acts of the legislature singling out one or more people and finding them to be guilty of a crime, without benefit of trial. In England, bills of attainder were permissible, but under the founding document, Congress is prohibited from ruling, by law, that a crime has been committed (by the head of some major company, the leader of a labor union, or the president). The delegates agreed that trials are needed and that guilt must be determined by courts, not legislatures. Mason did not contest that principle, but he insisted that it created a problem, because it deprived Congress of an important tool with which to contest presidential wrongdoing. In the absence of that tool, the grounds for impeachment had to be broadened beyond treason and bribery.

When Mason withdrew the term "maladministration" and substituted "high crimes and misdemeanors," he appeared to think that the phrase would simultaneously meet both Madison's concern and his own. Whatever the precise meaning of "high crimes and misdemeanors," the term includes "great and dangerous offenses."[63] That's important.

At this point, you might still be wondering, along with

some of the delegates, about why the separation of powers and the presidential election cycle aren't enough. If the real problem is one of accountability and the avoidance of monarchy, doesn't the rest of the Constitution do the job? After all, Congress makes the laws, and the president is obliged to take care that the laws are faithfully executed. He's elected, and once he's in office, he's hardly there for eternity. What does impeachment deliver that cannot be provided through other means?

From the standpoint of American history, that's a fair question. As we will see, impeachment has been exceedingly rare; if we focus only on presidents, we have a really small sample. But the founding generation insisted on the importance of taking precautions against unlikely scenarios. They were acutely concerned about the risk of serious abuse in year one, two, three, or four of a presidency.

They also knew about the value of deterrence. Consider the old tale of the Sword of Damocles, about which it was said, "The value of the sword is not that it falls, but rather, that it hangs." The importance of the sword of impeachment is that it sometimes falls. But for We the People, it is also important that it hangs.

chapter 4

What We the People Heard

While the debates in the Constitutional Convention are profoundly illuminating, they were kept secret during the ratification process. That means that the people who ratified the Constitution had no access to those debates.[1] In this light, there is a strong argument that if we really want to know the meaning of the impeachment provision, we should focus on the public ratification debates, which help explain how We the People understood the document.

In any effort to answer questions of interpretation, the constitutional text has priority. But the phrase "high crimes and misdemeanors" does not have a self-evident meaning, and the English understanding, while helpful, is far from conclusive. As we have seen, the Americans had been developing their own, distinctly republican understandings of why and when to remove high-level officials. What is more important is that those who defended the Constitution, and tried to explain what it meant, spoke of impeachment in ways that fit exceedingly well with the views of Madison and Mason, and the ultimate drift of the discussions at the Constitutional Convention.

The idea of "great and dangerous offenses" is an excellent shorthand for the views of the ratifiers—at least if we understand such offenses as including egregious abuses or misuses of official authority. At the same time, bad decisions, or politically objectionable decisions, are not sufficient grounds for impeachment, even if much of the nation is up in arms. The United States, unlike some other democracies, does not allow votes of no confidence.

Those who argued in favor of ratification seemed to suggest a pretty broad understanding of the legitimate grounds for impeachment—a bit broader than those who framed the provision in Philadelphia. That's no surprise. Their goal was to defend the document and to suggest that it was sufficiently republican and did not come close to creating a monarchy. To get the document ratified, it was necessary to convince the public that it did not betray the goals of the Revolution and that We the People would have enough control over the president. Opposition was fierce.

Those who rejected the proposed constitution argued that it represented a repudiation of the ideals for which Americans had fought; to them, it was a wholesale departure from the political commitments of 1776.[2] One way to answer that charge was to emphasize the power of impeachment. If we are interested in knowing what reasonable readers of the Constitution thought that it meant in 1787, the arguments in defense of ratification are probably the best source.

While the voices in the ratification debates were not entirely consistent and often less than precise, they can be fairly summarized in this way: if a president were to engage in some egregious violation of the public trust while in office, he could be impeached, convicted, and removed from office. To be sure, the violation would have to take the form of some action or omission that could count as a high crime or misdemeanor. And to be sure, we have to specify what is meant by this idea—but the ratification debates are helpful there as well.

Hamilton and More

As always, Hamilton is a terrific place to start. In *Federalist* No. 65, he explained that the "subjects" of impeachment involve "the abuse or violation of some public trust. They are of a nature which may with peculiar propriety be denominated POLITICAL, as they relate chiefly to injuries done immediately to the society itself."[3]

That might seem vague and bland, but it has real content. "High crimes and misdemeanors" are abuses or violations of what the public is entitled to expect. Moreover, we are speaking not of private misconduct (theft, assault, failure to pay rent) but of distinctly political offenses. In that way, Hamilton's claims should be taken as an echo of the textual idea, on which the delegates were unanimous at a late date, that the relevant high crimes and misdemeanors must run "against the United States."

Note too that Hamilton, who was never casual with words, was respecting Mason's concerns. He did not say that impeachment could be based only on treason, bribery, or a criminal offense. He scrupulously avoided any claim of that kind. Far more broadly, he emphasized "the abuse or violation of some public trust." In his account, the phrase appeared to work as a simple summary of the technical term "high crimes and misdemeanors."

The Constitution's supporters, defending the new executive in the ratification debates in various states, generally spoke in the same terms. They described impeachment as a check on serious presidential wrongdoing, taking the form not of mistakes of judgment or of controversial political choices but of terrible abuses of power.

Some people were worried about the possibility that the president might be too friendly to other nations. They emphasized that impeachment would serve as a check on corruption and corrupt treaties (that is, treaties that would be favorable, by design, to other nations and not the United States). One of the Constitution's defenders went so far as to urge that "the president is amenable himself for his conduct, and liable, like any other public officer, to be impeached for bad a[d]ministration."[4] In light of the debates at the Convention, and the bulk of comments during ratification, that is too broad, but it captures some of what We the People were hearing.

In Virginia, Madison responded to the concern that a president might seek to secure ratification of a treaty by exploiting the quorum requirement (two-thirds of the senators who are present), thus allowing senators from a small number of states to injure others, whose senators were not in attendance. Madison said, "Were the President to commit any thing so atrocious as to summon only a few states, he would be impeached and convicted, as a majority of states would be affected by his misdemeanor."[5] From the modern standpoint, the particular hypothetical might seem a bit crazy, but it reflects a broader principle. No crime is necessary. If the president is acting in an "atrocious" way that harms most of the states, he is committing a "misdemeanor," even if no violation of the law is involved.

George Mason worried over the breadth of the president's pardon power: "He may frequently pardon crimes which were advised by himself. . . . If he has the power of granting pardons before indictment, or conviction, may he not stop inquiry and prevent detection?" Madison answered: "There is one security in this case to which gentlemen may not have adverted: if the President be connected, in any suspicious manner, with any person, and there be grounds to believe he will shelter him, the House of Representatives can impeach him; [and] they can remove him if found guilty."[6] In Madison's view, "This is a great security." If the president uses the pardon power in a corrupt way, by pardoning crimes that he has himself advised (and thus sheltering the wrongdoer), impeachment is the remedy.

Also in Virginia, Edmund Randolph explained his judgment that the Constitution did not make the president unduly powerful. "At the end of four years, he may be turned out of office." Pointedly, he added, "If he misbehaves he may be impeached, and in this case he will never be re-elected. I cannot conceive how his powers can be called formidable."[7] In a brief remark a week later, he linked impeachment with the emoluments clause, emphasizing "another provision against the danger . . . of the President receiving emoluments from foreign powers. If discovered he may be impeached."[8] From the standpoint of the founders, the link made perfect sense. The emoluments clause protects the nation against officials who have been compromised by receiving gifts from foreign nations. Impeachment supplies the remedy in the event of a violation.[9]

There was also significant discussion in North Carolina. The most informative remarks came from James Iredell, a highly respected lawyer who was later appointed to the Supreme Court. Iredell said, "I suppose the only instances, in which the President would be liable to impeachment, would be where he had received a bribe, or had acted from some corrupt motive or other."[10] But he also stated that any man who was "a villain" should be "ignominiously punished" and indeed that a "president must certainly be punishable for giving false information to the Senate." He added: "He is to regulate all intercourse with foreign powers, and it is his duty to impart to the senate every material intelligence he receives." If he "has concealed important information which he ought to have communicated, and by that means induced them to enter into measures injurious to their country," he has committed a misdemeanor.[11]

Iredell stressed that with respect to the power of impeachment, "the occasion for its exercise will arise from acts of great injury to the community."[12] But he also emphasized limits on that power: "God forbid that a man, in any country in the world, should be liable to be punished for want of judgment. This is not the case here. . . . Whatever mistake a man may make, he ought not to be punished for it, nor his posterity rendered infamous."[13]

In New York, a delegate spoke in broadly Hamiltonian terms: "For the abuse of these powers he alone is answerable, and by the representatives of the people he may at any time be impeached."[14] In Massachusetts, where the American Revolution began, some defenders of the Constitution drew a different connection, seeing the impeachment power as a means to protect liberty. James Sullivan, writing influential essays under the name of "Cassius," proclaimed: "Thus we see that no office, however exalted, can protect the miscreant, who dares invade the liberties of his country, or countenance in his crimes the impious villain who sacrilegiously attempts to trample upon the rights of freemen."[15] In my view, this point is central, even defining, because it connects the power of impeachment with the American Revolution itself. On this account, a violation of liberty or rights is an impeachable offense—even if it is not itself a crime.

Elbridge Gerry, George Mason, and Edmund Randolph, who refused to sign the Constitution in Philadelphia (in part because it lacked a Bill of Rights), published letters under the joint pseudonym "Americanus." The first of the collected Americanus essays broadly asserts that the president's power "is limited in such a manner as to preclude every apprehension of influence and superiority. Should he, however, at any time be impelled by ambition, or blinded by passion, and boldly attempt to pass the bounds prescribed to his power, he is liable to be impeached and removed from office; and afterwards he is subject to indictment, trial, judgment, and punishment according to law."[16]

That's informative—but again, it goes beyond what most people were saying. Almost every American president has, on more than one occasion, passed the bounds of his power, in the sense that his administration has done something that it is not lawfully entitled to do. Some of those actions were probably a product of ambition or passion. President Franklin Roosevelt unlawfully sent arms to England to help that nation defend itself against Hitler's aggression. President Truman unlawfully seized the nation's steel mills to maintain production during the Korean War. Americanus was speaking rhetorically, and not really capturing the meaning of the constitutional text. But the rhetoric is informative; it tells us what the American people were being told.

Post-Ratification Clues

We also have some important clues after ratification. During the first Congress, there was widespread fear that a president would abuse his authority by removing executive officers without adequate reason. Madison responded that if he did so, "he will be impeachable by the House before the Senate for such an act of maladministration; for I contend that the wanton removal of meritorious officers would subject him to impeachment and removal."[17]

Whoa. That's a broad conception of the legitimate grounds for impeachment. It also creates a puzzle: Wasn't Madison the one who specifically opposed the idea that the president could be impeached for "maladministration"?

The best way to resolve the puzzle is to emphasize that Madison was speaking not of maladministration generally, but of a specific act of maladministration, in the form of "wanton" discharge of executive officers who were "meritorious." In Madison's view, that would be a misdemeanor. Again, it wouldn't be a crime—but as we have seen, a president can be impeached for offenses that are not crimes.

Others spoke in the same vein. In his great 1791 *Lectures on Law*, James Wilson observed, "In the United States and in Pennsylvania, impeachments are confined to political characters, to political crimes and misdemeanors, and to political punishments."[18] He added that under the Constitution, "impeachments, and offenses and offenders impeachable" should not be thought to come "within the sphere of ordinary jurisprudence. They are found on different principles; are governed by different maxims; and are directed to different objects."[19] Justice Joseph Story wrote in similar terms, describing as impeachable those "offences which are committed by public men in violation of their public trust and duties.... Strictly speaking, then, the power partakes of a political character, as it respects injuries to the society in its political character."[20]

William Rawle, another early commentator, went so far as to say that the "legitimate causes of impeachment . . . can have reference only to public character, and official duty.... In general, those offences which may be committed equally by a private person, as a public officer, are not the subjects of impeachment." In his view, "Murder, burglary, robbery, and indeed all offenses not immediately connected with office . . . are left to the ordinary course of judicial proceeding."[21]

This was a contested view (and I shall contest it), and in light of the history, it is plausible to say that murder and the like would be a legitimate basis for impeachment. But there was general agreement that impeachment was designed to initiate a process to remove from office those who had abused their public power.

Where We Are

From the founding era, the central ingredients of a framework are now in place. Impeachment is available for egregious abuses of official authority. Some crimes do not count as such, because they are essentially private (failing to pay taxes, punching someone, speeding) or because they are not sufficiently serious. Some offenses that are not crimes are nonetheless impeachable—punishing political enemies, trampling on liberty, deciding to take a year off, systematically lying to Congress and the American people. Such actions count as "high misdemeanors."

In some cases, we can say that bad conduct just isn't impeachable, because it is outside of the category of acts that qualify as such. (Some presidents have been awful administrators, but they were not impeachable for that reason.) In some cases, we can say that bad conduct is unquestionably impeachable, because it is obviously inside that category. In the hardest cases, we have to make a judgment of degree: Is the misconduct or the abuse serious enough? But even then, the concerns of the founding period give us orientation.

With respect to the Constitution, it's best to avoid two mistakes. The first is to think that words are more precise and more conclusive than they actually are. The Constitution protects "the freedom of speech" and makes the president "Commander-in-Chief," and those words have real meaning. But still, life turns up tough problems. Even in its republican context, the phrase "high crimes and misdemeanors" leaves some unanswered questions. You can stare at those words all you want, and read Hamilton, Madison, Mason, and all the rest, and you won't squeeze out enough meaning to solve every puzzle.

The second mistake is to conclude, from the existence of unanswered questions, that we are really at sea, or that high crimes and misdemeanors are whatever the House of Representatives says they are. We aren't, and they aren't. Steeped in republicanism, and with the monarchical legacy in mind, the framers and ratifiers gave us a framework. That's a lot.

chapter 5

Interpreting the Constitution:
An Interlude

Does the understanding of the founding generation really matter? Should twenty-first century Americans really care about what people believed in the late eighteenth century? Why should we pay such close attention to dead people? Isn't that a form of ancestor worship?

For some people, the answer to such questions is obvious: *the Constitution's meaning is settled by the understandings of those who ratified it.* If you are confident about that answer, you might think that you do not need to explore controversies about how to interpret the Constitution. True, you might acknowledge that the understandings of the ratifiers leave some questions open. Even so, those understandings are the place to start. But for other people, the historical inquiry is puzzling. In their view, the Constitution's meaning should be settled by *us,* not by people from the eighteenth century, and it is for current generations to decide on the meaning of the impeachment clause.

To understand the role of history, we need to offer a few words about some of the deepest debates in constitutional law, which separate people who are both smart and reasonable. During those debates, people who are usually quite calm can get pretty angry with one another. At the very least, they disagree intensely.

For example, Justice Thurgood Marshall thought it entirely clear that the meaning of the Constitution was not frozen in time. As he wrote in 1987, "I plan to celebrate the bicentennial of the Constitution as a living document."[1] He didn't think that we should answer constitutional questions by asking what people thought at the time of ratification.

To Justice Antonin Scalia, by contrast, the very idea of a "living document" was anathema. He believed that the meaning of constitutional provisions was fixed when they were ratified. As he said in 2008, "If you somehow adopt a philosophy that the Constitution itself is not static, but rather, it morphs from age to age to say whatever it ought to say—which is probably whatever the people would want it to say—you've eliminated the whole purpose of a constitution. And that's essentially what the 'living constitution' leaves you with."[2]

For orientation: everyone agrees that the *text* of the Constitution is binding.[3] Almost everyone thinks that we should be interested in the original meaning of the text. But some people, like Justice Scalia, purport to make the original meaning authoritative, and others, like Justice Marshall, feel free to depart from it. With respect to our rights and the operations of American government, there's a big difference between the two camps.

If these debates seem a bit academic, they also give life to the question of what it means to keep a republic. Sincerely and in good faith, Marshall and Scalia answered that question very differently. For impeachment, Scalia's view makes things relatively straightforward. And for impeachment, I think that Marshall would agree with him. But it's going to take a few pages to explain why.

"The Dead Have No Rights"

Those who believe in a living Constitution claim that the document contains abstract and open-ended terms whose meaning legitimately evolves in ways that the founding generation could not have imagined. Sometimes they enlist one of the greatest thinkers of that very generation, Thomas Jefferson, to support their argument:

> Some men look at constitutions with sanctimonious reverence, and deem them like the arc of the covenant, too sacred to be touched. They ascribe to the men of the preceding age a wisdom more than human, and suppose what they did to be beyond amendment. I knew that age well; I belonged to it, and labored with it. It deserved well of its country. It was very like the present, but without the experience of the present; and forty years of experience in government is worth a century of book-reading; and this they would say themselves, were they to rise from the dead. . . . I know also, that laws and institutions must go hand in hand with the progress of the human mind. As that becomes more developed, more enlightened, as new discoveries are made, new truths disclosed, and manners and opinions change with the change of circumstances, institutions must advance also, and keep pace with the times. . . . [T]he dead have no rights.[4]

Since 1787, Americans have learned an unfathomable amount, and our manners and our opinions have dramatically changed. Institutions and rights have advanced. Slavery has been abolished. Women can vote.

To be sure, those changes came through constitutional amendments, but even without changes in the text, our understandings of the Constitution's eighteenth-century words go far beyond what the founding generation thought. The Constitution now protects women against discrimination at the hands of the federal and state governments—even though the founding generation had no objection to such discrimination, and even though the constitutional amendments that followed the Civil War were not believed, at the time, to ban it. The Constitution now forbids the federal government from discriminating on the basis of race—even though no provision of the document, as originally understood, forbids such discrimination. (Alert readers will immediately ask about the equal protection clause, ratified after the Civil War—but that clause applies only to the states, and not the federal government. And by the way, the better view is that the equal protection clause, as originally understood, did not forbid school segregation at the state level.)

Our free speech principle is far more expansive than the founding generation believed. The text didn't change, but our understanding of the text did, and as a result, we're a lot freer. The very broad protection now given to political dissent almost certainly goes beyond the understandings of the founding period. Our Constitution protects the right to use contraceptives, the right to choose abortion, and the right to same-sex marriage, even though none of its provisions was originally understood to protect any of those things. If constitutional provisions were interpreted to fit with the original judgments of those who ratified them, our constitutional system would be radically different, barely recognizable, and much worse.

Maybe we would do lots better if we abandoned all that history and decided on our own what should count as high crimes and misdemeanors. Why not?

Originalists

A popular answer comes from the many people, including Justice Scalia, who have been drawn to the idea of "originalism." Most originalists insist that the *original public meaning* of constitutional provisions is indeed decisive. In their view, future generations, and courts, have no authority to go beyond it.

The original public meaning refers to the common understanding of constitutional terms at the time that they were ratified. Some originalists believe that what governs is *the intentions of the framers*—but they are in the minority. Justice Scalia and those who follow him do not speak of anyone's intentions, but instead ask what the terms were originally understood to mean. That might seem like a subtle distinction, but it matters. Intentions are what can be found inside people's heads. By contrast, public meaning is an objective social fact. In chapter 2, I said a fair bit about intentions, but most originalists would downplay what happened at the Convention (because it was secret) and emphasize instead the ratification debates insofar as they offer evidence about the original meaning of the impeachment clause.

If originalism is the right approach, a lot of constitutional questions get easier to answer. Suppose that the original public meaning of the words "the freedom of speech," back in the late eighteenth century, would have authorized the government to ban commercial advertising and obscenity. Originalists insist that in the twenty-first century, unelected judges should be bound by that judgment of We the People.[5] They have no license to go beyond the original meaning to invoke their own judgments about how "we" should understand "the freedom of speech." That would be an abuse of judicial authority, a violation of the rule of law. Originalists think that the first task of interpretation is *historical.* In many cases, that might turn out to be the only task. If We the People want to change the Constitution, of course we can do that. But constitutional change cannot legitimately occur through interpretation.

On the current Supreme Court, Justices Clarence Thomas and Neil Gorsuch embrace originalism. True, their approach leaves many questions open, because history can be murky, but it seems to be an honorable position. What's wrong with it?

The Living Constitution

Many of those who reject originalism argue that *the founding generation did not intend to freeze the specific judgments of their own time.* So originalism turns out to be self-defeating. The framers and the ratifiers—it is claimed—were not originalists. They had the foresight to know what Jefferson knew. The best evidence is that they chose broad terms (the freedom of speech, liberty, due process of law) whose particular meaning would necessarily change over time, with new circumstances and fresh learning. According to Justice Anthony Kennedy, writing in the 2015 case that ruled that all states must recognize same-sex marriages:

> The nature of injustice is that we may not always see it in our own times. The generations that wrote and ratified the Bill of Rights and the Fourteenth Amendment did not presume to know the extent of freedom in all of its dimensions, and so they entrusted to future generations a charter protecting the right of all persons to enjoy liberty as we learn its meaning. When new insight reveals discord between the Constitution's central protections and a received legal stricture, a claim to liberty must be addressed.[6]

Many people admire these sentences. (Many abhor them.) Right or wrong, Kennedy is offering a large idea here, and he is hardly the first to do so. The time-honored claim is that the founders "entrusted to future generations a charter," and so the specific meaning of that charter is up to us, not them. There's more than an echo here of Franklin's answer to Mrs. Powel.

One way to keep the republic is by being faithful to the text, but by specifying our own understandings about the precise meaning of "liberty." As some constitutional theorists put it, the text sets out a broad "concept," not a particular "conception." The concept does not change, but the conception does.

Kennedy is connecting his view of constitutional interpretation with democratic values. When the meaning of constitutional rights evolves, it is because society's understandings evolve, and judges are alert to those evolving understandings. After all, we do not see liberty now as they saw it centuries ago. The same is true of the Constitution's structural provisions, such as the grant to Congress of the power to "declare war." Such provisions can be interpreted in a way that is faithful to the document's words, but not necessarily to eighteenth-century understandings of the meanings of those words. The world has dramatically changed since then, and so has the role of the United States in the world. Perhaps we should understand Congress's power in a way that recognizes those dramatic changes—for example, by allowing the president, on his own, to use military force, at least if his use falls short of full-scale "war."

Is Kennedy right? Note that his argument seems to be about history and about what the founding generations actually meant to do. Among professional historians, that argument is deeply controversial. Did the founding generations really want future generations—and unelected judges—to reinterpret the Constitution by reference to what they "learn" about the meaning of liberty? Or did they seek to limit posterity, and judges, to the original understanding of the document that they wrote? Did they mean the idea of "high crimes and misdemeanors" to evolve, or did they mean to freeze the concept? In view of their concerns, there's a pretty good argument that they meant to freeze it!

Many of those who reject originalism have a different argument, and it's more fundamental. They contend that their objection isn't really about what members of the founding generations meant to do. They don't rely on Kennedy's claim about the judgments and understandings of long-dead people. They don't believe in time machines. They insist that the basic question is how to interpret the Constitution, and we can't resolve that question by asking about history. That is inescapably a question *for us*.

Suppose, for example, that the founding generation had a narrow view of "the freedom of speech." Suppose they believed, hoped, and expected that future generations would be bound by that narrow view. Are we bound? Certainly not. *Whether we are bound by the original understanding depends on whether we conclude, on principle, that we should be bound by the original understanding.* Those who reject originalism believe that our constitutional order is far better if we conclude that we are not bound. They believe that at least with respect to individual rights (where circumstances and values change), and perhaps with respect to constitutional structure more broadly (where again, circumstances and values change), we do much better to follow the text and pay respectful attention to the original understanding —without being rigidly constrained by it.

In my view, that's Justice Kennedy's best argument. He is claiming that our system of rights is better if we take the Constitution to set out broad principles whose particular content changes over time. Maybe that's true of the impeachment clause as well.

Tradition, Democracy, Morality

If we are loosened from the views of the founding generation, what do we do? Does anything go? Hardly. Recall that we are bound by the text. The question is where to turn when the text is vague or ambiguous.

Some people, like Justice Felix Frankfurter, have emphasized the importance of paying close attention to national traditions as they unfold over time. Traditionalists do not focus only on the founding generations. They ask about American practices over the decades and centuries. They insist that practices have a lot of weight.

Suppose that Congress and the president have agreed for many decades that the president has the authority to use military force on his own, and so does not need congressional approval, as long as the use is limited and falls far short of full-scale war. Sure, the Constitution gives Congress the authority to "declare war." But if presidents have long used military force without congressional approval, that's relevant to our interpretation of the Constitution. As Frankfurter had it, traditions can serve as a gloss on the text. For many questions that involve the powers of Congress and the president (such as when the president can make recess appointments), traditions turn out to be highly relevant to constitutional decisions. In Frankfurter's view, long-standing traditions can help us interpret ambiguous text, and they can even overcome the original understanding.

Others give less weight to traditions and more to the idea of self-government itself. Justice Stephen Breyer argues that an animating constitutional ideal is "active liberty," meaning active self-governance by We the People.[7] In Breyer's view, we should interpret ambiguous constitutional provisions with that ideal in mind. The general idea of "active liberty" can trump the original understanding. Breyer himself is no originalist—in fact he is a strong critic of Scalia's approach—and in the face of ambiguity in the text, he would invoke democratic ideals.

Believers in active liberty would be especially suspicious of any restriction on people's right to vote. They would be inclined to think that any deviation from the idea of "one person, one vote" should be invalidated under the equal protection clause; they would want to strike down efforts to make it harder for people to register to vote. And if We the People were to embrace some institutional reform expanding or contracting the power of the president, those who believe in active liberty would want to uphold it.

Still other people, most prominently Professor Ronald Dworkin, argue for a "moral reading" of the U.S. Constitution. What this means is that we must follow the Constitution's words, but in a way that makes best moral sense of them. In Dworkin's view, we have an obligation to be faithful to the Constitution's text. If we are not, we are not interpreting it at all. But when it is vague or ambiguous, we should not try to be historians and attempt to figure out what the founding generation thought. Instead we should think, for ourselves, about what makes the constitutional provision as good as it can be—on moral grounds.

If, for example, the equal protection clause is interpreted to forbid racial segregation, it is a lot more appealing, from the moral point of view, than it would otherwise be. If the cruel and unusual punishment clause is taken to forbid torture, it is a better safeguard of human rights.[8] Dworkin freely acknowledges that if judges are "moral readers," they will sometimes disagree. In his view, that's fine. They're disagreeing about exactly the right thing.

Three Dead Ends

Frankfurter, Breyer, and Dworkin offer powerful arguments about constitutional interpretation in general. But in the context of impeachment, their approaches are not promising. They are dead ends.

If you are a traditionalist, you will ask: With respect to impeachment, what have Americans actually done? How have we understood high crimes and misdemeanors since 1787? These are fair questions, but as we will soon see, traditions do not give clear answers. The total number of impeachments is low, and the number of presidential impeachments is very low. And if we wanted to understand our traditions, we would need to include cases in which the House of Representatives did *not* pursue impeachments even though there were arguments that it should have done so. The problem is that we cannot discern, from history, anything like a clear understanding of the idea of high crimes and misdemeanors. As Gertrude Stein wrote of Oakland, "there is no there there." (Okay, that's unfair to Oakland. But still.)

If you believe in active liberty, you might be inclined to think that We the People should be allowed to define high crimes and misdemeanors however we want. But for Madison's reasons, that would be a horrendous mistake. It would allow impeachment because of intense political disagreements. It would go far beyond "maladministration," which was already too broad. It would make hash of the system of the separation of powers.

If you believe in moral readings, you will want to ask: What's the morally best understanding of high crimes and misdemeanors? Good luck with that one. The question is a recipe for chaos. People will disagree, and their disagreements will inevitably reflect their enthusiasm, or their lack of enthusiasm, for the current occupant of the White House. That's no way to run a government.

Impeaching History

For those who embrace originalism, the historical materials are conclusive. To the extent that they give guidance, they tell us what we need to know. True, some hard cases will remain. But for an originalist, those cases must always be explored under the founding generation's framework, rather than one made up by current members of the House of Representatives, by the president's fiercest defenders, by the president's fiercest critics, or by some op-ed writer or law professor.

But even if you don't love originalism in general, you might love it for impeachment. That might seem like an opportunistic position, but it has unmistakable logic. In their different ways, Frankfurter, Breyer, and Dworkin are concerned with changes in circumstances and values. With respect to words like "liberty," "equal protection," and "due process," they do not want to freeze old understandings; they want to incorporate new learning. Fair enough. But with respect to impeachment, the problems confronted way back in 1787 are not so different from those we confront today. Sure, the president is far more powerful, and sure, he can commit "misdemeanors" that the founding generation could not have imagined: uses of drones and nuclear power, surveillance of email, abuses of authority under the Clean Air Act. But the abstract concerns that motivated them—treason, bribery, corruption, egregious abuse of public trust or misuse of presidential authority—are no different from those that concern us. *They are exactly the same.*

There is a further point. Much of constitutional law, including the understanding of constitutional rights, has unfolded through a careful process of case-by-case decisions, in which elaborate principles are built up over a period of many decades. That's what has happened for freedom of speech, for protection against unreasonable searches and seizures, for the equal protection of laws. After decades, the law often makes a lot of sense. The American people live with it, and sometimes even revere it. It would be pretty radical to tear down the whole edifice of constitutional law as it has been constructed over time by insisting that historical research shows that it is inconsistent with what Alexander Hamilton, James Madison, and Ephraim Wood thought as of 1791. Never a radical, Justice Scalia once proclaimed that he was a "faint-hearted" originalist, which meant that he had a lot of respect for precedent, and if the Court had developed stable principles, he would usually be prepared to go along. Faint-hearted originalism is wise, and it's courageous too.

But for impeachment, we don't have a lot of judicial rulings. We have none—and we never will.[9] (An explanation will come in due course.) If you have nothing else to work with, you might be inclined to think: *Let's not make it up. Let's not start from scratch. Let's figure out the original meaning of the impeachment clause.* That's an excellent thought.

The conclusion is strengthened once we focus on the content of the original meaning, and on how very unlikely it is that we could improve on it if we tried to interpret "high crimes and misdemeanors" by our own lights. Those who fought the American Revolution, preferred liberty to death, defeated a king, lived through the Articles of Confederation, and settled on a powerful, elected, removable executive knew what they were doing. They threaded a needle. They accomplished a miracle. There's no reason to depart from their understanding of their framework. We can't do better than they did, and if we tried, we would probably do worse.[10]

To be sure, some people might think that a narrow understanding of high crimes and misdemeanors—limited to actual crimes—would avoid a lot of trouble. But would it really make sense to say that the president could not be impeached if he announced that he would not defend the country against attack or enforce the civil rights laws—or that he is going to spend a year on vacation in Rome?

True, some people might think that a broad understanding, allowing the House of Representatives to define high crimes and misdemeanors however it wishes, would prevent a lot of mischief, while allowing more control by We the People. But such an understanding would breach the separation of powers. It would create the problems that Madison rightly feared. If these considerations are right, it makes sense to stick with the framework that the founding generation devised, very much as they understood it.

Let's use that framework to explore concrete problems. I am betting that the exploration will increase rather than reduce our admiration for the founding generation's understanding—and our desire to follow it.

chapter 6

Impeachment, American-Style

Andrew Johnson and Bill Clinton were impeached by the House—but the Senate refused to convict either of them. Richard Nixon resigned before he could be impeached (as he almost certainly would have been). The other forty-two presidents never faced a serious impeachment threat. Well, one did, but let's not spoil the surprise.

You might think that three is a pretty trivial number and that we can't learn a lot from such a small number of impeachment proceedings. But history has a lot to offer. In fact, the small number may itself be the largest lesson.

One of the best ways to keep faith with the founding document is to avoid resorting to the impeachment mechanism without sufficient cause. Use of the mechanism can transform political disagreement into charges of criminality or egregious wrongdoing. ("Lock him up!") It can be a way of stirring up the ugliest forces of anger and destruction. It can be a product of, and fuel, scandal-mongering and fake news. It can jeopardize the separation of powers. It can be profoundly destabilizing. It focuses the nation's attention on whether to remove its leader—rather than how to promote economic growth, reduce premature deaths, increase national security, or cut poverty. It can increase partisan rage, with the suggestion that the principal figure in one of the nation's political parties, and the winner of a national election, is not merely a bad president but guilty of terribleness and horrors. It leads political opponents to focus obsessively on how to prove that terribleness and those horrors, whether or not they exist.

It's a national nightmare, a body blow to the republic, even if it is also the best or the only way to keep it. Using the impeachment mechanism only when its use is warranted is as important as any other instruction from the founding period—and the United States has generally followed that instruction.

The Worst Presidents

Periodically, historians are asked to rank the nation's presidents. Washington, Lincoln, and Franklin Delano Roosevelt are almost always at the top. But I'm not interested in the best. Here's a list of the fifteen worst, according to a survey of presidential historians in 2017.[1] I've put them in reverse order of badness:

15. James A. Garfield

14. Benjamin Harrison

13. Zachary Taylor

12. Rutherford B. Hayes

11. George W. Bush

10. Martin Van Buren

9. Chester Arthur

8. Herbert Hoover

7. Millard Fillmore

6. William Henry Harrison

5. John Tyler

4. Warren G. Harding

3. Franklin Pierce

2. Andrew Johnson

1. James Buchanan

Thirteen of the fifteen avoided any kind of impeachment inquiry. Harding, Pierce, and Buchanan are almost always ranked among the worst of the bad, and they were exceedingly unpopular in their time. But there was no serious effort to get rid of them. The essential point is clear: intense political opposition, and even a general sense that the president is a failure, is not sufficient cause for impeachment. In the post-Nixon era, Jimmy Carter is sometimes regarded as the least successful president, and for him, impeachment talk would have been ridiculous.

It is also noteworthy that in the first forty years of the republic, the House of Representatives made no serious impeachment attempt, even though that period saw some pretty bad presidents. To be sure, we can find noises and sputtering. During early debates over the relationship between the United States, England, and France, George Washington sent Supreme Court Chief Justice John Jay to London, where negotiations led to a controversial treaty (the Jay Treaty). Republican legislators in Kentucky and

Virginia didn't much like the treaty, and they supported impeachment of Jay and perhaps Washington himself.[2] But their efforts never went anywhere. The absence of any serious impeachment process is informative, because it suggests a clear understanding, on the part of the founding generation and its successor, that truly egregious misconduct was required.

The First Impeachment Attempt

It's not widely known, but the first real attempt at impeachment did involve one of the worst presidents: John Tyler in 1842.

The precipitating offense was Tyler's use of the presidential veto. In the early days of the republic, vetoes were quite unusual, and they were generally based on constitutional objections rather than objections from the standpoint of policy. Tyler departed from that practice: he used vetoes on prominent occasions and solely on policy grounds. His opponents initiated an investigation with the aim of impeaching him. By a narrow majority, the House endorsed a select committee report that condemned his use of the veto and laid the groundwork for possible impeachment, finding him a "fit subject" for that without specifically recommending it.[3]

The steam went out of the effort in the mid-term elections, when the Whigs, who were leading the whole effort, lost their majority in the House. But early in 1843, John Minor Botts of Virginia gave a barn burner of a speech, accusing Tyler of "corruption, malconduct, high crimes and misdemeanors," and asking for the formation of an investigating committee on the basis of an astoundingly long list of specified transgressions. Here's a taste (feel free to skim):

First. I charge him with gross usurpation of power and violation of law, in attempting to exercise a controlling influence over the accounting officers of the Treasury Department, by ordering the payment of amounts of long standing, that had been by them rejected for want of legal authority to pay, and threatening them with expulsion from office unless his orders were obeyed; by virtue of which threat, thousands were drawn from the public treasury without the authority of law.

Second. I charge him with a wicked and corrupt abuse of the power of appointment to, and removal from, office; first, in displacing those who were competent and faithful in the discharge of their public duties, only because they were supposed to entertain a political preference for another; and, secondly, in bestowing them on creatures of his own will, alike regardless of the public welfare and his duty to the country.

Third. I charge him with the high crime and misdemeanor of aiding to excite a disorganizing and revolutionary spirit in the country, by placing on the records of the State Department his objections to a law, as carrying no constitutional obligation with it; whereby the several States of this Union were invited to disregard and disobey a law of Congress, which he himself had sanctioned and sworn to see faithfully executed, from which nothing but disorder, confusion, and anarchy can follow.[4]

A roll call vote was called, and a strong majority rejected the proposal to take an initial step toward impeachment: 127 to 83.[5]

Without going through Botts's long list, let me make three observations. First, the case he laid out for impeachment was at least in the very general ballpark of the concerns of the impeachment clause. Botts spoke in terms of what he saw as egregious abuse of presidential authority. Second, it would be impossible to defend the claim that Tyler was impeachable because of his use of the veto; Tyler had a perfectly reasonable argument, vindicated by subsequent history, that the president has the authority to veto legislation on policy grounds. Third, most and perhaps all of Botts's charges, however colorfully made, were really about acute policy disagreements. It is no wonder that a number of Whigs joined Democrats to defeat the motion.

Politics

The largest lesson of the three serious impeachment efforts is simple: in each case, it was an overwhelmingly partisan affair. It was sought and engineered by people who were determined to bring down a president they despised. As always, Hamilton was prescient, noting in *Federalist* No. 65 that in many cases, the trial of impeachments in the Senate "will connect itself with the pre-existing factions, and will enlist all their animosities, partialities, influence, and interest on one side or on the other; and in such cases there will always be the greatest danger that the decision will be regulated more by the comparative strength of parties, than by the real demonstrations of innocence or guilt."[6] Right.

It is ironic that the two successful presidential impeachments were unconstitutional, even farcical—case studies in what the United States should avoid. But the third impeachment proceeding, halted with Nixon's resignation, was a profile in constitutional courage, even if "the comparative strength of parties" played a massive role.

Watergate

President Richard Nixon was smart and shrewd. He mastered the details. He saw the big picture. He did great things, which continue to define our nation. He was a Republican and a conservative, but he was tough to pigeonhole. He created the Environmental Protection Agency, claiming that clean air and clear water are "a birthright for every American."[7] He created the Occupational Safety and Health Administration. He promoted self-determination for Native-Americans. He signed the great civil rights law that prohibited sex discrimination in higher education. He reoriented the Supreme Court. He calmed tensions between the United States and the Soviet Union. He went to China. If you are listing the five most consequential presidents in American history, you could make a good argument that Nixon belongs on the list.

His enemies called him "Tricky Dick." He lacked charm and charisma. On camera, he would sweat at inopportune moments. In private, he could be brutal. Washington, he said, "is full of Jews." In his view, that was a problem, because "most Jews are disloyal." One of his campaigns was based on three words: "law and order." But he didn't seem to care so much about obeying the law. He lied to the American people. He kept an enemies list.

If you were born before 1965, you probably remember the

Watergate controversy. If you were born after 1985, you might not know why so many controversies have "gate" at the end—as in Irangate, Russiagate, Troopergate, Travelgate, Traingate, Spygate, Tigergate, TaylorSwiftgate. (Okay, I made up the last one, but still.) In a nutshell, here's what happened.

In May 1972, several people broke into the Democratic National Committee's headquarters in the Watergate complex, in Washington, DC. They planted "bugs" in the headquarters' phones and photographed documents. The break-in was successful in the sense that no one even knew about it at the time. But evidently the bugs were faulty. A month later, there was another break-in at the same place. This time, a security guard noticed that the lock on a basement door had been taped over. He called the police, who spotted and arrested the burglars.

At first, the whole event seemed random, even bizarre. The burglars were interested in neither jewelry nor money. They were trying to install microphones in the phones. A puzzle: Why were burglars interested in listening in on conversations in the headquarters of the Democratic National Committee?

It turned out that they had a link to President Nixon. Copies of the White House phone number of Nixon's re-election committee were found in the burglars' belongings. Was the White House behind the criminal action? To alleviate suspicions, the president spoke to the nation in August, reassuring the public that White House employees were not responsible for the break-in. I remember that speech, and it was convincing. Under pressure, Nixon usually delivered.

He won a smashing victory that November, obtaining more than 60 percent of the vote and carrying no fewer than forty-nine of the fifty states. His opponent, George McGovern, was crushed in the Electoral College, 520 to 17. (He won Massachusetts and the District of Columbia.)

It later emerged that there was indeed a connection between the burglary and Nixon's White House. Whether or not Nixon and his team had in some sense authorized the break-in, they had arranged to pay "hush money" after the fact to the burglars, and his White House apparently tried to enlist the Central Intelligence Agency to help counteract the FBI's investigation into the burglary. At its heart, the Watergate scandal is a tale of a cover-up—not the worst thing in the world, but not good. Impeachable? We will get to that.

The investigation—by the media, by the Department of Justice, and by Congress—ended up revealing more and worse. Nixon was abusing presidential authority in ways that involved far more than snooping on Democratic political figures. In view of Nixon's extraordinary skills, his defining achievements, and his genuine sense of patriotism, it is an enduring puzzle how he and his White House could have ended up doing what they did.

My own speculation is that it was a product of the intense political polarization of the time, following the 1960s, in which many millions of people admired Nixon, and many millions of people utterly despised him. Republicans and Democrats saw one another as enemies, producing gross abuse and illegality, on the part of the White House, not all at once but by increments—drip, drip, drip. The president's acute sense of mission and his own rectitude, combined with his fear and loathing of what his (often hate-filled and in some cases nutty) enemies stood for and might do, led to a White House culture that produced, by degrees, a series of measures that (I like to think) would have appalled and horrified Nixon himself at the start of his presidency. The whole story is long and sordid, and you can read all about it elsewhere.

Let's focus instead on the alleged grounds for impeachment. Formally, impeachment proceedings start with the drafting of "articles of impeachment," which are written and voted on by the designated committee within the House of Representatives. If the committee votes in favor, the articles proceed to a vote in the full House. In the case of Nixon, several articles received serious consideration by the Judiciary Committee of the House of Representatives. Because of his resignation, there was no vote in the full House. As we will now see, one of the articles provided a very weak basis for impeachment.[8] One of them, however, offered a very strong basis and two of them were in the middle, but strong enough.

No

The Internal Revenue Service ruled that in his first years in office, Nixon underpaid his taxes by a total of more than $400,000. Note that he did that as president, not as private citizen.

That's a lot of money (especially if you adjust for inflation). You could argue that such a large underpayment, from a president with access to the finest legal advice, was a product of something much worse than mere negligence. But tax evasion isn't an impeachable offense. It's not an abuse of official authority. It's in a wholly different category from the high crimes and misdemeanors that concerned Madison and Hamilton, and that would justify impeachment. The vote against proceeding was 26 to 12.[9] It should have been 38 to 0. (To the twelve Democrats who voted in favor: not good.)

Probably

The House and Senate are fiercely protective of their own prerogatives, not least when they are seeking materials from the executive branch. They take their investigations seriously (even if their principal or sole motivation is political). They do not like to be thwarted. For its part, the executive branch is deeply suspicious of investigations, thinking that they are efforts to make political hay. Its officials do not love to hand over documents. They are fiercely protective of their own deliberative processes, and that is true whether the president is Republican or Democratic.

If White House officials are speaking to one another behind closed doors, the president's lawyers will not want Congress or the public to know what they have said. And if the president himself is involved in the conversations, the executive branch will vigorously resist disclosure. There is a legitimate reason for that resistance: if advisers are to be candid, and to venture their arguments and express concerns, it is important for them to know that they can speak in confidence. With this point in mind, the executive branch will probably even claim that the Constitution itself protects the president's right to keep things confidential.

In 1974, the Supreme Court agreed with that claim, ruling that the president has a presumptive right not to disclose his conversations. (The case had a terrific name: *United States v. Nixon*.) The Court emphasized the need for candor. In its view, a presidency cannot function if the boss and his advisers are unable to keep their discussions private. At the same time, the Court ruled that the presumption could be overcome by a showing of a demonstrated, specific need for evidence in a pending criminal trial. (And so the United States won, not Nixon.[10]) The *Nixon* holding does not speak to legislative investigations. But you could read the Court's opinion to suggest that if Congress believes that the president has committed a crime, if that belief has some evidentiary basis, and if Congress can make a strong showing that it has a critical need for specific information for legitimate purposes, it can probably get the information it seeks.[11]

Before the Court's decision, Nixon refused to comply with the Committee's subpoenas. By a narrow vote of 21 to 17, the Judiciary Committee found, in that very refusal, a basis for impeachment. (Democrats voted in favor, 19 to 2; Republicans voted against, 2 to 15.) In its third article of impeachment, it made this charge:

Richard M. Nixon . . . has failed without lawful cause or excuse to produce papers and things as directed by duly authorized subpoenas issued by the Committee . . . and willfully disobeyed such subpoenas. The subpoenaed papers and things were deemed necessary by the Committee in order to resolve by direct evidence fundamental, factual questions relating to Presidential direction, knowledge or approval of actions demonstrated by other evidence to be substantial grounds for impeachment of the President.[12]

That seems pretty grave. In a way, it certainly is. But by itself, disobedience of a subpoena is not necessarily an impeachable offense. Everything depends on what the subpoena is *for*. Consider three categories of cases:

∷ A subpoena asks for all emails between the president and his advisers on a specific topic, and his lawyers claim executive privilege. To the extent that the president has a constitutional basis for resisting a subpoena, or even a good-faith argument that he is entitled to do that, there is no legitimate basis for impeachment.[13] The reason is that, in such a situation, the president has not done anything that comes close to a high crime or misdemeanor. We are not speaking of a large-scale abuse of presidential power. Instead we are dealing with a conflict between the branches.

∷ A subpoena is based on suspicion of wrongdoing—calling for all emails from the president relating to his allegedly unlawful income-tax evasion—and the White House refuses to comply. It has no good-faith argument that executive privilege is available, but the underlying offense is not impeachable. Here as well, there is no legitimate basis for impeachment. Presidents should cooperate with legitimate investigations, but it is not a high crime or misdemeanor to refuse to cooperate with a congressional investigation into an offense that is not independently impeachable. Congress cannot gin up an impeachable offense by investigating an offense that is not impeachable, and then encountering presidential resistance. The theory here is simple: if the underlying conduct is not impeachable, it is not impeachable for the president to resist an investigation of that conduct. (We could imagine a more elaborate cover-up that would test this proposition; I will get to that issue in due course.)

∴ A subpoena is based on suspicion of independently impeachable wrongdoing—say, treason or bribery—and the White House refuses to comply, even though the president lacks executive privilege, or even a good-faith justification for asserting it. It is tempting to think that the answer is easy. Surely the president can be impeached for unlawfully refusing to cooperate when Congress is investigating impeachable misconduct on his part!

Almost surely so, but there are arguments on both sides. On the one hand, the failure to comply with a subpoena that stems from (mere) suspicion of independently impeachable actions is hardly as grave as those actions. Maybe the suspicion is unfounded. Maybe the actions never took place. Maybe the president thinks that he is being subjected to a witch hunt, or at least a politically motivated effort to damage him.

On the other hand, the Constitution certainly gives the House the authority to investigate whether impeachable wrongdoing has occurred. If the president declines to cooperate with a lawful investigation, and if he has no good-faith argument that he is legally entitled to do so, there is a strong argument that he has committed a misdemeanor within the meaning of the impeachment clause. And this, in fact, appears to be the claim in what formally became the third article of impeachment against Nixon, part of which is reprinted above.

My own vote would be in favor of impeachment. If the president refuses to cooperate with a lawful investigation into whether he has done something impeachable, he is abusing his power. But it's not the easiest question, so I will leave it at a firm "probably."

Yes

The article of impeachment that the Judiciary Committee placed first in its final draft referred to the Watergate controversy itself—to the unlawful entry into the headquarters of the Democratic National Committee "for the purpose of securing official intelligence."[14] There was no claim that Nixon had directed the unlawful inquiry. In the words of the article itself, he had been behind an elaborate conspiracy to cover it up by:

1. Making false or misleading statements to lawfully authorized investigative officers and employees of the United States;
2. Withholding relevant and material evidence or information from lawfully authorized investigative officers and employees of the United States;
3. Approving, condoning, acquiescing in, and counselling witnesses with respect to the giving of false or misleading statements to lawfully authorized investigative officers

and employees of the United States and false or misleading testimony in duly instituted judicial and congressional proceedings;

4. Interfering or endeavouring to interfere with the conduct of investigations by the Department of Justice of the United States, the Federal Bureau of Investigation, the office of Watergate Special Prosecution Force, and Congressional Committees;

5. Approving, condoning, and acquiescing in, the surreptitious payment of substantial sums of money for the purpose of obtaining the silence or influencing the testimony of witnesses, potential witnesses or individuals who participated in such unlawful entry and other illegal activities;

6. Endeavouring to misuse the Central Intelligence Agency, an agency of the United States;

7. Disseminating information received from officers of the Department of Justice of the United States to subjects of investigations conducted by lawfully authorized investigative officers and employees of the United States, for the purpose of aiding and assisting such subjects in their attempts to avoid criminal liability;

8. Making or causing to be made false or misleading public statements for the purpose of deceiving the people of the United States into believing that a thorough and complete investigation had been conducted with respect to allegations of misconduct on the part of personnel of the executive branch of the United States and personnel of the Committee for the Re-election of the President, and that there was no involvement of such personnel in such misconduct; or

9. Endeavouring to cause prospective defendants, and individuals duly tried and convicted, to expect favoured treatment and consideration in return for their silence or false testimony, or rewarding individuals for their silence or false testimony.[15]

The Judiciary Committee voted in favor of this article by a whopping margin of 27 to 11. But the margin conceals a big partisan difference. All twenty-one Democrats on the Committee supported it; only six of seventeen Republicans did so. Let's underline that. The Democrats were unanimous. By a strong majority, the Republicans voted the other way.[16]

This article almost certainly established an impeachable offense. The president's own campaign committee committed unlawful acts to promote his reelection (a patent violation of democratic norms, itself impeachable if undertaken at the president's direction). When those unlawful acts came to light, the president did not disclose them, as he should have, but instead used official power, sometimes in violation of the law, to prevent people from knowing about them. The sheer accumulation of charges (nine of them!) makes that argument compelling.

It is true that under the framework that we are using, there is another view: *It is not impeachable to use official power to cover up an action that is not itself impeachable.* Suppose that the president committed some clearly nonimpeachable offense—say, tax evasion, speeding, occasional use of recreational drugs. Suppose that he used the apparatus of the federal government to reduce the likelihood that anyone would find out about it. By analogy to the failure to respond to a subpoena, it could be urged that there has been no high crime or misdemeanor. But the analogy probably fails. Active, thoroughgoing use of the apparatus of the federal government—at least on the scale reflected in charges one through nine above—looks like a plenty high-enough misdemeanor.

We should acknowledge that the question would be tougher if we took some of those items in isolation. By itself, charge eight, while plenty awful, may not have the magnitude that would justify impeachment. The worst is probably charge six. Everything depends on the details, but efforts to engage the CIA to prevent disclosure of wrongdoing by the president's campaign committee is unquestionably a misdemeanor in the constitutional sense.

Emphatically Yes

Nixon was separately charged with offenses that fall within the core of the impeachment clause. In what became the second article, the vote of the Judiciary Committee was the same as for the cover-up article, with the identical partisan breakdown. If we assume that the second article accurately stated the facts, the vote should have been unanimous; partisanship prevented many Republicans from doing their constitutional duty.

Here are the three strongest charges:

1. He has, acting personally and through his subordinates and agents, endeavoured to obtain from the Internal Revenue Service, in violation of the constitutional rights of

citizens, confidential information contained in income tax returns for purposes not authorized by law, and to cause, in violation of the constitutional rights of citizens, income tax audits or other income tax investigations to be initiated or conducted in a discriminatory manner.

2. He misused the Federal Bureau of Investigation, the Secret Service, and other executive personnel, in violation or disregard of the constitutional rights of citizens, by directing or authorizing such agencies or personnel to conduct or continue electronic surveillance or other investigations for purposes unrelated to national security, the enforcement of laws, or any other lawful function of his office; he did direct, authorize, or permit the use of information obtained thereby for purposes unrelated to national security, the enforcement of laws, or any other lawful function of his office; and he did direct the concealment of certain records made by the Federal Bureau of Investigation of electronic surveillance.

3. He has, acting personally and through his subordinates and agents, in violation or disregard of the constitutional rights of citizens, authorized and permitted to be maintained a secret investigative unit within the office of the President, financed in part with money derived from campaign contributions, which unlawfully utilized the resources of the Central Intelligence Agency, engaged in covert and unlawful activities, and attempted to prejudice the constitutional right of an accused to a fair trial.[17]

It's tough to argue about those three.[18] Indeed, they get at the core of the concerns expressed during the ratification debates in Massachusetts back in 1787, when the impeachment provision was directly linked with the preservation of liberty. If a president uses the apparatus of government in an unlawful way, to compromise democratic processes and to invade constitutional rights, we come to the heart of what the impeachment provision is all about.

If we ever get there again, let's keep the republic.

Sex and Lies

In the two actual impeachments of American presidents, no impeachable offense was committed. In a sense, the founding document worked: the Senate refused to convict. Still, the nation was badly served.

Decades after it happened, the impeachment of Bill Clinton is almost incomprehensible, at least if it is explored in light of the debates in the late eighteenth century. You would have to work really hard to make a minimally plausible argument that Clinton committed an impeachable offense. But he gave his political opponents an opening, and they were willing to work really hard.

Clinton had an extraordinary ability to connect with people. He was also a successful president, with a quick mind and a capacity to listen and to compromise. His was an era of peace and prosperity. But he had something in common with Nixon: he provoked implacable political opposition. Long before serious allegations were made, his opponents hated him, and they wanted to impeach him. For years, they were in search of plausible grounds. In their opposition to him, they were relentless.

One reason was his political genius. The first two-term

Democratic president since Franklin Delano Roosevelt, he was agile and flexible, and a terrific improviser. But from the start, his opponents distrusted him. They thought that he was a liar, interested in political success but unprincipled. They called him "Slick Willie," and they accused him of every imaginable form of wrongdoing. He was definitely slick, but as it happened, he was innocent of almost all of the charges. But as he said on television during his initial presidential campaign, he had "caused pain in his marriage," and he continued to cause his marriage pain while serving as president.

The process began with a 1994 investigation into real estate investments made by Bill and Hillary Clinton. The two invested in the Whitewater Development Corporation, which ended up failing. The investigation was eventually overseen by Kenneth Starr, a distinguished lawyer and former judge. No one ever charged the Clintons with wrongdoing in connection with Whitewater, but Starr's authority was repeatedly expanded, to the point where he was investigating a wide range of controversies, including the firing of travel personnel at the White House and a sexual harassment lawsuit brought against Clinton by Paula Jones, an Arkansas employee who alleged that Clinton propositioned her. As part of the Jones investigation, Starr ended up exploring alleged wrongdoing in connection with Clinton's sexual relationship with Monica Lewinsky, a White House intern whose name arose in the early stages of Jones's lawsuit.

Eventually Starr produced a lengthy report on that relationship, including salacious details and a series of claims about violations of the law by the president. There has never been a prosecutor's report quite like Starr's. If it were a movie, you wouldn't bring your children. But it was also written like a legal brief. It contained these words: "There Is Substantial and Credible Information that President Clinton Committed Acts that May Constitute Grounds for an Impeachment."[19] Starr's focus was entirely on Clinton's relationship with Lewinsky and his various efforts to cover it up, not only by lying to his wife, his staff, the cabinet, and the American people, but also by perjuring himself and obstructing justice.

Did Clinton commit high crimes or misdemeanors? In Starr's report, it would be difficult to find any.[20] Nonetheless, Starr himself seemed to think so, and the president's opponents in the House of Representatives tried to build directly on the Nixon precedent. They spoke of perjury and of obstruction of justice. Focusing on perjury, the first article of impeachment included the following charge:

Contrary to [his] oath, William Jefferson Clinton willfully provided perjurious, false and misleading testimony to the grand jury concerning one or more of the following:

1. the nature and details of his relationship with a subordinate Government employee;
2. prior perjurious, false and misleading testimony he gave in a Federal civil rights action brought against him;
3. prior false and misleading statements he allowed his attorney to make to a Federal judge in that civil rights action; and

4. his corrupt efforts to influence the testimony of witnesses and to impede the discovery of evidence in that civil rights action.[21]

If the claims are true, Clinton did commit perjury in connection with his efforts to cover up a sexual relationship. That's unlawful. But under the constitutional framework, it's not close to a basis for impeachment, because it's not an egregious abuse of presidential authority. Nonetheless, the House voted to impeach, 228 to 206.[22] As in the Nixon case, the vote was along partisan lines—but even more so. Only five Democrats voted for that article, and only five Republicans against it.

The second article focused on obstruction of justice, with particular reference to the Paula Jones lawsuit. It alleged a "course of conduct or scheme" including various acts:

1. On or about December 17, 1997, William Jefferson Clinton corruptly encouraged a witness in a Federal civil rights action brought against him to execute a sworn affidavit in that proceeding that he knew to be perjurious, false and misleading.

2. On or about December 17, 1997, William Jefferson Clinton corruptly encouraged a witness in a Federal civil rights action brought against him to give perjurious, false and misleading testimony if and when called to testify personally in that proceeding.

3. On or about December 28, 1997, William Jefferson Clinton corruptly engaged in, encouraged, or supported a scheme to conceal evidence that had been subpoenaed in a Federal civil rights action brought against him.

4. Beginning on or about December 7, 1997, and continuing through and including January 14, 1998, William Jefferson Clinton intensified and succeeded in an effort to secure job assistance to a witness in a Federal civil rights action brought against him in order to corruptly prevent the truthful testimony of that witness in that proceeding at a time when the truthful testimony of that witness would have been harmful to him.[23]

There's more, but it's all in this vein. No one should trivialize obstruction of justice. If you're sued, you shouldn't engage in anything like these acts, and if you do, you might feel the force of the criminal law.

But recall the context. Paula Jones sued Clinton for sexual harassment, based on his alleged conduct well before he became president. Clinton was charged with undertaking a variety of unlawful steps to reduce her chances of victory. Most of those steps involved efforts to persuade Monica Lewinsky to lie. That's not good, but it is hardly close to the kind of thing that concerned Hamilton, Madison, and their colleagues. We aren't speaking here of systematic violation of civil liberty, or acquisition of the office by unlawful means, or the grave misuses of official authority that triggered impeachment proceedings in the American colonies.

The House voted to impeach by a count of 221 to 212. Yet again, nearly all Republicans favored impeachment, and nearly all Democrats didn't. On the perjury charge, the Senate voted to acquit by a margin of 55 to 45. On the obstruction charge, the vote was 50 to 50. Yet again, partisanship mattered; all 45 Democratic senators voted to acquit. Only

ten of the 55 Senate Republicans voted to acquit on the perjury charge, and only five on the obstruction charge.

The Unitary Executive Again

Andrew Johnson was impeached in 1868 for just one reason:
he fired Edwin Stanton, the secretary of war (now called the
secretary of defense), and he tried to replace Stanton with
someone he preferred. You might well ask: Isn't the president allowed to choose the Secretary of Defense? Doesn't he
get to fire members of his own cabinet?

Excellent questions. You will remember that the framers
created a unitary presidency. That is generally taken to mean
that under the Constitution, the president can get rid of
members of his own cabinet. Congress has no authority to
limit that power. That's certainly what Johnson believed.
And ultimately, the Supreme Court agreed with him.[24]

Nonetheless, Congress enacted a law that it called the
Tenure of Office Act, which was specifically designed to forbid the president from removing certain executive officials,
including the secretary of war, without the Senate's approval. The law said that those officials "shall hold their offices respectively for and during the term of the President by
whom they may have been appointed and for one month
thereafter, subject to removal by and with the consent of the
Senate."[25] Believing that the Tenure of Office Act was unconstitutional, Johnson ignored it. So the House impeached
him.

Of course there was a dramatic political background.
Johnson had become president only because of the assassi-

nation of Abraham Lincoln. After the Civil War, the nation was embroiled in a debate about how to reconstruct the defeated South, and how to reunify the nation. Although Johnson was from the South, many in a group within the Republican Party, sometimes described as the Radical Republicans, hoped and believed that he would adopt an aggressive set of programs during Reconstruction, designed above all to protect and assist the newly freed slaves. Johnson badly disappointed them. He proved far more cautious than they expected, and as they saw it, far more solicitous of the defeated South.

Emboldened by electoral success, the Radical Republicans enacted the Tenure of Office Act specifically to protect Stanton, who generally shared their views. More than that, the Tenure of Office Act was designed to threaten and to trigger impeachment. It explicitly said that if the president violated it, he would be committing a "high misdemeanor." Gosh. As far as I am aware, nothing like that has ever happened in American history, either before or since. Johnson paid no attention.

In response, the House passed no fewer than eleven articles of impeachment. They're endless as well as redundant. The first article complained about Johnson's order to dismiss Stanton:

Which order was unlawfully issued, and with intent then and there to violate the act entitled "An act regulating the tenure of certain civil office," passed March 2, 1867, and contrary to the provisions of said act, and in violation thereof, and contrary to the provisions of the Constitution of the United States, and without the advice and consent of the Senate of the United States, the said Senate then and there being in session, to remove said E. M. Stanton from the office of Secretary for the Department of War, whereby said Andrew Johnson, President of the United States, did then and there commit, and was guilty of a high misdemeanor in office.[26]

Saying so doesn't make it so. Johnson had a good-faith argument that he was acting in accordance with his constitutional authority.[27] For those who sought to impeach Johnson, things were even worse. As I have noted, the Supreme Court eventually ruled that Johnson was exactly right on the Constitution, which forbids Congress from requiring the president to obtain the Senate's consent before firing members of his cabinet.[28]

In the House, the vote against Johnson was overwhelming: 126 to 47.[29] Johnson narrowly avoided conviction in the Senate, whose 35 to 19 vote to convict fell just one short of a two-thirds majority.[30] All nine Democrats voted Not Guilty; just ten of the 45 Republicans joined them. Johnson was a terrible president, but his impeachment violated the constitutional plan.

Non-Presidential Impeachments

In American history, the House of Representatives has impeached just nineteen officials. The Senate found eight guilty and acquitted seven. One impeachment was dismissed for technical reasons. Three officials who were impeached ended up resigning.[31] The U.S. House of Representatives has published a full accounting, reproduced below.[32]

As we can see, only one United States senator was impeached, in 1797: William Blount, who had fought in the Revolutionary War. Strapped for cash, Blount conspired with the British to help England conquer parts of Spanish Louisiana and Florida. After the impeachment, the Senate voted to expel him by a two-thirds vote. The impeachment trial in the Senate was dismissed on the grounds that the Senate lacked the authority to impeach its own members. (There was also an objection that he had already been removed from office and for that reason may not have been impeachable.)

Justice Samuel Chase was impeached in 1804 for allegedly engaging in arbitrary and oppressive treatment of parties before his court.[33] In one case, he was said to have acted as a prosecutor rather than a judge. In another, he refused to discharge a grand jury after it declined to indict a printer who had allegedly engaged in seditious behavior. Chase was widely regarded as a highly partisan judge. William Belknap, the secretary of war, was impeached in 1876 for bribery. In 1912, a judge on the United States Commerce Court, Robert Archibald, was impeached for influence-peddling with litigants.

A strong majority of impeached officials—thirteen of the nineteen—have been federal district court judges. Of the fifteen non-presidential impeachments, only eight were convicted: Pickering, Humphreys, Archibald, Ritter, Claiborne, Hastings, Nixon, and Porteous. Delahay, Belknap, English, and Kent resigned before the Senate vote.

CHART I

History of Impeachments by the House of Representatives

Individual	Position	House Action / Charges
William Blount	U.S. senator from Tennessee	Impeached July 7, 1797, on charges of conspiring to assist in Great Britain's attempt to seize Spanish-controlled territories in modern-day Florida and Louisiana
John Pickering	Judge, U.S. district court, District of New Hampshire	Impeached March 2, 1803, on charges of intoxication on the bench and unlawful handling of property claims
Samuel Chase	Associate justice, U.S. Supreme Court	Impeached March 12, 1804, on charges of arbitrary and oppressive conduct of trials
James H. Peck	Judge, U.S. district court, Western district of Tennessee	Impeached April 24, 1830, on charges of abuse of the contempt power
West H. Humphreys	Judge, U.S. district court, Western district of Tennessee	Impeached May 6, 1862, on charges of refusing to hold court and waging war against the U.S. government
Andrew Johnson	President of the United States	Impeached February 24, 1868, on charges of violating the Tenure of Office Act by removing Secretary of War Edwin Stanton from office

Senate Trial	Result
December 17, 1798–January 14, 1799	Charges dismissed for want of jurisdiction; Blount had been expelled from the U.S. Senate before his trial
March 3, 1803–March 12, 1804	Found guilty; removed from office
December 7, 1804–March 1, 1805	Acquitted
April 26, 1830–January 31, 1831	Acquitted
June 9, 1862–June 26, 1862	Found guilty; removed from office and disqualified from future office
February 25–May 26, 1868	Acquitted

Individual	Position	House Action / Charges
Mark H. Delahay	Judge, U.S. district court, Kansas	Impeached February 28, 1873, on charges of intoxication on the bench
William W. Belknap	U.S. Secretary of War	Impeached March 2, 1876, on charges of criminal disregard for his office and accepting payments in exchange for making official appointments
Charles Swayne	Judge, U.S. district court, Northern district of Florida	Impeached December 13, 1904, on charges of abuse of contempt power and other misuses of office
Robert W. Archibald	Associate judge, U.S. Commerce Court	Impeached July 11, 1912, on charges of improper business relationship with litigants
George W. English	Judge, U.S. district court, Eastern district of Illinois	Impeached April 1, 1926, on charges of abuse of power
Harold Louderback	Judge, U.S. district court, Northern district of California	Impeached February 24, 1933, on charges of favoritism in the appointment of bankruptcy receivers
Halsted L. Ritter	Judge, U.S. district court, Southern district of Florida	Impeached March 2, 1936, on charges of favoritism in the appointment of bankruptcy receivers and practicing law as a sitting judge

Senate Trial	Result
No trial held	Resigned prior to trial
March 3–August 1, 1876	Acquitted
December 14, 1904– February 27, 1905	Acquitted
July 13, 1912–January 13, 1913	Found guilty; removed from office and disqualified from future office
April 23–December 13, 1926	Resigned November 4, 1926; proceedings dismissed December 13, 1926
May 15–24, 1933	Acquitted
March 10–April 17, 1936	Found guilty; removed from office

Individual	Position	House Action / Charges
Harry E. Claiborne	Judge, U.S. district court of Nevada	Impeached July 22, 1986, on charges of income tax evasion and of remaining on the bench following criminal conviction
Alcee L. Hastings	Judge, U.S. district court, Southern district of Florida	Impeached August 3, 1988, on charges of perjury and conspiring to solicit a bribe
Walter L. Nixon	Judge, U.S. district court, Southern district of Mississippi	Impeached May 10, 1989, on charges of perjury before a federal grand jury
William J. Clinton	President of the United States	Impeached December 19, 1998, on charges of lying under oath to a federal grand jury and obstruction of justice
Samuel B. Kent	Judge, U.S. district court for the Southern district of Texas	Impeached June 19, 2009, on charges of sexual assault, obstructing and impeding an official proceeding, and making false and misleading statements
G. Thomas Porteous, Jr.	Judge, U.S. district court, Eastern district of Louisiana	Impeached March 11, 2010, on charges of accepting bribes and making false statements under penalty of perjury

Senate Trial	Result
October 7–9, 1986	Found guilty; removed from office
October 18–20, 1989	Found guilty; removed from office
November 1–3, 1989	Found guilty; removed from office
January 7–February 12, 1999	Acquitted
June 24–July 22, 2009	Resigned June 30, 2009, before the completion of the trial; H. Res. 661 ended the proceedings
December 7–8, 2010	Found guilty; removed from office and disqualified from holding future office

Of Judges and Presidents

In American history, there have been more than three thousand federal judges, and some of them have proved highly controversial—usually because of their rulings, which have alienated large segments of the population, and sometimes because of their actions on and off the bench, which have ranged from the unseemly to the unsavory to the unlawful. Since the 1950s, justices on both the left and the right have upset a lot of people; consider Chief Justices Earl Warren and William Rehnquist, and also Justices William Brennan and Antonin Scalia. Even so, we have not seen a lot of politically motivated impeachment proceedings.

In general, Americans respect and even revere the idea of judicial independence, and controversial, even despised rulings have not triggered serious impeachment inquiries. To that extent, the House of Representatives has shown impressive restraint, and judicial impeachments have usually satisfied the constitutional standard. Under the constitutional text, acceptance of a bribe is easy, and if judges are randomly disbarring lawyers or refusing to hear witnesses, they are committing misdemeanors. But in some of the cases, the grounds invoked by the House of Representatives were pretty shaky. Harry Claiborne was not shown to have abused distinctly judicial powers, and you could make the same argument about Walter Nixon. Some of the grounds for impeaching Mark Delahay and Charles Swayne also seem to fall short of the constitutional standard. What should we make of this?

One answer is to say that some of the judicial impeachments have a feature in common with the Clinton and Johnson impeachments: they are clear deviations from the Constitution. That's probably right. After all, the constitutional standard for impeachment and conviction of federal judges is exactly the same as the standard for the president.[34]

But there is another and more interesting answer, which is that there is a real difference between judicial and presidential impeachments. Even though the constitutional text is the same, the structure of the Constitution and its surrounding context suggest possible reasons for taking special caution before impeaching presidents, and for allowing a mildly different and somewhat lower bar for impeaching federal judges.

Begin with history: one of the framers' particular concerns, voiced in the Constitutional Convention, was the need to protect the president from the authority of Congress; they sought to insulate him in particular. Sure, they much wanted to ensure judicial independence as well, but the debates focused on the importance of ensuring that the president would not be within the control of Congress. As we have seen, essentially all of their debates were about the president, not federal judges, and the ratification debates were also preoccupied with the relationship between the president and Congress.

Turn to pragmatic considerations: impeachment of the president is uniquely destabilizing. Sure, it's a grave act to impeach a federal judge, and doing so can endanger judicial independence, but outside of the most unusual situations, it does not exactly threaten a national crisis. It's relevant that federal judges have life tenure. If judges can be impeached only for the most horrific abuses, then the nation will be stuck with terrible judges for their whole lives. The president has only a four-year term, which means that he can be thrown out, which argues for a higher bar for impeaching him.

I do not mean to make too much of these suggestions. Again, the constitutional standard is the same. The largest point is that with just a few exceptions, the House of Representatives has shown immense respect for the standards established by the constitutional framework, even though the controversial role of the federal judiciary must have made it tempting, on many occasions, not to do so.

chapter 7

Twenty-One Cases

Many first-year law students are surprised to see that in their early classes, most professors don't lecture. Instead they offer an infuriating and seemingly endless stream of "hypotheticals"— specific problems, real or imagined, about legal problems. They try to elicit students' judgments, and they use those judgments as the foundation for discussion.

From one point of view, this way of thinking about law and public policy is pretty silly. If you put people on the spot in a classroom, they'll consult their intuitions and tell you their immediate reactions. Should policy and law be based on intuitions and immediate reactions? The entire constitutional order can be seen as an emphatic answer: "NO!"

Hamilton, Madison, and their colleagues made one truly original contribution to political thought, which was to reject the long-standing view, shared by some of history's greatest thinkers (including Montesquieu himself), that republics should be small and homogenous. They suggested instead that *a large republic, with diverse people, would be the best way to produce a deliberative democracy*. In their conception of democracy, as Justice Louis Brandeis put it, "the deliberative forces should prevail over the arbitrary"—and deliberation would entail circumspection, not intuition.

Theirs was a republic of reasons. They didn't think that law and policy should result from people's immediate reactions to a long series of hypothetical questions.

At the same time, the approach in law school classrooms does have one big virtue: it avoids premature resort to abstractions, which can produce big trouble. The great British poet William Blake once scribbled in a margin, "To Generalize is to be an Idiot; To Particularize is the Alone Distinction of Merit."[1] To be sure, that's itself a generalization, so in a sense, Blake's claim is self-contradictory and self-defeating. But let's not be fussy. Blake was right.

On some issues, an excellent way to make progress is by offering an assortment of problems and asking how best to deal with them. Of course you can't do that in the dark. Some kind of orienting framework is necessary to discipline the analysis. But with respect to impeachment, history provides us with a framework, under which the central question is whether we have an egregious abuse of official power.

My strategy will be to begin with a set of easy cases, in which impeachment is obviously legitimate. From there I turn to cases that are also easy, but for the opposite reason: impeachment would be obviously unconstitutional, even if the American public wants it, and even if the president has done something terribly wrong. I conclude with a series of harder cases, where reasonable people can differ. In such cases, I suggest, an institutional resolution is not a terrible idea: *Where the constitutional issue is reasonably debated, and where no resolution is clearly correct, We the People, acting through our elected representatives, get to decide.*

Easy Cases: Impeachable

1. A president has admiration and sympathy for a foreign nation that wishes to do harm to the United States. While in office, he reveals classified information to leaders of that nation, with the clear intention of strengthening it and of weakening his own country.

    The president can be impeached. He may have committed treason. The Constitution offers a definition: "Treason against the United States, shall consist only in levying war against them, or in adhering to their enemies, giving them aid and comfort." We would need to do some work to know whether the president's action fits within the technical definition, which would require interpretation of the words "enemies," "adhering," and "aid and comfort." But whether or not it's treason, it clearly counts as a high crime or misdemeanor.

2. A president is overseeing the development of his budget, which will be submitted to Congress. Makers of electric cars promise him that if he supports a tax credit for their vehicles, they will put a lot of money into his personal bank account, either immediately or after he leaves office. He agrees.

    The president can be impeached. He has accepted a bribe in connection with his exercise of presidential authority.

3. A president is seeking to obtain public support for his health reform plan. A prominent insurance company dislikes his plan. The president tells the head of the company: "If you support the plan, I will find a way to send

some of my own money your way. Maybe not now, maybe not while I am president, but eventually. You won't be sorry."

The president can be impeached. He has tried to bribe someone in connection with his exercise of presidential authority.

We could complicate this case by reimagining it as one of deal-making, involving not the president's personal funds, but a more informal kind of you-scratch-my-back-and-I'll-scratch-yours. Deal-making is hardly impeachable. A president is entitled to tell the head of a company that if it supports health care reform, he will not proceed with some other plan that the company dislikes. That is not bribery in the constitutional sense. But some deals are out of bounds: if a president tells a company that if it supports his plan, he will make sure that it receives a government contract (whether or not it deserves it), we seem to have a case of bribery—and if so, the president can be impeached.

4. (a) A president orders one of his subordinates to murder a political opponent, because he is a political opponent. (b) A president orders one of his subordinates to beat up a political opponent, because he is a political opponent. (c) A president orders the Internal Revenue Service to investigate a political opponent, because he is a political opponent.

In all of these cases, the president can be impeached. In (a) and (b), he has almost certainly committed a crime, and a high one, but whether or not that is so, he has committed a misdemeanor within the meaning of the Constitution: the use of physical force against a political opponent is an egregious abuse of presidential power. The same conclusion is appropriate for (c) if we stipulate that the president has no basis for thinking that the opponent has violated the tax laws. If so, we have a misdemeanor in the constitutional sense.

To make things more complicated, suppose that the political opponent has, in fact, violated tax laws, and the president is aware of that—but his desire to punish a political opponent is really what motivates him to exercise what he sees as his authority over the Internal Revenue Service. That's a bit trickier, but in the end, it's not all that hard. It's a misdemeanor, in the constitutional sense, for the president to use his authority to single out political opponents for law enforcement activity. Use of official power to punish political opponents is near the core of the category of impeachable offenses.

5. A president decides to spend six months in London. He explains that he adores London, and the history, and the shopping, and he needs a break. There is no reason to think that he is disloyal to the United States. He simply needs a break. He adds that he will discharge the duties of his office "when he has time," and he expects to have time.

The president can be impeached. He has committed no crime, but he is neglecting his constitutional duties in a patently egregious way. A president is allowed to have plenty of golf weekends and even some vacations. But he cannot decide that he needs six months in a foreign country, even if he asserts that while there, he will do what he needs to do as president.

6. A president likes police officers—a lot. He believes that they have been unfairly treated. He announces that if any

police officer is accused of murder or assault, he will exercise his pardon power, and pardon that officer in full.

The president can be impeached. He has essentially said that he will authorize murder and assault. He is exercising his official authority in a way that promotes grotesque misconduct. He may or may not have committed a crime, but that doesn't matter. He has abused distinctly presidential powers in an egregious manner.

7. A president is elected as a result of a secret plan with a nation that is unfriendly to the United States. As part of that plan, the president has worked closely, and personally, with leaders of that nation to disseminate false information about his political opponent. There is no quid pro quo, but the president's election has unquestionably been facilitated by an explicit plan.

The president can be impeached. To be sure, the relevant action occurred before the president assumed office. On the basis of the constitutional text and context, it might be tempting to argue that impeachable offenses *are limited to those that occur while the president is in office.* But the debates at the Convention suggest that if the president procures office by objectionable means, impeachment is available. Indeed, the debates suggest that cases of this kind are defining examples of what impeachment is for. Recall George Mason's words: "Shall the man who has practiced corruption & by that means procured his appointment in the first instance, be suffered to escape punishment, by repeating his guilt?"

This view has logic on its side. The Constitution aspires to governance by We the People. If the president obtains office through illicit means—and worse, by collaborating with a foreign country—self-governance has been compromised. Impeachment is available.

8. A president uses the FBI and the CIA in order to obtain incriminating evidence about, and in an attempt to punish, political adversaries. He orders them to engage in various forms of surveillance, and he plans to use whatever he learns in order to embarrass those adversaries through the press, and possibly to initiate criminal proceedings.

   The president is impeachable. Whether or not such conduct involves a technical violation of the criminal law, it amounts to an impeachable offense, in the form of an egregious abuse of the power of the office. Recall the ratification debates in Massachusetts, which pointed to violations of liberties as impeachable offenses. In the problem at hand, we might have a technical violation of the First and Fourth Amendments. Even if we don't, we have a violation of the most basic democratic principles.

9. During a war or a domestic crisis, a president fails to perform the basic tasks of his job, not because he makes choices with which many people disagree, but because he has essentially defaulted. The default may be a result of stress, drunkenness, mental illness, boredom, physical problems, or sheer laziness.

   The president is impeachable. Here, too, there is no crime, but he has committed a misdemeanor and can be removed from office. Recall that Madison pointed to "neglect of duty" as a basis for impeachment, and here we have an egregious neglect of duty. True, we have to be careful with the whole idea, lest political disagreement, or public disappointment or outrage, be transformed into a claim of impeachable neglect. And true, this case requires an amendment of our governing principle, which reads high crimes and misdemeanors as egregious abuses of public power. That principle captures the core of the concept, but not all of it. A failure to do one's job is a misdemeanor too.

Easy Cases: Not Impeachable

10. A president issues an executive order requiring his Environmental Protection Agency to issue certain regulations under the Clean Air Act. In the view of most informed observers, the regulations are in clear violation of the Clean Air Act and therefore unlawful. True, some people believe that the regulations are lawful, but they are in a small minority. The Supreme Court unanimously strikes down the regulations that the president ordered.

The president cannot be impeached. Every president—Reagan and Clinton, Bush and Obama, Roosevelt and Truman and Eisenhower—has suffered and will suffer significant losses in court. The president is perfectly entitled to act in a way that defies the majority view among legal specialists. So long as a legal defense can be mounted in good faith, there is no plausible basis for impeachment, even if the Supreme Court unanimously agrees that the president is wrong. The reason is that a president who acts in accordance with a good-faith legal argument is not engaging in an egregious abuse of presidential authority, even if he is wrong.

11. In the aftermath of a terrorist attack, a president issues a series of executive orders designed to combat terrorism. Some of those orders strike many Americans as draconian, severe, and "un-American." One of them imposes aggressive new security restrictions at airports, which include intrusive personal questions to people who have been "profiled" as potentially suspicious. Another order authorizes what some people consider to be torture (for example, waterboarding). Several of them are invalidated in court on constitutional grounds. In the face of those rulings, the president's opponents argue that he has acted unconstitutionally and violated his oath of office, and that he has ordered his subordinates to commit crimes.[2] His opponents add that the president is constitutionally obliged to "take care that the laws be faithfully executed"—and he has not done that.

The president cannot be impeached. This case is harder than the last case, and perhaps it cannot fairly be counted as easy, because it involves a series of unlawful actions rather than merely one, and also human rights violations. But it is not all *that* hard, at least if the president has a good-faith argument that his orders are lawful. It is not an impeachable offense to reach a series of legal conclusions that both courts and international law reject. Violation of the oath of office (the claim of the first article proposed during the Clinton impeachment) is a red herring—a form of foolishness. The Constitution does not make any such violation a reason for impeachment. It requires a high crime or misdemeanor.

To be sure, we can revise this case in a way that moves it into the realm of the difficult or even the obviously impeachable. If the draconian measures reach a certain level of severity, such that a good-faith argument in their defense is unavailable, we have a misdemeanor, on the same theory invoked in Massachusetts during the ratification debates. The case would be hard (I think) if (1) the measures are very extreme by any mesure (involving, say, unambiguous torture and gross violations of civil rights), but (2) the president believes, wrongly but in good faith and with a plausible argument (under existing law), that he has legal authorization to order them. In such a case, it makes sense to say that the impeachment clause does not give authoritative guidance, and so We the People, acting through the House and Senate, can do as we think best.

12. Before his election, a president cheated on his taxes. He failed to report significant income. He has committed a serious crime.

    The president cannot be impeached. He has not abused his official authority in any way. It follows that however egregious his actions might have been before becoming president, the commander-in-chief cannot be impeached for those actions—with just one exception, captured in case 7 above.

13. While in office, a president cheats on his taxes by failing to report significant income. In doing so, he commits a serious crime.

    The president cannot be impeached. He did not abuse his official authority in any way. It is true that he committed a crime, but because there was no abuse of his authority, impeachment is unavailable. (See the discussion of the Nixon case in chapter 6.) He can be prosecuted—after he leaves office.

14. A president fires members of the Federal Communications Commission, the Federal Trade Commission, and the Federal Reserve Board. Those members were appointed by his predecessor. They are in the midst of their five-year terms. The law protects them from discharge unless they have engaged in "malfeasance, neglect of duty, or inefficiency in office."

The president does not contend that the members have engaged in any of those things. Instead he argues that under the Constitution, the executive branch is "unitary," and so he is allowed to fire anyone whose job is to execute the law. In other words, he thinks that the statutes intrude on his constitutional authority—and so he ignores the intrusion. The Supreme Court has rejected the president's view of the Constitution, by ruling that Congress can make these agencies independent of the president's control, but he wants to test the legal waters again.

The president is not impeachable. He has acted on the basis of a good-faith understanding of his constitutional powers. Even if he is wrong, he has not committed a high crime or misdemeanor. This case is a cartoon version of the principal grounds for impeaching Andrew Johnson. As we have seen, those grounds were illegitimate; the impeachment was unconstitutional. This case is a bit stronger for impeachment than the Johnson case, because the president is almost certainly wrong on the law. (Recall that Johnson was right.) But so long as he has a good-faith argument, impeachment is off the table. We do not have a high crime or misdemeanor. Once more: it is not a misdemeanor for a president to act on the basis of a reasonable belief that he had the authority to act as he did.

Harder Cases

15. In the context of a war effort, a president repeatedly deceives the American people. When publicly justifying the decision to go to war, he misstates what the evidence is, in an effort to suggest that if he did nothing, the American people would be at serious risk. The misstatement is at least reckless and probably willful. During the prolonged hostilities, the president does not tell the truth about the progress of the war. He is far too optimistic about what is happening on the ground—again, in a way that is at least reckless and probably willful. He makes statements about the enemy and its conduct that are inconsistent with the facts.

    This is not an easy case. The president is commander-in-chief, and when a war is ongoing, his principal task is to win. In the midst of a war, no president is likely to tell the whole truth and nothing but the truth. True, the president has committed no crime. Reasonable people could urge that even a series of falsehoods, during a war, is not legitimate grounds for removing a president from office. The goal is to do what is necessary to win.

    Nonetheless, he is impeachable (in my view). Even in the midst of war, a sustained pattern of lying to the American public can be counted as a misdemeanor—an abuse of public trust with respect to a matter central to governance. Lying to Americans about extramarital affairs is bad. But lying to Americans about the rationale for a war, and for putting human lives on the line, is impeachable. Even with respect to war, We the People are ultimately in charge. If a president does not care about the truth, and repeatedly lies in ways material to the fulfillment of the duties of his office, he is abusing his authority. (Recall that during the founding era, lying to the Senate was singled out as a legitimate basis for impeachment.)

16. In the aftermath of a serious terrorist attack in Chicago, a president engages in a host of actions that are widely seen as unlawful violations of civil rights and civil liberties. He supports, and authorizes, the detention of suspected sympathizers with the enemy; his test for suspicion includes an inquiry into people's religious convictions. (Muslims are at special risk.) He supports, and authorizes, a crackdown on speech that is (in his view) injurious to the war effort and in particular the recruitment of soldiers. He supports, and authorizes, widespread surveillance of American citizens (including of cell phones and emails); he believes that "privacy is now a threat to national security." Several of these actions have been struck down in federal courts.

This is a more severe version of case 11, and it might seem to be easy, but it isn't. Two of our nation's greatest presidents—I would rank them at the very top—engaged in serious violations of civil rights and civil liberties in the midst of war: Abraham Lincoln and Franklin Delano Roosevelt. Lincoln suspended the writ of habeas corpus. Roosevelt ordered the internment of 117,000 people of Japanese descent living on the West Coast, two-thirds of whom were native-born citizens of the United States.

If the nation faces a serious threat, the president's most important job is to avert that threat, and there can be good arguments that civil rights and civil liberties have to yield. On the other hand, Japanese-Americans did not pose a threat to our security, civil rights and civil liberties are foundational to our constitutional order and our democracy, part of what we fight for—and in the example, I am stipulating that the president has acted unlawfully.

In such cases, we lack hard-and-fast lines, and so there is no escaping a judgment about matters of degree. Categorical statements make little sense. Relevant questions: Under the law, does the president have a good-faith argument, or not? How egregious, exactly, are the violations? How many are there? If the president is systematically ignoring constitutional restrictions on government's power, impeachment is a legitimate response.

17. A president makes a host of erratic decisions, and they lead to domestic and international turmoil. The economy is suffering badly; markets are collapsing; the world is a far more dangerous place. The problem is not that the president is literally incompetent. It is that his judgment is so terrible, and so terrible so often, that there is a bipartisan consensus, more or less, that he needs to go.

Reasonable people can differ about whether the president is impeachable. Of course policy disagreement is not a legitimate basis for impeachment. Intense unpopularity should not trigger impeachment. Presidents are allowed to make mistakes—a lot of them. The United States does not allow votes of no confidence; impeachment is not about that.

Here again, what is necessary is a judgment of degree. If there is a bipartisan consensus, more rather than less, that a president needs to go because of a host of genuinely erratic decisions, we can fairly speak of gross neglect of duty, to a degree that makes impeachment legitimate.

Wise people tread cautiously here, but if the facts are awful enough to establish constitutionally unacceptable misdemeanors, he is impeachable. Recall my institutional suggestion: in the hardest cases on the constitutional issue, We the People, acting through the constitutional channels, get to define "misdemeanors" as we see fit.

18. The nation is not in the midst of war, but a president lies, constantly and on important occasions, to the American people. The lies involve the budget, taxes, and foreign policy. We are not speaking of "spinning," even in its least attractive forms. We are speaking of lies.

    This case is comparable to case 15, and in a way it is easier: impeachment is available. It is easier in the sense that the president does not have the justification that is arguably provided by an ongoing war effort. At the same time, the line between spinning and lies can be less than clear, and if a president is impeachable whenever he crosses that line, we are going to see a lot of impeachments. In addition, it is plausible to say that even a lot of lying is not anything like treason or bribery, or the high crimes and misdemeanors on which the Constitution focuses. Again, if the pattern of lying is repeated enough and egregious enough, so that we are speaking of an abuse of trust, impeachment is on the table.

19. Terrible things happen on a president's watch. White House officials are involved in a variety of illegal activities. Members of the president's cabinet also violate the law, and a number of them engage in actions that are struck down in court—regulating when they lack authority to regulate, deregulating when they lack authority to deregulate. It's a mess. (OMG.)

What makes this a tough one is that the objectionable conduct is not directed by the president himself. Can the commander-in-chief be impeached if his underlings do unlawful or terrible things? The founding-era debates do not resolve that question, which should be answered by asking exactly how terrible they are. As Harry Truman famously said, "The buck stops here," and because the president is in charge of the executive branch, he is the one to blame if horrible decisions are made. Of course the president cannot be impeached if the secretary of transportation issues an unlawful regulation or if the secretary of state commits some kind of crime. Recall that "maladministration" is not a legitimate basis for impeachment. But if the executive branch is engaged in systematic misconduct, if it occurred on the president's watch, and if he failed to do anything about it, we have likely crossed the threshold into misdemeanors within the meaning of the Constitution.

20. Congress is engaged in an investigation of alleged presidential wrongdoing. The president strenuously resists the investigation. He refuses to turn over documents. He asserts executive privilege. He also threatens a special prosecutor, appointed by his own Department of Justice. "If you don't back off," he makes clear, "I am going to make life miserable for you." He says to the Director of the Federal Bureau of Investigation: "You work for me, and one thing that you're *not* going to do is to investigate your own boss. That's an order."

This case presents a continuum of actions, and the proper conclusion depends on where we are on the continuum. A president's refusal to turn over documents is certainly not impeachable if he has a good-faith argument that he is not required to turn them over. (See chapter 6.) Congressional investigations are often motivated by politics, and turn out to be a form of grandstanding. Within limits, the president is entitled to resist those investigations. We can go further. Even if the president's refusal to cooperate is a clear violation of the law, there may be no impeachable offense. As we have seen, a *cover-up of activity that does not amount to a high crime or misdemeanor may not itself amount to a high crime or misdemeanor.* I put that in italics because it is both important and easy to overlook.

In the cases of Nixon and Clinton, the public debated whether the president engaged in obstruction of justice, under the apparent assumption that the answer to that question simultaneously answers the question of impeachment. That is a major mistake. Obstruction of justice need not be a high crime or misdemeanor. If the president obstructs an investigation into his own illegal investments before becoming president, there is probably no impeachable offense. (I use the word "probably," and the phrase "may not" in the italicized sentence, because large-scale misuse of the apparatus of the federal government could be a misdemeanor.) And if the president obstructs justice with respect to use of marijuana by White House staff, impeachment would be absurd (unless large-scale misuse of that apparatus is involved).

If, on the other hand, the president engages in actions that fall short of obstruction of justice, we might nonetheless have a misdemeanor within the meaning of the Constitution, depending on the substance of the investigation. If the FBI is investigating an act of presidential treason or bribery, themselves impeachable, then serious interference with the investigation could count as a misdemeanor. That conclusion holds whether or not the interference meets the technical standards for obstruction of justice.

21. A president hires a gunman to murder someone simply because he does not like him. There is no political motivation; the dispute is entirely personal.

It is surprising but true that this is not a simple case. On one view, there is no abuse of distinctly presidential powers, and hence no impeachable offense. (If the president has used the power of the office to arrange for the murder, then the case becomes easy.) On another view, the president can be impeached for this level of private misconduct, on the theory that murder is an exceptionally serious crime and the president is not likely to be able to govern after committing such a crime.

The Constitution would not make a lot of sense if it did not permit the nation to remove murderers from the highest office in the land. We should interpret the Constitution to make sense.

chapter 8

The Twenty-Fifth Amendment

If impeachment is available only for serious offenses, criminal or otherwise, then a large gap remains. What if a president has not committed any such offense, but suffers from a disability (physical or mental), such that he is unable to serve as commander-in-chief, or is otherwise unfit to continue in office? Suppose that he is stricken by Alzheimer's disease or crippling depression, or is showing some kind of emotional or cognitive decline.[1] Suppose that he is acting more than a little crazy. Can a president be removed if, as a result, he is unable to do his job? Who gets to remove him? Recall James Madison's claim that a president could be impeached if he suffered from "incapacity." But unless incapacity leads to a high crime or misdemeanor, the impeachment mechanism isn't the right one. What else is there?

In 1981, I was privileged to work as a young lawyer in the Office of Legal Counsel in the Department of Justice. OLC, as it is called, serves as the president's legal brain trust. I joined OLC in 1980 under President Jimmy Carter, when his administration was winding down. I continued to work there after the election of President Ronald Reagan, who was brimming with new plans and ideas, some of which raised serious legal issues.

Just a few weeks after Reagan's inauguration, my terrific

and farsighted boss, Theodore Olson, brought me into his massive, wood-paneled office on the famous fifth floor of the Department of Justice, and asked me to write a detailed, formal memorandum on the third and fourth sections of the Twenty-Fifth Amendment. I prided myself on knowing something about the Constitution, but I had to stay quiet. The reason? I had no idea what that amendment said.

I didn't confess my ignorance. Instead I told Olson that I would get right to work. After I left his office, I immediately looked up the text, and here's what I found:

Section 3.

Whenever the President transmits to the President pro tempore of the Senate and the Speaker of the House of Representatives his written declaration that he is unable to discharge the powers and duties of his office, and until he transmits to them a written declaration to the contrary, such powers and duties shall be discharged by the Vice President as Acting President.

Section 4.

Whenever the Vice President and a majority of either the principal officers of the executive departments or of such other body as Congress may by law provide, transmit to the President pro tempore of the Senate and the Speaker of the House of Representatives their written declaration that the President is unable to discharge the powers and duties of his office, the Vice President shall immediately assume the powers and duties of the office as Acting President.

Thereafter, when the President transmits to the President pro tempore of the Senate and the Speaker of the

House of Representatives his written declaration that no inability exists, he shall resume the powers and duties of his office unless the Vice President and a majority of either the principal officers of the executive department or of such other body as Congress may by law provide, transmit within four days to the President pro tempore of the Senate and the Speaker of the House of Representatives their written declaration that the President is unable to discharge the powers and duties of his office. Thereupon Congress shall decide the issue, assembling within forty-eight hours for that purpose if not in session. If the Congress, within twenty-one days after receipt of the latter written declaration, or, if Congress is not in session, within twenty-one days after Congress is required to assemble, determines by two-thirds vote of both Houses that the President is unable to discharge the powers and duties of his office, the Vice President shall continue to discharge the same as Acting President; otherwise, the President shall resume the powers and duties of his office.[2]

Oh.

I was amazed by what I read, not because the text was entirely unfamiliar, but because that was what Olson wanted me to write about. The provisions are intriguing, and they have plenty of mysteries, but Olson's request for a full-scale memorandum seemed bizarre.

The reason is that as a general rule, OLC's work was (and is) focused on immediately pressing legal issues, sometimes even crises. Maybe the Department of State disagrees with the Department of Defense on some legal question. Who's right? Or the president's base wants him to stop abortion, without amending the Constitution. Is that possible? Or the president wants to use military force in some distant land, and lacks congressional authorization. Can he do that?

By contrast, these sections of the Twenty-Fifth Amendment seemed to deal with an entirely hypothetical problem. President Reagan was about to have his seventieth birthday, but he was the picture of good health. Why was I asked to write that memorandum? It seemed like pretty academic work. As Olson explained it, my memorandum was for general background, in the unlikely event of a catastrophe.

Almost exactly one month later, John Hinckley, Jr. shot Reagan.

In the Cockpit

On the fifth floor of the Justice Department, about ten of OLC's lawyers sat crowded around a big television set, watching the news anchors, who explained that the president was in the hospital but apparently fine. Though the shooting was dramatic, traumatic, and riveting, the commander-in-chief was not in serious trouble. National crisis averted. As I sat in the little group, I felt a tap on my shoulder. It was Olson, who needed to speak with me privately. He took me into a hallway, where his voice lowered to a whisper.

"The president is in much worse shape than they're saying," he explained, in a cool, steady voice. "We don't know what will happen, but we need to be prepared. You remember the details of your Twenty-Fifth Amendment memorandum, don't you? You know what to do?" He explained that of the countless lawyers in the building, I was the only

Twenty-Fifth Amendment expert. I needed to get to work immediately.

The top officials at the department left for the White House, and for two hours or so I was manning the fort, sitting alone in Olson's office, in front of those huge desks. My entire hall looked empty, so it seemed as if no one else was in the entire Justice Department. Just three years out of law school, I had been asked, in the strictest confidence, to write two memoranda to remove the recently elected Reagan from the presidency.

The first, to be signed by Reagan himself (if he was able), would comply with Section 2 of the Twenty-Fifth Amendment. It would be a written declaration that he was unable to discharge the powers and duties of his office. The second, to be signed by Vice President Bush and the cabinet, would make the same declaration.

On an old manual typewriter, I typed out the two memoranda. The need for secrecy was such that no secretary could be involved. In the second memorandum, I left black lines for the relevant signatures (those seemed the most momentous parts), and I typed out all their names, letter by letter. As I recall, my hands did not tremble; it must have been the adrenaline. The task was mechanical, but I have never been more intensely focused. I remember that typing as if it were yesterday.

I sealed the two memoranda tightly in a yellow envelope, and a messenger hand-delivered them to the White House.

Of course members of the press were constantly calling the department, and no one important was there to answer their questions. Trying to seem authoritative, but actually in a mild panic, I told the secretaries I would not speak to anybody. I had no idea what I could or should say. But the *New York Times* must have been particularly insistent, because its reporter was put through to me. He had one question: "We have a report that the department has just sent over two memoranda, by which the vice president would assume the presidency. Can you confirm that?" I was flabbergasted. How on earth did they know that?

I still have no idea. As the reporter waited for an answer, time seemed to stand still. What to say? Instead of confessing or falling apart, my mind seized upon two words that I had learned from old television shows: "No comment."

What the Amendment Is All About

As it turned out, Reagan recovered well, and no one needed to invoke the Twenty-Fifth Amendment. But the tale helps to show what the amendment is all about. Added in 1967 in the aftermath of the assassination of President John F. Kennedy, and sometimes described as a memorial to the fallen president, the amendment explains, in its first section, what happens if the president dies, is removed, or resigns: the vice president takes over.[3] Its second section specifies what happens if the office of the vice president becomes vacant: "The President shall nominate a Vice President who shall take office upon confirmation by a majority vote of both Houses of Congress."

All that is straightforward. The remaining two sections deal with the much harder cases of incapacity. The test is simple, deceptively so: the president's inability to discharge the powers and duties of the office.

Importantly, the president himself is given the opportunity to declare that inability. A president who has been severely wounded, or who is grappling with some debilitating health problem, can transfer power to the vice president, either permanently or during the time of his convalescence. But whether or not he wants to continue to serve, the president can be bypassed. That's important, because a president might be unable to make a declaration (perhaps because he is unconscious), or even if he is capable of doing that, he might be unwilling to acknowledge the existence or the extent of his disability. If the vice president concludes that the president cannot discharge the powers and duties of the office, and if a majority of the cabinet agrees, the presidency is over—unless and until the president protests and potentially causes a contest in Congress.

Recall just who gets to bypass the president. The relevant part of section 4: "the Vice President and a majority of either the principal officers of the executive departments or of such other body as Congress may by law provide." I will return to these critical words. They show a radically different choice from that made by the framers of the impeachment clause, back in Philadelphia.

One Word

The central question of the Twenty-Fifth Amendment, of course, is the meaning of one word: "unable." (Note that under the third and fourth sections, the standard—"unable to discharge the powers and duties of his office"—seems to be the same.) On the basis of the amendment's text, we can imagine a continuum of understandings. At one extreme, a president is "unable" only if he is *literally unable to make decisions*—perhaps because he is not conscious, perhaps because he has suffered a severe mental breakdown of some sort. Call this Twenty-Fifth Amendment minimalism. At the other end of the continuum, the vice president and the cabinet are authorized to declare the president "unable" for whatever reasons they like. If they say he is unable, he is unable. That's Twenty-Fifth Amendment maximalism.

Members of Congress were alert to the ambiguity in the text. During their debates on the constitutional text, several of them emphasized its lack of clarity.[4] But they failed to offer a definition, perhaps because they could not agree on one. Nonetheless, the background of the Twenty-Fifth Amendment offers helpful guidance, especially insofar as it shows where the legislators' attention was focused.[5]

Several members emphasized four cases, three real and one hypothetical. The real ones were the prolonged deathbed experience of James Garfield, shot in 1881; the two years that Woodrow Wilson remained in office after his massive stroke in 1919; and Dwight Eisenhower's period of convalescence after a serious heart attack and while suffering other heart problems. The hypothetical case posited a situation in which President Kennedy managed to survive the assassination attempt in Dallas in 1963, but ended up incapacitated by his injuries.

For the legislators, the cases of Garfield and Wilson presented the precise problems that the Twenty-Fifth Amendment was intended to solve. Those cases were defining. As noted by Lewis Powell, then president-elect of the American Bar Association and later a member of the Supreme

Court, their inability to carry out their duties resulted in "a virtual void in Executive leadership."[6] Senator Birch Bayh, who played a critical role in the debates, observed that in the eighty days between Garfield's shooting and death, his "only official act . . . was the signing of an extradition paper."[7] He also pointed to the considerable control that Woodrow Wilson's wife and doctor exerted over his schedule in the aftermath of his stroke.[8]

During the discussions, some legislators focused on greatly diminished cognitive capacity, stemming from physical disability, severe psychological problems, or some other source. At one point, Senator Bayh spoke quite broadly, saying that the text spoke of "any type of inability, whether it is from traveling from one nation to another, a breakdown of communications, capture by the enemy, or anything that is imaginable."[9] Because of Senator Bayh's central role, his statements deserve careful attention, but the words "any type of disability" seem to overshoot the mark. At another point, Senator Bayh said more crisply that "the ability to perform the job would be the prime evidence that would determine whether a president were disabled or not."[10]

That may not seem to be the most helpful formulation, because it essentially restates the constitutional text. But it does offer a purposive account of "unable"; the question is always whether he can carry out his constitutional functions. If a president's physical or cognitive problems make it very difficult or impossible for him to do what he is supposed to do, the Twenty-Fifth Amendment should be triggered. One week before Congress passed the recommended text of the amendment, Senator Bayh and Senator Edward M. Kennedy spoke of the president's "total disability," understood as "physical or mental inability to exercise the powers and duties of his office."[11]

Consistent with that view, some comments pointed to situations in which "the president by reason of some physical ailment or some sudden accident is unconscious or paralyzed," or "by reason of mental debility, is unable or unwilling to make any rational decision, including particularly the decision to stand aside."[12] But other comments suggested a somewhat broader view than might be signaled by the term "total disability." Former Attorney General Herbert Brownell pointed to situations in which "the president might be going to have an operation" or in which "his doctors recommend temporary suspension of his normal governmental activities, to facilitate his recovery."[13] In particular, both illness and surgery were taken to be potential bases for invocation of section 3.

Too Strong

Congress's focus on relatively extreme cases rules the maximalist interpretation out of bounds. The vice president and cabinet cannot just decide to declare a president unable. The context, after all, is set by the first two sections of the Twenty-Fifth Amendment, which deal with death or removal from office. That context is underlined by the obvious motivation of section 4, which is to provide a solution in cases of incapacitation. Terrible judgment, laziness, incompetence, and even impeachable acts do not justify invocation of the Twenty-Fifth Amendment.[14] The amendment's reference to the president's inability to discharge his duties requires a very serious impairment, whether physical or mental.

It follows that to invoke the amendment, the vice president and the cabinet have to be able to point to some such impairment. They cannot remove the president from office simply because that is what they want to do. In particular, they cannot remove him because they do not like his decisions, because he is unpopular, because he is hurting his party, because he has an awful temper, because he is going to war (or not going to war), because he is ruining the economy, because he has committed a crime or crimes, or because he is impossible to deal with. In ordinary language, they might say and even believe that he is "unable" to perform his constitutional functions, but that is not what the amendment is about.

We should note here that even though Twenty-Fifth Amendment maximalism is wrong, it would probably not produce a ton of mischief. After all, the president chooses his own team, and the members of that team are likely to be intensely loyal to him. In a dramatic departure from the impeachment provision, the Twenty-Fifth Amendment lets the president's people run the show (unless Congress decides to give the authority to some other body, and it has not yet done that). The real risk is not that the Twenty-Fifth Amendment will be invoked when it shouldn't, but that it won't be invoked when it should.

If we wanted to exercise our imaginations, perhaps we could foresee some kind of coup, in which an ambitious vice president, eager to obtain power, turns out to be able to get the cabinet on his side, and thus to wrest power from a president who is not really unable to do his job. But that seems like a television show, not reality. (*House of Cards,* anyone?) We could also imagine a truly bizarre political context, in which a sitting president is destroying his own party's prospects, or in which his decisions seem, even to his own people, to be so damaging and eccentric that he has to be relieved of his duties. In such a case, the argument for removing him might well seem overwhelming. But even so, the maximalist position is wrong. The constitutionally specified remedy is the ballot box or possibly impeachment, not the Twenty-Fifth Amendment.

Too Weak

In a similar spirit, we should acknowledge that the minimalist position is just too weak, and so it too must be rejected. That is a really important conclusion—more important, in fact, than the rejection of maximalism.

Notwithstanding the reference to "total disability," a president might be unable to discharge his duties even if he is not literally unable to make decisions. A serious cognitive impairment—say, a certain stage of Alzheimer's disease—might not produce such a literal inability, but could entail a loss of memory and of functional capacity. Such a loss could easily disable a president from doing his job. In a case of that kind, the Twenty-Fifth Amendment is best read to allow the president's team to relieve him of his responsibilities.

We could also imagine cases of acute depression, crippling anxiety, paranoia, or otherwise serious emotional breakdown, which would also prove debilitating, even if the president is not literally unable to make decisions. The debilitation could take the form of highly erratic behavior (as some people feared in the cases of Johnson and Nixon). Or it could take the form of indecisiveness. If the condition is sufficiently severe, it could render the president "unable" to do his job within the meaning of the Twenty-Fifth Amendment.

At least if it does not become extreme, physical incapacitation could produce hard cases. True, a state of unconsciousness, even if temporary, would justify use of the amendment, and if a strong anesthetic is administered to the president, there might also be a good occasion for its use. These points bear on routine, or less than routine, medical procedures. In 2002, President George W. Bush invoked the Twenty-Fifth Amendment, transferring power to Vice President Dick Cheney during a colorectal screening, and in 2007, he did so for a few hours when doctors removed benign polyps from his large intestine.

A continuing inability to travel, domestically or abroad, would make it harder for the president to do his job, but in spite of one of Senator Bayh's comments ("any type of inability, whether it is from traveling from one nation to another"), it need not render him "unable." For Twenty-Fifth Amendment purposes, everything would depend on the extent of the incapacitation. The cases of Garfield and Wilson are straightforward, and if a president suffers from an impairment that is even close to theirs, the Twenty-Fifth Amendment is available. Physical disabilities that do not rise to that level could present tough questions.

Easy and Hard

Extreme unpopularity, bad character, corruption, and disastrous decisions are easy; the Twenty-Fifth Amendment cannot be triggered. That's not what it's about. Literal inability to make decisions is also easy; the Twenty-Fifth Amendment can and should be triggered. That's what it's about.

The hard cases involve a diminished capacity as a result of a serious physical or mental impairment. In such cases, there are no hard-and-fast rules. The best solution, invited by the text of the Twenty-Fifth Amendment, is institutional: If the president's own team points to such an impairment, and concludes that he has to go, well, then—he has to go.

chapter 9

What Every American Should Know

We now have a clear sense of the fundamentals of impeachment—its relationship to the American Revolution, its place in the constitutional structure, the historical practice, and the legitimate and illegitimate grounds for removing the president from office. We know that the focus is on egregious abuses of power.

But plenty of questions remain. Let's ask and answer the most important ones. We've encountered some of them before, but crisp answers can be clarifying.

Who can be impeached?

The president, the vice president, and all civil officers of the United States.

"Civil officers" is a broad term; it includes federal judges and appointed officials of the federal government, whether their positions are high or low. The attorney general certainly can be impeached, and so can the secretary of state, and so can the chief justice of the United States. (During the Obama administration, I served as administrator of the Office of Information and Regulatory Affairs, and I certainly could have been impeached.) To keep things simple, I am going to refer throughout this chapter to the president, but most of the answers would be the same for the vice president and all civil officers.

It is generally agreed that members of Congress are not civil officers of the United States and so are not subject to impeachment. Officers of the army and navy, and other parts of the armed forces, are not considered civil officers of the United States.

Who impeaches the president?

The House of Representatives. It does so by a simple majority vote.

Why did the drafters of the Constitution choose the House?

Its members are elected every two years, and so the House is more popularly responsive than the Senate. Because republican principles put a premium on self-government, the House is the institution that gets to initiate the process for removing the president.

Why a simple majority?

The framers and ratifiers did not want to make impeachment too hard. Hard, but not too hard.

Does impeachment mean that the president has to leave office?

No! Impeachment is roughly analogous to an indictment, and then the Senate, acting as a kind of court, conducts a trial and decides whether to "convict." If the Senate convicts the president, he is removed. If he is acquitted, he gets to stay in office, even though he has been impeached.

A little more detail: under the Constitution, a vote in favor of impeachment moves the national debate from the House to the Senate, which can remove the president, but only by a vote of two-thirds. That is a very high threshold. Because it is so high, any impeachment might turn out to be futile, at least if it is based on a desire to remove the president from office. On some occasions, the potential futility of impeachment has probably deterred the House from proceeding even when many of its members were pretty unhappy with the president.

To appreciate the role of the Senate in the whole process, note also that under the Constitution, the senators must take an oath, which is to "do impartial justice according to the Constitution and laws."[1] That oath is separate from the senators' oath of office. It signals the unique gravity of the occasion. Let's underline the word "impartial," which suggests that the senators are supposed to act like judges, not politicians.

If the president is impeached and the Senate conducts a trial, members of the House continue to have an important role, which is to select "managers," who act like prosecutors. They are in charge of presenting the arguments for conviction. Because of their role, it makes good sense for the House to select members who are excellent lawyers. And indeed, the tradition, in the few cases that have come up, is to try to do exactly that. (The word "try" is deliberate; in the Clinton impeachment proceedings, for example, the lawyering may have fallen short of excellent.)

*What's the purpose of this pretty complicated
institutional arrangement?*

The delegates who supported the power to impeach and remove the president wanted to thread a needle. They sought
to create a safety valve while also maintaining the separation of powers and ensuring that the president would not be
Congress's lackey.

The "high crimes and misdemeanors" threshold was the
first way to promote those goals. The second was to create
institutional safeguards, assuring that a president would not
have to leave office unless there were something close to a
national consensus that he should do so. The two-thirds majority in the Senate is an important and strong safeguard—
as the Johnson and Clinton cases reveal.

Because the Senate, whose members enjoy six-year terms,
is the less populist body, the framers assumed that it would
be the more deliberative one—slower, calmer, less passionate, more reflective. This was an emphatically republican
answer to the question of how to remove the commander-
in-chief. As one careful historical account puts it, "The Constitution assigned this labor to the Senate because the delegates expected the upper house to rely upon its own wisdom,
information, stability, and even temper. . . . The American
impeachment trial, with its two-thirds requirement, was
thus a hybrid of native origin, expressing truly republican
compromises."[2]

According to an old story, Thomas Jefferson, always an
enthusiastic fan of self-government, questioned George

Washington for having supported the idea of two legislative chambers, with the Senate potentially serving as a brake on the judgments of We the People.

Washington's response was simple: "Why did you just now pour that coffee into your saucer, before drinking?"

"To cool it," answered Jefferson, "my throat is not made of brass."

"Even so," rejoined Washington, "we pour our legislation into the senatorial saucer to cool it."[3]

For the whole process of impeachment and removal, the senatorial saucer cools it.

Is the standard for conviction in the Senate the same as the standard for impeachment in the House?

Technically, yes. In practice: close, but not quite.

Yes, because for impeachment, as for conviction, it is necessary to show treason, bribery, or some other high crime or misdemeanor. It's the same standard for both.

Not quite, because all by itself, impeachment has no material consequences, whereas conviction results in removal. In light of that fact, the Senate will likely demand clearer and stronger proof than will the House. Recall that the Senate is acting essentially as a court.

Are the constitutional procedures really republican?

You could argue about that one.

Republicanism is a pretty abstract commitment. If you insist on rule by the people, you might insist that if a majority of the House of Representatives thinks that someone should be removed from office, that ought to be plenty enough. But there is another view, well stated by Hoffer and Hull. "The two-thirds requirement for conviction in the Senate was the capstone of the republicanization of impeachment and trial procedure," they write. "It ensured that the Senate would be as thoughtful and deliberate in its hearing and determining of cases as the House of Lords, without any of the aristocratic trappings of that English body."[4]

Is impeachment a criminal proceeding?

Not really, in the sense that even if a president is impeached and removed for criminal activity, he faces no criminal punishment. He loses his job, not his liberty. If he is impeached for criminal activity and then convicted, he is subject to criminal prosecution in ordinary courts after he leaves office. (See below.) And as we have seen, the president may be impeached for actions that are not crimes.

Suppose that an impeachment is unconstitutional. Can federal courts stop it? Can the Supreme Court intervene?

No. The Constitution puts impeachment and conviction in the hands of Congress, not the judiciary. If an impeachment and conviction violate constitutional standards, there is no legal remedy.

I say this with a lot of confidence, but candor compels an acknowledgment: it's not quite 100 percent clear. (More than 99 percent, but not quite 100 percent.) Suppose that a president is impeached on grounds that obviously fall short of the constitutional requirements, and suppose he goes to federal court for a declaratory judgment, saying exactly that and asking the court to intervene. Why, you might ask, can't courts vindicate the Constitution? Isn't that their job?

The technical answer is that some issues are treated as "political questions," which means that the Constitution commits them to resolution by other branches of the government. The Court has come very close to ruling, and may even be taken to have ruled, that impeachment is an example.[5] Of course we should all fervently hope that no president will ever be impeached or removed from office on grounds that fail to meet the constitutional standard. American history suggests that such a removal, at least, is unlikely, and so the political safeguards of the impeachment process have worked. (As we have seen, the Clinton and Johnson impeachments violated the constitutional standard, but neither president was convicted.)

What is the role of the chief justice of the Supreme Court?

Under the Constitution, the chief justice has no role in the impeachment proceedings in the House, but he does preside over the trial in the Senate. In the Johnson impeachment, Salmon Chase was the presiding judge; William Rehnquist presided over the Clinton impeachment. But the role of the presiding judge is quite limited. He oversees the trial, and he can resolve technical questions, but he is not likely to have any authority to push the outcome in his preferred direction.

In the two presidential impeachment proceedings in American history, the chief justice was a pretty minor player.

Because it is such a landmark event to see the chief justice presiding in the Senate, people pay a lot of attention to him, but the crucial decisions are made by the senators.

Suppose that the president is incapacitated. Maybe he has suffered some terrible physical injury, illness, or impairment; maybe he is losing his mind. Can he be impeached?

No.

It's hazardous and usually foolhardy to disagree with James Madison on a point of constitutional law, but I'm doing just that. You may recall that at the Convention, Madison pointed to incapacity as one of the grounds for impeachment. But when he did that, he was speaking of an earlier version of the text, one that might well have accommodated that interpretation. By itself, incapacity is not treason, bribery, or any other high crime or misdemeanor.

If a president is incapacitated, you might ask, can *anything* be done? The simple answer is that the Twenty-Fifth Amendment was designed for exactly that problem. But you might persist: suppose that the president and his team refuse to invoke the Twenty-Fifth Amendment, even though to any objective observer, it's clear that the president is unable to perform the duties of the office. What then?

The answer is that impeachment might well turn out to be available, not because of presidential incapacity as such, but because of egregious abuse or neglect of duty (a high misdemeanor), which can be shown by actions and omissions. If a president is unable to make decisions, or to make rational decisions, and if a pattern of terrible misconduct demonstrates that fact, then the House can impeach him.

Does the prospect of impeachment affect presidents while they are in office?

A good question, on which we don't have a lot of evidence, but the answer is almost certainly yes.

During the Iran–Contra affair in the Reagan era (look it up, if you like), the specter of impeachment was raised in Reagan's presence. In a 1984 meeting in the White House Situation Room, members of his national security team discussed whether, how, and how much money could be channeled to the Nicaraguan Contra rebels. (Congress had forbidden direct funding.) Secretary of State George Schultz repeated a warning he had heard from James Baker that "if we go out and try to get money from third countries, it is an impeachable offense."[6]

A personal anecdote: while I was in the Obama administration, Congress threatened not to raise the debt limit, which could have created serious economic difficulties for the United States and the world. If the debt limit had not been raised, the United States might have defaulted on its debts, potentially causing chaos in the international economic system. Some lawyers have argued that if Congress fails to act, the president has the authority to raise the debt limit on his own. I was involved in some discussions in the White House about this question, and in my view that argument has force (even though most constitutional specialists do not accept it).

But some of the president's legislative advisers warned that if President Obama did raise the debt limit on his own, he might be subject to a serious impeachment inquiry, especially with Republicans in the majority in the House. I have no idea whether President Obama was affected by that speculation or not, but the possibility certainly did get his advisers' attention.

Here, as always, our framework is helpful. If a president raised the debt limit on his own, there would be a plausible argument for impeachment *only if he had no good-faith legal argument that he was entitled to do that.* In my view, any president would have such a good-faith argument. Still, the prospect of impeachment is likely to concentrate the presidential mind.

If the president has committed an impeachable offense, are members of the House of Representatives obliged to vote to impeach him? Are senators obliged to vote to convict him?

Yes and yes. I think.

The reason for the two yeses: in my view, the Constitution contemplates that if the president really has committed treason, bribery, or some other high crime or misdemeanor, he must be impeached and then removed from office. Even if the president is a terrific person and has done terrific things, he cannot stay in office if he has been bribed or committed treason.

The reason for "I think": prosecutors have discretion. If you have violated the law, a prosecutor might not proceed against you if, in the circumstances, it just doesn't make sense for her to do so. For citizens, that is a great guarantor of liberty. (Ask whether you have violated the law over the last twenty years—any law at all. Maybe you have?) By way of analogy, We the People, acting through our elected representatives, might have prosecutorial discretion with regard to the impeachment power as well. Maybe we can decide: he did a terrible thing, but we won't exercise our discretion to remove him from office. Maybe we can think: he's a bum, but he's our bum, and we kind of like him.

But under the constitutional plan, we can't make that decision. I think.

Isn't impeachment just a matter of politics, and if so, why should we focus so much on the legal standard?

What a cynical question.

Sure, a Democratic House is more likely to impeach a Republican president than to impeach a Democratic president. Sure, a Democratic House might impeach a Republican president for constitutionally inadequate reasons, and a Republican House might refuse to impeach a Republican president even if the constitutional test is clearly met. Because any president is likely to enjoy loyal support from his own party and a significant percentage of voters, there will be a large political dimension to any impeachment inquiry. As we have seen, that's an unmistakable lesson of history. (By the way, the rise of political parties followed ratification of the Constitution; the framers did not anticipate it.)

But let's not overreact. Ours is a Rule of Law, which means that the law matters, which means that the legal standard matters, even if it is not always obeyed. During the

Clinton impeachment, those who violated the legal standard, and made hash of it, nevertheless worked hard to show that they were obeying it. The French thinker Francois de La Rochefoucauld proclaimed: "Hypocrisy is the tribute vice pays to virtue."[7] If the Rule of Law sometimes produces hypocrisy, at least we know what counts as vice and what counts as virtue.

An understanding of the legitimate grounds for impeachment imposes a disciplining effect on the political process. It is in part because the standard is high that political opponents of presidents have so rarely resorted to the impeachment mechanism. Despised presidents, and bad presidents, have hardly ever been impeached, which is a tribute to the Rule of Law.

Can a president be subject to a civil lawsuit on the basis of his official acts?

No, he cannot.

The Supreme Court ruled in favor of absolute immunity in *Nixon v. Fitzgerald,* decided by a 5 to 4 vote in 1982.[8] Emphasizing that the president "occupies a unique position in the constitutional scheme," the Court concluded that in light of "the singular importance of the President's duties, diversion of his energies by concern with private lawsuits would raise unique risks to the effective functioning of government." It follows that the president enjoys full immunity so long as he is being sued for actions taken within the domain of his official responsibilities. This rule applies to both sitting and former presidents. Pointedly, the Court added: "A rule of absolute immunity for the President will not leave the Nation without sufficient protection against misconduct on the part of the Chief Executive. There remains the constitutional remedy of impeachment."

Can a president be subject to a civil lawsuit while in office, when the basis for the lawsuit does not involve his official acts?

Yes, he can.

The Supreme Court so ruled in *Jones* v. *Clinton,* decided unanimously in 1997.[9] The theory of the decision is that nothing in the Constitution explicitly forbids such civil actions against the president; that presidential immunity from such actions would have to be an inference from more general provisions of the Constitution; and that there is no provision from which immunity can appropriately be inferred. The Court reconciled its conclusion with that in *Nixon* v. *Fitzgerald* by emphasizing that in that case, official acts were the basis for the lawsuit: "In context, however, it is clear that our dominant concern was with the diversion of the President's attention during the decision-making process caused by needless worry as to the possibility of damages actions stemming from any particular official decision."

It's not absolutely clear that the Supreme Court was right in *Jones* v. *Clinton.* As in *Nixon* v. *Fitzgerald,* so too here: in light of "the singular importance of the President's duties, diversion of his energies by concern with private lawsuits would raise unique risks to the effective functioning of government." Whether or not the lawsuit involves official acts, there is a reasonable argument that it would seriously interfere with his ability to perform his constitutionally specified duties. Handling a lawsuit is a significant burden. For many people, it can be a full-time job. Can the president really do what he is supposed to do, if he is facing a lawsuit?

The Supreme Court acknowledged the concern. It referred to "the risk that our decision will generate a large volume of politically motivated harassing and frivolous litigation, and the danger that national security concerns might prevent the President from explaining a legitimate need for a continuance." But it answered that the risks were not that serious and that the legal system could handle them: "Although scheduling problems may arise, there is no reason to assume that the district courts will be either unable to accommodate the President's needs or unfaithful to the tradition—especially in matters involving national security—of giving 'the utmost deference to Presidential responsibilities.'"

It's true that many years after *Jones* v. *Clinton,* we cannot be absolutely sure that the current Supreme Court would allow lawsuits against a sitting president. But the Court is reluctant to overrule its own precedents, and so we can be sure enough.

Can a president be criminally prosecuted while in office?

The Supreme Court has not answered that question, so the technical answer is: unclear. My own answer is different: no. Admittedly, it's a tough one, a kind of constitutional brainteaser.

The Constitution's impeachment provisions can be read to suggest that, in the context of presidential wrongdoing, the appropriate response is removal from office, not criminal prosecution, at least while the president is serving. Recall the text: "Judgement in Cases of Impeachment shall not extend further than to removal from Office, and disqualification to hold and enjoy any Office of honor, Trust or Profit under the United States: but the Party convicted shall nevertheless be liable and subject to Indictment, Trial, Judgement and Punishment, according to Law." You could easily take this language to suggest a temporal separation: first impeachment, then judgment and removal, then prosecution.

In *Federalist* No. 69, Alexander Hamilton seemed to read the provision exactly that way: "The President of the United States would be liable to be impeached, tried, and, upon conviction of treason, bribery, or other high crimes or misdemeanors, removed from office; and would afterwards be liable to prosecution and punishment in the ordinary course of law." The word "afterwards" seems to mean you can't indict and try a sitting president. He has to be impeached and removed first.

True, this interpretation isn't inevitable. You could read the text to mean only that the consequence of conviction is removal from office, and that a convicted president can be prosecuted—but to be silent on, and so not to resolve, the question whether a president can be prosecuted for crimes while he in office. On that interpretation, nothing in the Constitution rules out a prosecution of the president for, say, obstruction of justice or for perjury. He could be subject *both* to prosecution and to impeachment.

Maybe. But even if this view is convincing, there is another reason, building on *Nixon* v. *Fitzgerald,* to say that the president cannot be criminally prosecuted while in office. Unlike a civil action, a criminal prosecution imposes a unique kind of stigma and threat, such that the president's ability to undertake his constitutionally specified tasks really would be at risk. Under *Nixon* v. *Fitzgerald,* there is an argument that this conclusion is right if a president is being prosecuted on the basis of official acts: if a president cannot be subject to a civil lawsuit for such acts, it might follow that he cannot be criminally prosecuted for them.

If so, the real question, raised by *Jones* v. *Clinton,* is whether he can be criminally prosecuted for *unofficial* acts —say, those in which he engaged before becoming president, or those that were not part of his official responsibilities. My own conclusion is that, because of the unique nature of a criminal prosecution, a president should have absolute immunity in such cases as well—at least while he is president.

True, we could imagine cases that would call this conclusion into question. Suppose that the president is prosecuted for income-tax evasion or for disorderly conduct. Suppose too that he could not be impeached for such offenses. In that event, impeachment is not the alternative remedy. And would such a prosecution really jeopardize the president's ability to undertake his constitutional responsibilities? These are testing cases, but sometimes bright lines are a lot better than case-by-case judgments.

Can the president be indicted while in office?

I don't think so.

This is also an unresolved question, at least if the indictment is brought on the basis of unofficial acts. (*Nixon* v.

Fitzgerald is probably best read to settle the issue, and to answer "no," with respect to official acts.) Suppose that a prosecutor seeks an indictment but acknowledges that the president cannot be tried while in office. In other words, the prosecutor wants to get an indictment in place, but urges that the proceedings should be stayed during the time of the presidency.

On the one hand, it could be argued that nothing in the impeachment provisions forbids an indictment itself, and that so long as the president is not subject to a criminal trial, he can certainly do his job. In support of that argument, the prosecutor could contend that he is not speaking of impeachable offenses, so impeachment cannot be the exclusive remedy. On the other hand, the text might be read to suggest that impeachment is the constitutionally specified way to "indict" a president who is in office—and that it excludes criminal indictments. And while such an indictment is far less of an intrusion than an actual trial, it is not easily ignored.

Though reasonable people can differ, my conclusion is that the president cannot be indicted while in office. (We're getting pretty technical here.)

Can a president be prosecuted after leaving office, for crimes committed either before becoming president or while serving as president?

Let's take this question in three different ways. First: If the president is impeached and removed for criminal activity, can he be prosecuted for the crimes that led to his removal? Absolutely. The text of the impeachment provision makes that unmistakably clear.

Second: Can a former president be prosecuted for criminal actions in which he engaged outside of the context of his official duties? Absolutely. Nothing in the Constitution immunizes a former president from prosecution for income tax fraud or unlawful drug use.

Third: Can a former president be prosecuted for criminal actions in which he engaged as part of his official duties? It's not clear, but maybe not. As we have seen, *Nixon* v. *Fitzgerald* creates a rule of absolute immunity from civil lawsuits for actions undertaken as part of a president's official duties, and it may follow that if official duties really are involved, a former president enjoys absolute immunity from criminal prosecution as well. (You might not love that conclusion—I am not sure that I do—but there we are.)

Can the president pardon himself?

Probably not. What the heck, let's go for broke: no.

The Constitution says, "The President . . . shall have Power to grant Reprieves and Pardons for Offences against the United States, except in Cases of Impeachment." You could easily read that provision to say that the president can pardon anyone for anything (except in impeachment cases) —and that would allow self-pardons. That's the theory to beat.

One qualification to the theory is that, if the president exercises the pardon power in certain ways, he might be impeachable *for that very reason*. The president could be impeached if he said that he would pardon anyone accused or convicted of rape. And if a president is under investigation for serious wrongdoing and pardons himself, as a way of eliminating any risk of prosecution, there is a good argument that he has committed a misdemeanor in the constitutional sense. That would seem to be an abuse of power.

But that doesn't answer the question. The best argument against self-pardons would emphasize the old maxim that "no one can be judge in his own cause," and add that if a president is pardoning himself, he's violating that maxim. Surely—you might insist—the drafters and ratifiers of the Constitution, deeply hostile to the whole idea of a king, could not have wanted to allow the president to place himself above justice. True, the pardon clause seems to give the president unlimited authority (outside of impeachment cases), but in view of the background and the context, it should not be read to allow him to insulate *himself* from the force of the criminal law.

Sounds right to me.

With respect to impeachment, what should contemporary Americans be worried about?

Two things.

The first is that a combination of extreme partisanship, rapid spread of false information (especially online), and various behavioral biases will result in unjustified, harmful, and destabilizing efforts to impeach the president. The problem of fake news is certainly relevant here.

Social scientists speak of "group polarization," which means that when like-minded people get together, they often go to extremes. Social scientists also speak of "informational cascades," which occur when information, even if false, quickly spreads from one person to another, with the result that numerous people end up believing something, not because they have independent reason to think that it is true, but because other people seem to believe it. Because of "confirmation bias," people are inclined to believe things that fit with what they already believe or want to believe. That means that people can get pretty charged up even if the facts, which would calm them down, are freely available.

Group polarization, informational cascades, and confirmation bias all played big roles in the Nixon and Clinton impeachments. We could easily imagine wildly unjustified and highly destabilizing impeachments, rooted in those mechanisms, whenever the presidency is held by someone from a political party other than that which holds the House and the Senate.

But I think that we shouldn't worry about that too much, thanks to the Constitution, and to the fact that we live in a free society. Because the president won an election (after all), because his own party is likely to support him (unless he has done something quite terrible), because he has so many ways to defend himself in public, because the impeachment process is so difficult, and because conviction is even more difficult, we have plenty of safeguards against unjustified efforts to get rid of the commander-in-chief.

The second thing to worry about is the failure to use the impeachment mechanism in circumstances in which it really is justified. Imagine that the president systematically overreaches in his use of executive authority, paying no attention to the law and making a mockery of the system of separation of powers. Or imagine that he takes steps to violate civil rights and civil liberties, without anything like a good-faith argument that he was entitled to do that. In extreme cases, would We the People start to consider impeachment in a serious way?

Maybe not. The constitutional safeguards are one reason. Another is party loyalty. History suggests that Republicans will be exceedingly reluctant to abandon a Republican president, and Democrats are no different. That means that impeachment is highly unlikely whenever the president's party controls the House, and that conviction is essentially impossible unless the country is nearly unified against its leader. If a president systematically overreaches in his use of executive authority, or puts civil rights and civil liberties seriously at risk, he is likely to have, or to be able to get, the backing of a lot of Americans—at the very least, a big chunk of the electorate. Will We the People end up doing anything in response?

I don't know. That's worth worrying about.

chapter 10

Keeping the Republic

When I was growing up in Waban, Massachusetts, my family celebrated four holidays: Christmas, Easter, Thankgiving, and the Fourth of July. For a child, Christmas and Easter were the most fun. But even for a child, Thanksgiving and the Fourth of July were the most meaningful.

On Thanksgiving, my mother would go around the dinner table, asking each of us what we were most thankful for. I didn't love that, because I suspected that we were supposed to cry out, "Our parents!" But my mother's question got under my skin, and in a good way. Behavioral scientists report that if you think about what you're grateful for, you'll feel happier and more peaceful. My mother knew what she was doing.

But the Thanksgiving holiday was mostly about country, not family. When I was very young, my mother told me about the Pilgrims, who celebrated Thanksgiving. In her account, the Pilgrims came to our shores long before there even was a United States. They had some kind of celebratory dinner, in Massachusetts no less, in which they expressed their gratitude for being where they were, and for the food that had been placed before them. Her account was essentially right. The first Thanksgiving, as it is called, was celebrated by the Mayflower Pilgrims in 1621, though there were forerunners in the very young American colonies.

In school—first grade, I think—it was imprinted on us that during the Revolutionary War, Americans celebrated Thanksgiving too. In 1777, the Continental Congress issued the first National Proclamation of Thanksgiving. On October 3, 1789, President George Washington established the first Thanksgiving Day for the nation under its new Constitution. I didn't know that level of detail, but I did know something important and joyful about Washington: "First in peace, first in war, and first in the hearts of his countrymen!"[1]

For me, the Fourth of July was the perfect family bookend to Thanksgiving Day. My father, a Naval lieutenant, fought in the Philippines during World War II. The fighting was brutal and he was nearly killed—twice. (His most harrowing tale: he was driving a car though a remote area when he spotted a Japanese sniper, taking direct aim at him. He kneeled down as he drove. Unable to see where he was going, he managed not to get hit by several shots fired at him.) He wasn't sentimental, but the nation's birthday meant everything to him. At baseball games, he always stood up for the national anthem, and when he did so, he put his hand over his heart.

But it was my mother who told me about Thomas Jefferson and some "declaration" that he had written. Thankfully, the holiday was mostly about ice cream and tennis, not dead people and declarations. But on the day itself, that old text was everywhere, and it seemed like a prayer: "We hold these truths to be self-evident, that all men are created equal, that they are endowed by their Creator with certain inalienable rights, that among these are Life, Liberty, and the pursuit of Happiness."

If you read the text today, you might be surprised. A lot of it consists of a list of grievances against "the present King of Great Britain," whose history is one "of repeated injuries and usurpations, all having in direct object the establishment of an absolute Tyranny over these states." It's like a criminal indictment, or articles of impeachment. A flavor:

∷ "He has refused his Assent to Laws, the most wholesome and necessary for the public good."

∷ "He has made Judges dependent on his Will alone for the tenure of their offices, and the amount and payment of their salaries."

∷ "He has endeavored to prevent the population of these States; for that purpose obstructing the Laws for Naturalization of Foreigners; refusing to pass others to encourage their migrations hither; and raising the conditions of new Appropriations of Lands."

The authors of the Declaration did not like monarchs: "A Prince, whose character is thus marked by every act which may define a Tyrant, is unfit to be the ruler of a free people." They closed with a pledge: "And for the support of this Declaration, with a firm reliance on the protection of Divine Providence, we mutually pledge to each other our Lives, our Fortunes, and our sacred Honor."

They acted in accordance with that pledge. Nine of the fifty-six signatories died in battle. Two lost their sons. The homes of at least a dozen were pillaged and burned.

On Thanksgiving, and every other day, Americans have much to be thankful for. That star-spangled banner yet waves. Before long, the Declaration will celebrate its 250th birthday. All over the world, the nation has been a beacon of liberty. America's citizens have had no tyrants, in part because of the constitutional design. The Constitution is still in force. It has been amended repeatedly, almost always for the better, and so it's even greater than it was. But the essential framework, and most of the choices of Madison, Hamilton, and their colleagues remain unaltered.

It's true that we could tell plenty of tales of oppression, cruelty, and betrayal. It took a Civil War to abolish slavery. Until 1920, women could be forbidden from voting. Until 1954, the Constitution allowed states to segregate people by race. Freedom of speech did not flower until the 1960s. But many of the hardest-won victories can be understood as a product of the American Revolution itself—a revolution that put a principle of the equal dignity of human beings at the center of national aspirations.

When the Revolution overthrew a king, and when the Constitution prohibited titles of nobility, they reflected, and unleashed, a set of commitments that continues to ignite fires. Defending the civil rights movement, Martin Luther King, Jr., insisted, "If we are wrong, the Constitution of the United States is wrong."[2] More fires are to come. As John Dewey put it, "The United States are not yet made; they are not a finished fact to be categorically assessed."[3]

The power of impeachment provides a unique window onto the American republic. It helps to define American exceptionalism. In the eighteenth century or the twenty-first, no large nation can flourish without some kind of executive authority. For Hamilton's reasons, that authority needs to be powerful. At the same time, the executive is, by far, the most dangerous of the three branches, because it can do so much, for better or for ill, in such a short time.[4] As the framing generation saw it, there are inextricable links among the creation of a powerful presidency, the four-year term, electoral control, and the power of impeachment. You can't allow the first without the latter three.

In an echo of Franklin's plea, Supreme Court Justice Louis Brandeis, attempting to vindicate the freedom of speech, warned that "the greatest menace to freedom is an inert people."[5] If the American constitutional system is working well, or at least well enough, We the People can cast our votes and love our families and live our lives. We do not need to focus on the impeachment mechanism. But if we are going to keep our republic, we do need to know about it. It's our fail-safe, our shield, our sword—our ultimate weapon for self-defense.

And it's a lot more than that. It's a symbol and a reminder of who is really in charge, and of where sovereignty resides. As much as any provision of our founding document, it announces that Americans are citizens, not subjects. It connects each and every citizen—wherever your parents, or you, were born—to Concord's embattled farmers and to those difficult, inspired days in the middle and late 1770s, when republicanism was literally on the march. Whenever Americans strike a blow against some form of tyranny, large or small, we are honoring our nation's highest ideals, and those who were willing to live and die for them.

AFTERWORD

This book was inspired by a day: April 19, 1775.

That was the day of the Battles of Lexington and Concord, which marked the beginning of the Revolutionary War. At dawn, seven hundred British troops arrived in Lexington, where they encountered seventy-seven militiamen gathered on the town green. A British major called out, "Throw down your arms! Ye villains, ye rebels!" The British promptly routed the militiamen, killing eight. But when they came to Concord, things didn't go so well for them. On North Bridge, Major John Buttrick, leading a group of "embattled farmers," gave that fateful order: "Fire, fellow soldiers, for God's sake, *fire*!" The war was on.

April 19, 1775, was the culmination of decades of republican thought, opposing the whole idea of monarchy and reflecting this way of thinking:

> We hold these truths to be sacred & undeniable; all men
> are created equal & independant, that from that equal cre-
> ation they derive rights inherent & inalienable, among which
> are the preservation of life, & liberty, & the pursuit of hap-
> piness; that to secure these ends, governments are instituted
> among men, deriving their just powers from the consent of
> the governed; that whenever any form of government shall
> become destructive of these ends, it is the right of the people
> to alter or to abolish it, & to institute new government, laying

it's foundation on such principles & organising it's powers in such form, as to them shall seem most likely to effect their safety & happiness.

If that sounds familiar but a little discordant, it should. It's Thomas Jefferson's "original Rough draught" of the Declaration of Independence. It's less elegant than the final version, but it has its own charm.

The final version of the Declaration, adopted in 1776, reads a lot like articles of impeachment. That is no accident. The idea of impeachment played a major role in the decades that led to the fight for independence. The idea became a defining part of republicanism, American-style—and part and parcel of the attack on the claims of monarchs and monarchy, and an insistence on the equal dignity of human beings.

The system of checks and balances, the protection of freedom of speech, the commitment to free exercise of religion, the ban on titles of nobility, the protection of property rights, the very words "We the People," opening the Constitution—all this, and much more, emerged from that day in April. So did the Constitution's impeachment provisions. When Bob Dylan sang, "Goodness hides behind its gates / But even the president of the United States / Sometimes must have to stand naked," he was recalling the spirit of American republicanism.

Almost immediately after the election of Donald Trump, many people called for his impeachment. They did so not because they could point to impeachable offenses, but because they disliked him and they strongly opposed his policies. I recall one conversation with a prominent impeachment advocate who was trying to launch a campaign, in which I asked quietly, "On what grounds do you think President Trump should be impeached?" The answer came back immediately: "Climate change!"

That's not a good answer. To say the least, I do not agree with President Trump's actions with respect to climate change. But they do not amount to a high crime or misdemeanor. One of the original motivations for this book—not the driving force, but still—was to counteract what seemed to me to be reckless and irresponsible arguments for the impeachment of President Trump before his presidency even got started.

My much larger goals were to correct some recurring misunderstandings of the impeachment clause, which have played a significant role in debates over impeachment at least since the 1990s. Some of those misunderstandings are harmful to any president, including President Trump. Some of the misunderstandings are helpful to any president, including President Trump. In the current period, five of them have been especially prominent. Far too many people believe them.

1. If the president has not committed a crime, he cannot be impeached.
2. If the president has committed a crime, he can be impeached.
3. The constitutional phrase "high crimes or misdemeanors" is deliberately open-ended. It is a kind of punt, meant to give broad discretion to the House of Representatives.
4. Impeachment is a political act, unbounded by law.
5. Even if the president has committed a clearly impeachable act, the House of Representatives has discretion to refuse to impeach him.

Each of these claims is worse than wrong; it is a betrayal of the constitutional settlement. And each of them is relevant to the discussion of Special Counsel Robert Mueller's report in 2019, and to debates over the possible impeachment of President Trump. I am going to restrict the discussion here to impeachment questions raised by that report. (Of course, some people argue that there are others.) My hope is that an understanding of the Constitution's impeachment provisions will help readers to develop their own answers to those questions.

The report, called *Report on the Investigation into Russian Interference in the 2016 Presidential Election*, comes in two volumes. The first involves Russia's actions and the Trump campaign's connection to those actions. The second involves the possible obstruction of justice on the part of President Trump.

One of the distinctive features of the report, taken as a whole, is its care and caution. It does not shout. In that respect, it is a remarkable contrast from the most recent historical analogue, which is Judge Kenneth Starr's lengthy report on the investigation of President Bill Clinton. Judge Starr's report announces: "There Is Substantial and Credible Information that President Clinton Committed Acts that May Constitute Grounds for an Impeachment." It lists eleven such grounds, including these:

- "There is substantial and credible information that President Clinton lied under oath as a defendant in *Jones* v. *Clinton* regarding his sexual relationship with Monica Lewinsky."
- "There is substantial and credible information that President Clinton endeavored to obstruct justice by engaging

in a pattern of activity to conceal evidence regarding his relationship with Monica Lewinsky from the judicial process in the *Jones* case."

- "There is substantial and credible information that President Clinton endeavored to obstruct justice by helping Ms. Lewinsky obtain a job in New York at a time when she would have been an adverse witness against him were she to tell the truth during the *Jones* case."

- "There is substantial and credible information that President Clinton endeavored to obstruct justice during the federal grand jury investigation. While refusing to testify for seven months, he simultaneously lied to potential grand jury witnesses knowing that they would relay the falsehoods to the grand jury."

By contrast, the Mueller report is nearly silent on the topic of impeachment. Much of it makes for riveting reading, but it is generally focused on recitations of facts and relatively technical analysis of law (as in "The Text of Section 1512(c)(2) Prohibits a Broad Range of Obstructive Acts" and "Congress Has Power to Protect Congressional, Grand Jury, and Judicial Proceedings Against Corrupt Acts from Any Source").

Let's take the two volumes in sequence.

Russia

Mueller's report offers a detailed account of Russia's role in the 2016 campaign and its aggressive effort to ensure the election of Donald Trump. The report describes Russia's interference as "sweeping and systemic." In its words: "The campaign evolved from a generalized program designed in 2014 and 2015 to undermine the U.S. electoral system, to a targeted operation that by early 2016 favored candidate Trump and disparaged candidate Clinton."

The first form of the election interference came largely from Russia's Internet Research Agency (IRA), which conducted extensive disinformation and social media operations in the United States in order to sow internal discord and to influence the outcome of the election. It began by addressing divisive issues of law and politics, with groups and accounts stating, falsely, that they were affiliated with U.S. political organizations or controlled by U.S. activists. For example, one IRA-controlled account, on Twitter, claimed to be connected to the Tennessee Republican Party. Others claimed to be anti-immigration groups, Black Lives Matter protesters, and Tea Party activists.

By early 2016, IRA operations moved to support candidate Trump and to disparage Hillary Clinton. In March 2016, the IRA bought an advertisement featuring Clinton with a caption reading, "If one day God lets this liar enter the White House as a president—that day would be a real national tragedy."

The IRA also bought many advertisements in Trump's favor, including the Facebook groups "Secured Borders" (with 130,000 followers) and "Being Patriotic" (with 200,000 followers). The report found that the IRA controlled many Facebook groups, Instagram accounts, and Twitter accounts. About 470 Facebook accounts, controlled by the IRA, made 80,000 posts. Ultimately, the IRA was able to reach 126 million people.

Also in 2016, the Russian government's Main Intelligence

Directorate of the General Staff (GRU) employed a second form of interference: cyber intrusions (hacking) and releases of hacked materials damaging to the Clinton campaign. Two of GRU's military units undertook intrusions into the Clinton campaign, the Democratic Congressional Campaign Committee, and the Democratic National Committee. The GRU stole tens of thousands of emails. It released stolen materials through two fictitious online personas that it created: "DCLeaks" and "Guccifer 2.0." Later it did so through the organization WikiLeaks.

What did the Trump campaign do or think about all that? A lot of the report is redacted, but there is no question that people associated with the campaign were glad. The campaign "showed interest in WikiLeaks's releases of documents and welcomed their potential to damage candidate Clinton." There were many "contacts between Trump Campaign officials and individuals with ties to the Russian government." The investigation found that "the Russian government perceived it would benefit from a Trump presidency and worked to secure that outcome, and that the Campaign expected it would benefit electorally from information stolen and released through Russian efforts."

At the same time—and this is important—"the investigation did not establish that members of the Trump Campaign conspired or coordinated with the Russian government in its election interference activities." The report is careful to note that its focus was on the law of conspiracy and coordination, not on the idea of "collusion," which "is not a specific offense or theory of liability" under national criminal law. In some important places, the report suggests that its conclusion not to seek a criminal indictment was based on the "beyond a reasonable doubt" standard, which is difficult to meet. For example, "the Office did not find evidence likely to prove beyond a reasonable doubt that Campaign officials such as Paul Manafort, George Papadopoulos, and Carter Page acted as agents of the Russian government—or at its direction, control, or request—during the relevant time period."

Two aspects of volume I are shocking. The first, and the most important for the future, is the sheer scale of Russia's efforts to interfere with the operations of the democratic process in the United States. For present purposes, it does not much matter whether those efforts actually made a difference to the outcome. For Russia to engage in these kinds of actions is not exactly an act of war. But let there be no doubt about it: This was an attack. Russian interference with American democracy is a clear and present danger. It requires sustained attention.

The second is the general receptivity of some people in the Trump campaign to Russian interference and Russian help. How could that happen? I had a modest role in the Obama campaign in 2008, and from my vantage point, the idea of taking a meeting with Russian officials, in the midst of a presidential campaign, is not even imaginable. If Russian agents seek to meet with people who are working with a campaign, the best step is to decline the meeting and to contact the Federal Bureau of Investigation. The second best step is to decline the meeting and to refuse any further contact.

With respect to impeachment, two propositions are clear. First: If a successful presidential campaign conspired or co-ordinated with a foreign government to interfere with the election, a president would be impeachable—at least if he knew about the interference. (See case 7 in chapter 7.) Second: If a foreign government helped a successful campaign, and the campaign did not coordinate or conspire with it in any way, there is no basis for impeachment. It is exceedingly difficult to argue that mere knowledge of what a foreign government did or was doing, without active engagement of some kind, counts as a high crime or misdemeanor.

It is true that the special counsel found much more than mere knowledge. Members of the Trump campaign had numerous contacts with people connected to the Russian government. But so far as the report found, the candidate himself was not working with Russian agents on the campaign, and he did not order any of his subordinates to do that. To be sure, there were improprieties and worse during the campaign. But on this count, the report does not identify an impeachable offense.

Obstruction

Volume II of the report describes numerous actions or sets of actions by President Trump, and asks whether they might count as obstruction of justice. The volume is largely dedicated to a careful description of these actions or sets of actions, followed by an analysis of whether the president did, in fact, obstruct justice.

While volume I is relatively straightforward, volume II is anything but that. It makes for challenging reading. One reason is inevitable: Obstruction of justice is a complicated subject. A more surprising reason is that it is not easy to figure out what the report is actually saying.

Much of volume II consists of an exhaustive catalog of

false statements by the president and his apparent efforts to interfere with or to derail the Russian investigation. For example, Trump "denied having any business in or connections to Russia, even though as late as June 2016 the Trump Organization had been pursuing a licensing deal for a skyscraper to be built in Russia called Trump Tower Moscow." His firing of FBI director James Comey appeared to be an effort to remove the pressure coming from the FBI's investigation of Russia's role in the 2016 campaign. The day after he fired Comey, he told Russian officials that he faced "great pressure because of Russia," and that the pressure had been "taken off" as a result of the firing. And after Trump removed Comey, he directed White House Counsel Donald McGahn "to call the Acting Attorney General and say that the Special Counsel had conflicts of interest and must be removed." He also tried to get McGahn to deny that he had ordered him to have the Special Counsel removed. And there is much more.

The most puzzling thing about volume II is a single sentence, appearing first in the executive summary and then repeated twice more:

"While this report does not conclude that the President committed a crime, it also does not exonerate him."

That is an opaque sentence. What does it mean? Unraveling the puzzle is a bit like reading a mystery novel.

A strong clue comes from the report's brisk outline of the considerations that guided the special counsel's investigation of the possibility that the president obstructed justice. The first, and perhaps the most critical, is that the special counsel "determined not to make a traditional prosecutorial judgment." The reason is that as a part of the Department of Justice, the special counsel "accepted" the department's conclusion that under the Constitution, a president cannot be indicted. (I agree with that conclusion, as stated in chapter 9.) And even if we put the Constitution to one side, "a federal criminal accusation against a sitting President would place burdens on the President's capacity to govern and potentially preempt constitutional processes for addressing presidential misconduct," including impeachment. The most important word here is "accusation." The special counsel was giving a clear signal that a mere "accusation" would burden the president's ability to do his job—and hence that he would be exceedingly reluctant to make it.

The report adds that if an indictment could not be brought, it would be uniquely unfair to offer a judgment, in public, that the president committed a crime. The reason is simple: There could be no trial, and so the president could not defend himself and clear his name. "The ordinary means for an individual to respond to an accusation is through a speedy and public trial." No president could take advantage of that means in this case. Hence "we determined not to apply an approach that could potentially result in a judgment that the President committed crimes."

That is a tangled sentence. In context, the best reading is that the special counsel decided that it would not offer "a judgment that crimes were committed," in part because the president could not defend himself in court, and in part because that very judgment could affect his ability to govern.

Then the report adds this crucial sentence: "[I]f we had confidence after a thorough investigation of the facts that the President clearly did not commit obstruction of justice, we would so state." But on the basis of the facts and the legal standards, "we are unable to reach that judgment." The evidence "about the President's actions and intent presents difficult issues that prevent us from conclusively determining that no criminal conduct occurred." Hence the report "does not exonerate him."

It would be possible to read the report's analysis in two different ways. First, Mueller believed that the president probably did obstruct justice, but because President Trump cannot be indicted, he declined to say that publicly. Second, Mueller was just not sure whether the president obstructed justice—the legal and factual issues are difficult—and so he decided merely to lay out the evidence and let readers (including members of Congress) make their own decision.

The first reading is far more damning, and on reflection, something like it is probably right. Consider again these all-important words: "[W]e determined not to apply an approach that could potentially result in a judgment that the President committed crimes." The report's emphasis on the president's immunity from prosecution, and hence the impossibility of having a trial, would make little sense if the special counsel were merely saying: "I don't know whether the evidence makes out a crime."

He was not merely saying that. Instead he was saying something close to this: "The evidence probably makes out a crime, but because the president cannot be indicted, and because there can't be a trial, I'm not going to say so." That, I think, is the solution to the mystery, and the clue to the meaning of those crucial words: "[W]hile this report does not conclude that the President committed a crime, it also does not exonerate him."

The best response would point to the report's statement that "the President's actions and intent presents difficult issues that prevent us from conclusively determining that no criminal conduct occurred." The reference to "difficult issues" might be taken to support the first reading: Mueller really wasn't sure whether criminal conduct occurred. Note, however, the context of the statement—not "difficult issues" period, but "difficult issues that prevent us from conclusively determining that no criminal conduct occurred." With the report's prefatory words, emphasizing that it would be inappropriate and unfair to say that criminal conduct did occur (even if it did), the reference to "difficult issues" is not best taken as a statement of agnosticism.

In this light, we can see why Mueller's staff is reported to have been so dissatisfied with Attorney General William Barr's initial summary of their report. Barr's conclusion was that under the normal standards, Trump did not commit obstruction of justice. Mueller pointedly refused to reach that conclusion. Though the question is not free from doubt, the best bet is that he thought otherwise. To put it plainly: The best bet is that Mueller believed that Trump obstructed justice with respect to the investigation into Russia's interference with the 2016 presidential election.

That leaves a large question: What is the constitutional duty of the House of Representatives?

Precedents

To answer that question, it is natural and fair to look to historical precedents. Two of them are worth considering.

First: We have seen that President Bill Clinton was impeached in part for obstruction of justice. One of the two articles of impeachment against him charged that he corruptly encouraged a witness (Monica Lewinsky) to give perjurious testimony, and also that he corruptly supported a scheme to conceal evidence that had been subpoenaed in a civil rights action brought against him. As we have also seen, the House of Representatives, in voting for that article, plainly violated its constitutional duty. Obstruction of justice was not, in that case, an impeachable offense under the founding document, because it did not involve an egregious misuse of distinctly presidential authority.

If a president uses that authority to obstruct justice with respect to an investigation of (say) his use of presidential powers to punish political opponents, the constitutional question would be easy; that would be a misdemeanor within the meaning of the impeachment clause. But the Clinton impeachment should not be taken as a precedent for anything, just because the obstruction of justice, in that case, was so wildly far afield from the concerns that animated the impeachment provisions.

Second: Recall that with respect to President Richard Nixon, the House Judiciary Committee voted in favor of (1) an article of impeachment that involved a refusal to respond to duly authorized subpoenas and (2) an article of impeachment that involved a conspiracy to cover up the Watergate break-in. The former article is not directly relevant to the Mueller report. The latter is closer. That article contended that Nixon "has prevented, obstructed, and impeded the administration of justice." More specifically, Nixon was charged with

- *making false or misleading statements to lawfully authorized investigative officers and employees of the United States;*
- *withholding relevant and material evidence or information from lawfully authorized investigative officers and employees of the United States;*
- *approving, condoning, acquiescing in, and counselling witnesses with respect to the giving of false or misleading statements to lawfully authorized investigative officers and employees of the United States and false or misleading testimony in duly instituted judicial and congressional proceedings;*
- *interfering or endeavouring to interfere with the conduct of investigations by the Department of Justice of the United States, the Federal Bureau of Investigation, the office of Watergate Special Prosecution Force, and Congressional Committees;*
- *approving, condoning, and acquiescing in, the surreptitious payment of substantial sums of money for the purpose of obtaining the silence or influencing the testimony of witnesses, potential witnesses or individuals who participated in such unlawful entry and other illegal activities; . . .*
- *making or causing to be made false or misleading public statements for the purpose of deceiving the people of the United States into believing that a thorough and complete investigation had been conducted with respect to allegations of misconduct on the part of personnel of the executive branch of the United States and personnel of the Committee for the Re-election of the President, and that there was no involvement of such personnel in such misconduct; or*
- *endeavouring to cause prospective defendants, and individuals duly tried and convicted, to expect favoured treatment and consideration in return for their silence or false*

testimony, or rewarding individuals for their silence or false testimony.

It's quite a list. There is no serious question that the House Judiciary Committee was right to conclude that these actions constituted an impeachment offense. Nixon's obstruction involved a lawful investigation into his campaign's abuses of the democratic process, through spying on the opposing political party. They were not the worst imaginable abuses, to be sure (and they were far less egregious abuses than those committed by Russia in connection with the 2016 presidential election). But they were abuses nonetheless.

In considering the Nixon precedent, we should note that the special counsel did not conclude that candidate Trump, or the Trump campaign, conspired or cooperated with Russia. It is also important to note that Mueller declined to say that Trump committed obstruction of justice (though for reasons sketched above, he probably thinks that he did). It is both instructive and fair for readers—whatever their political party, and whatever their conclusions—to compare the actions catalogued in volume II of the report with the actions described above.

The Duty of the House of Representatives

In an important statement, House Speaker Nancy Pelosi said, in response to an interview question, "I'm not for impeachment." Speaking more than a month before the release of the Mueller report, she explained: "Impeachment is so divisive to the country that unless there's something so compelling and overwhelming and bipartisan, I don't think we should go down that path, because it divides the country."

If we take her comment as stating a general proposition about impeachment, it makes a lot of sense. As the Constitution's framers and ratifiers were well aware, impeachment should not be a political weapon—a way for political losers to undo the effects of an election. Recall that the term "maladministration" was rejected at the Constitutional Convention, and that the debate over impeachment culminated in a standard that would forbid impeachment because a president's opponents intensely disliked him or disapproved of his policies. Pelosi's emphasis on what is "compelling and overwhelming and bipartisan" can be taken to speak for the founding generation.

At the same time, her statement can easily be read in a way that puts it at odds with the Constitution. It's best to assume that Pelosi did not mean it in that way. But on such a fundamental question, we should get very clear on what the founding document means and requires.

One last time: In the domain of impeachment, it is crucial to embrace a firm commitment to political neutrality. If you like a particular president and agree with his policies, you should assess an alleged basis for impeachment by asking: *How would I evaluate that claim if I disliked him and disagreed with his policies?* It is at least as important to say that if you dislike a particular president and abhor his policies, you should assess an alleged basis for impeachment by asking: *How would I evaluate that claim if I liked him and loved his policies?* It is even better to adopt a veil of ignorance and to ask: *If I knew nothing at all about a president, would I think that the claim against him made out an impeachable offense?*

Suppose that a president commits a clearly impeachable offense—by, say, committing treason or by using the apparatus of government to violate people's rights and liberties. Suppose, too, that many members of the president's party remain intensely loyal to him, thinking, "True, he's horrible in some ways, but he's good on a lot of other issues, and anyhow, he's our guy, the captain of our team." In those circumstances, the Constitution does not license members of the House of Representatives to refrain from impeachment, on the ground that it would not be "bipartisan" and would "divide the country."

We have seen that the impeachment mechanism was specifically designed as a response to those who feared that by establishing a powerful president, the new Constitution would re-create a kind of monarchy and thus betray the principles for which the Revolution had been fought. Without the impeachment mechanism, the nation would probably have refused to ratify the Constitution. To those who are inclined to take Pelosi's words at face value, it is worth recalling George Mason's critical words at the Constitutional Convention:

> No point is of more importance than that the right of impeachment should be continued. Shall any man be above Justice? Above all shall that man be above it, who can commit the most extensive injustice? . . . Shall the man who has practised corruption & by that means procured his appointment in the first instance, be suffered to escape punishment, by repeating his guilt?

In this light, it defies belief to think that the impeachment process is purely "political"—or that the House of

Representatives may decline to proceed against a president who has engaged in treason, produced "the most extensive injustice," or otherwise committed a clearly impeachable offense. If Pelosi meant to say otherwise—to suggest that the House can refrain from acting unless impeachment is "bipartisan" or not "divisive"—she was speaking in patent defiance of the constitutional plan. But it would be possible to understand her words more narrowly.

In some cases, reasonable people might agree on the constitutional standard while disagreeing on the facts. Pelosi might have meant that impeachment is not a good idea unless there is "compelling and overwhelming" evidence that the president actually engaged in actions that would amount to an impeachable offense. If so, her position is perfectly sensible.

In other cases, reasonable people might agree on the facts but disagree about whether the constitutional standard is met—about whether a president's actions count as a "high crime and misdemeanor." It is important to note that in their context, those words are far less ambiguous than they seem. They set out a pretty clear legal standard.

Some cases do fall within a gray area. We have seen that article III of the impeachment articles against President Richard Nixon, pointing to his failure to comply with congressional subpoenas, is an example. It is hardly crazy to insist that if it is not clear whether the president has committed what the Constitution deems to be an impeachable act, the House is entitled to refrain from acting, at least when the nation is sharply divided along political lines.

There is a much larger point here. During the outrage and battles of the moment, the Constitution provides a lodestar, focusing us instead on enduring ideals. In the eighteenth century, a lot of people put their lives on the line for those ideals. In the founding document, they turned one of their ideals into a principle, which deserves to be put in bold letters: **If a president has committed a clearly impeachable offense, the House of Representatives is obliged to impeach him—even if the process does not turn out to be "bipartisan," and even if it is "divisive."**

What Follows

The two volumes of the Mueller report run some 448 pages. Much of it makes for riveting reading—especially, perhaps, on Russia's actions during the 2016 campaign, and also on some of the actions of the president and his staff after the election. What follows is an effort to capture the highlights (with all footnotes omitted). In a sense, the authors of the report made that easy, because they included helpful and relatively comprehensive executive summaries (reprinted here in full). With respect to the question of obstruction of justice, however, it is not easy to get clarity on the underlying issues without more details. Some of the most important of them are supplied here. Interested readers are of course invited to consult the entire report.

Executive Summaries and Excerpts from the

Report on the Investigation into Russian Interference in the 2016 Presidential Election

Special Counsel Robert S. Mueller, III

Washington, D.C.

March 2019

N.B.: All footnotes from the full report have been omitted.

. . .

INTRODUCTION TO VOLUME I

This report is submitted to the Attorney General pursuant to 28 C.F.R. § 600.S(c), which states that, "[a]t the conclusion of the Special Counsel's work, he . . . shall provide the Attorney General a confidential report explaining the prosecution or declination decisions [the Special Counsel] reached."

The Russian government interfered in the 2016 presidential election in sweeping and systematic fashion. Evidence of Russian government operations began to surface in mid-2016. In June, the Democratic National Committee and its cyber response team publicly announced that Russian hackers had compromised its computer network. Releases of hacked materials—hacks that public reporting soon attributed to the Russian government—began that same month. Additional releases followed in July through the organization WikiLeaks, with further releases in October and November.

In late July 2016, soon after WikiLeaks's first release of stolen documents, a foreign government contacted the FBI about a May 2016 encounter with Trump Campaign foreign policy advisor George Papadopoulos. Papadopoulos had suggested to a representative of that foreign government that the Trump Campaign had received indications from the Russian government that it could assist the Campaign through the anonymous release of information damaging to Democratic presidential candidate Hillary Clinton. That information prompted the FBI on July 31, 2016, to open an investigation into whether individuals associated with the Trump Campaign were coordinating with the Russian government in its interference activities.

That fall, two federal agencies jointly announced that the Russian government "directed recent compromises of e-mails from US persons and institutions, including US political organizations," and, "[t]hese thefts and disclosures are intended to interfere with the US election process." After the election, in late December 2016, the United States imposed sanctions on Russia for having interfered in the election. By early 2017, several congressional committees were examining Russia's interference in the election.

Within the Executive Branch, these investigatory efforts ultimately led to the May 2017 appointment of Special Counsel Robert S. Mueller, III. The order appointing the Special Counsel authorized him to investigate "the Russian government's efforts to interfere in the 2016 presidential election," including any links or coordination between the Russian government and individuals associated with the Trump Campaign.

As set forth in detail in this report, the Special Counsel's investigation established that Russia interfered in the 2016 presidential election principally through two operations. First, a Russian entity carried out a social media campaign that favored presidential candidate Donald J. Trump and disparaged presidential candidate Hillary Clinton. Second, a Russian intelligence service conducted computer-intrusion operations against entities, employees, and volunteers working on the Clinton Campaign and then released stolen documents. The investigation also identified numerous links between the Russian government and the Trump Campaign. Although the investigation established that the Russian government perceived it would benefit from a Trump presidency and worked to secure that outcome, and that the Campaign expected it would benefit electorally from information stolen and released through Russian efforts, the investigation did not establish that members of the Trump Campaign conspired or coordinated with the Russian government in its election interference activities.

* * *

Below we describe the evidentiary considerations underpinning statements about the results of our investigation and the Special Counsel's charging decisions, and we then provide an overview of the two volumes of our report.

The report describes actions and events that the Special Counsel's Office found to be supported by the evidence collected in our investigation. In some instances, the report points out the absence of evidence or conflicts in the evidence about a particular fact or event. In other instances, when substantial, credible evidence enabled the Office to reach a conclusion with confidence, the report states that the investigation established that certain actions or events occurred. A statement that the investigation did not establish particular facts does not mean there was no evidence of those facts.

In evaluating whether evidence about collective action of multiple individuals constituted a crime, we applied the framework of conspiracy law, not the concept of "collusion." In so doing, the Office recognized that the word "collud[e]" was used in communications with the Acting Attorney General confirming certain aspects of the investigation's scope and that the term has frequently been invoked in public reporting about the investigation. But collusion is not a specific offense or theory of liability found in the United States Code, nor is it a term of art in federal criminal law. For those reasons, the Office's focus in analyzing questions of joint criminal liability was on conspiracy as defined in federal law. In connection with that analysis, we addressed the factual question whether members of the Trump Campaign "coordinat[ed]"—a term that appears in the appointment order—with Russian election interference activities. Like collusion, "coordination" does not have a settled definition in federal criminal law. We understood coordination to require an agreement—tacit or express—between the Trump Campaign and the Russian government on election interference. That requires more than the two parties taking actions that were informed by or responsive to the other's actions or interests. We applied the term coordination in that sense when stating in the report that the investigation did not establish that the Trump Campaign coordinated with the Russian government in its election interference activities.

• • •

EXECUTIVE SUMMARY TO VOLUME I

RUSSIAN SOCIAL MEDIA CAMPAIGN

The Internet Research Agency (IRA) carried out the earliest Russian interference operations identified by the investigation—a social media campaign designed to provoke and amplify political and social discord in the United States. The IRA was based in St. Petersburg, Russia, and received funding from Russian oligarch Yevgeniy Prigozhin and companies he controlled. Prigozhin is widely reported to have ties to Russian President Vladimir Putin, Harm to Ongoing Matter

In mid-2014, the IRA sent employees to the United States on an intelligence-gathering mission with instructions Harm to Ongoing Matter

The IRA later used social media accounts and interest groups to sow discord in the U.S. political system through what it termed "information warfare." The campaign evolved from a generalized program designed in 2014 and 2015 to undermine the U.S. electoral system, to a targeted operation that by early 2016 favored candidate Trump and disparaged candidate Clinton. The IRA's operation also included the purchase of political advertisements on social media in the names of U.S. persons and entities, as well as the staging of political rallies inside the United States. To organize those rallies, IRA employees posed as U.S. grassroots entities and persons and made contact with Trump supporters and Trump Campaign officials in the United States. The investigation did not identify evidence that any U.S. persons conspired or coordinated with the IRA. Section II of this report details the Office's investigation of the Russian social media campaign.

RUSSIAN HACKING OPERATIONS

At the same time that the IRA operation began to focus on supporting candidate Trump in early 2016, the Russian government employed a second form of interference: cyber intrusions (hacking) and releases of hacked materials damaging to the Clinton Campaign. The Russian intelligence service known as the Main Intelligence Directorate of the General Staff of the Russian Army (GRU) carried out these operations.

In March 2016, the GRU began hacking the email accounts of Clinton Campaign volunteers and employees, including campaign chairman John Podesta. In April 2016, the GRU hacked into the computer networks of the Democratic Congressional Campaign Committee (DCCC) and the Democratic National Committee (DNC). The GRU stole hundreds of thousands of documents from the compromised email accounts and networks. Around the time that the DNC announced in mid-June 2016 the

Russian government's role in hacking its network, the GRU began disseminating stolen materials through the fictitious online personas "DCLeaks" and "Guccifer 2.0." The GRU later released additional materials through the organization WikiLeaks.

The presidential campaign of Donald J. Trump ("Trump Campaign" or "Campaign") showed interest in WikiLeaks's releases of documents and welcomed their potential to damage candidate Clinton. Beginning in June 2016, ▇▇▇ Harm to Ongoing Matter ▇▇▇ forecast to senior Campaign officials that WikiLeaks would release information damaging to candidate Clinton. WikiLeaks's first release came in July 2016. Around the same time, candidate Trump announced that he hoped Russia would recover emails described as missing from a private server used by Clinton when she was Secretary of State (he later said that he was speaking sarcastically). ▇▇▇

▇▇▇ Harm to Ongoing Matter ▇▇▇

▇▇▇ WikiLeaks began releasing Podesta's stolen emails on October 7, 2016, less than one hour after a U.S. media outlet released video considered damaging to candidate Trump. Section III of this Report details the Office's investigation into the Russian hacking operations, as well as other efforts by Trump Campaign supporters to obtain Clinton-related emails.

RUSSIAN CONTACTS WITH THE CAMPAIGN

The social media campaign and the GRU hacking operations coincided with a series of contacts between Trump Campaign officials and individuals with ties to the Russian government. The Office investigated whether those contacts reflected or resulted in the Campaign conspiring or coordinating with Russia in its election-interference activities. Although the investigation established that the Russian government perceived it would benefit from a Trump presidency and worked to secure that outcome, and that the Campaign expected it would benefit electorally from information stolen and released through Russian efforts, the investigation did not establish that members of the Trump Campaign conspired or coordinated with the Russian government in its election interference activities.

The Russian contacts consisted of business connections, offers of assistance to the Campaign, invitations for candidate Trump and Putin to meet in person, invitations for Campaign officials and representatives of the Russian government to meet, and policy positions seeking improved U.S.-Russian relations. Section IV of this Report details the contacts between Russia and the Trump Campaign during the campaign and transition periods, the most salient of which are summarized below in chronological order.

2015. Some of the earliest contacts were made in connection with a Trump Organization real-estate project in Russia known as Trump Tower Moscow. Candidate Trump signed a Letter of Intent for Trump Tower Moscow by November 2015, and in January 2016 Trump Organization executive Michael Cohen emailed and spoke about the project with the office of Russian government press secretary Dmitry Peskov. The Trump Organization pursued the project through at least June 2016, including by considering travel to Russia by Cohen and candidate Trump.

Spring 2016. Campaign foreign policy advisor George Papadopoulos made early contact with Joseph Mifsud, a London-based professor who had connections to Russia and traveled to Moscow in April 2016. Immediately upon his return to London from that trip, Mifsud told Papadopoulos that the Russian government had "dirt" on Hillary Clinton in the form of thousands of emails. One week later, in the first week of May 2016, Papadopoulos suggested to a representative of a foreign government that the Trump Campaign had received indications from the Russian government that it could assist the Campaign through the anonymous release of information damaging to candidate Clinton. Throughout that period of time and for several months thereafter, Papadopoulos worked with Mifsud and two Russian nationals to arrange a meeting between the Campaign and the Russian government. No meeting took place.

Summer 2016. Russian outreach to the Trump Campaign continued into the summer of 2016, as candidate Trump was becoming the presumptive Republican nominee for President. On June 9, 2016, for example, a Russian lawyer met with senior Trump Campaign officials Donald Trump Jr., Jared Kushner, and campaign chairman Paul Manafort to deliver what the email proposing the meeting had described as "official documents and information that would incriminate Hillary." The materials were offered to Trump Jr. as "part of Russia and its government's support for Mr. Trump." The written communications setting up the meeting showed that the Campaign anticipated receiving information from Russia that could assist candidate Trump's electoral prospects, but the Russian lawyer's presentation did not provide such information.

Days after the June 9 meeting, on June 14, 2016, a cybersecurity firm and the DNC announced that Russian government hackers had infiltrated the DNC and obtained access to opposition research on candidate Trump, among other documents.

In July 2016, Campaign foreign policy advisor Carter Page traveled in his personal capacity to Moscow and gave the keynote address at the New Economic School. Page had lived and worked in Russia between 2003 and 2007. After returning to the United States, Page became acquainted with at least two Russian intelligence officers, one of whom was later charged in 2015 with conspiracy to act as an unregistered agent of Russia. Page's July 2016 trip to Moscow and his advocacy for pro-Russian foreign policy drew media attention. The Campaign then distanced itself from Page and, by late September 2016, removed him from the Campaign.

July 2016 was also the month WikiLeaks first released emails stolen by the GRU from the DNC. On July 22, 2016, WikiLeaks posted thousands of internal DNC documents revealing information about the Clinton Campaign. Within days, there was public reporting that U.S. intelligence agencies had "high confidence" that the Russian government was behind the theft of emails and documents from the DNC. And within a week of the release, a foreign government informed the FBI about its May 2016 interaction with Papadopoulos and his statement that the Russian government could assist the Trump Campaign. On July 31, 2016, based on the foreign government reporting, the FBI opened an investigation into potential coordination between the Russian government and individuals associated with the Trump Campaign.

Separately, on August 2, 2016, Trump campaign chairman Paul Manafort met in New York City with his long-time business associate Konstantin Kilimnik, who the FBI assesses to have ties to Russian intelligence. Kilimnik requested the meeting to deliver in person a peace plan for Ukraine that Manafort acknowledged to the Special Counsel's Office was a "backdoor" way for Russia to control part of eastern Ukraine; both men believed the plan would require candidate Trump's assent to succeed (were he to be elected President). They also discussed the status of the Trump Campaign and Manafort's strategy for winning Democratic votes in Midwestern states. Months before that meeting, Manafort had caused internal polling data to be shared with Kilimnik, and the sharing continued for some period of time after their August meeting.

Fall 2016. On October 7, 2016, the media released video of candidate Trump speaking in graphic terms about women years earlier, which was considered damaging to his candidacy. Less than an hour later, WikiLeaks made its second release: thousands of John Podesta's emails that had been stolen by the GRU in late March 2016. The FBI and other U.S. government institutions were at the time continuing their investigation of suspected Russian government efforts to interfere in the presidential election. That same day, October 7, the Department of Homeland Security and the Office of the Director of National Intelligence issued a joint public statement "that the Russian Government directed the recent compromises of e-mails from US persons and institutions, including from US political organizations." Those "thefts" and the "disclosures" of the hacked materials through online platforms such as WikiLeaks, the statement continued, "are intended to interfere with the US election process."

Post-2016 Election. Immediately after the November 8 election, Russian government officials and prominent Russian businessmen began trying to make inroads into the new administration. The most senior levels of the Russian government encouraged these efforts. The Russian Embassy made contact hours after the election to congratulate the President-Elect and to arrange a call with President Putin. Several Russian businessmen picked up the effort from there.

Kirill Dmitriev, the chief executive officer of Russia's sovereign wealth fund, was among the Russians who tried to make contact with the incoming administration. In early December, a business associate steered Dmitriev to Erik Prince, a supporter of the Trump Campaign and an associate of senior Trump advisor Steve Bannon. Dmitriev and Prince later met face-to-face in January 2017 in the Seychelles and discussed U.S.-Russia relations. During the same period, another business associate introduced Dmitriev to a friend of Jared Kushner who had not served on the Campaign or the Transition Team. Dmitriev and Kushner's friend collaborated on a short written reconciliation plan for the United States and Russia, which Dmitriev implied had been cleared through Putin. The friend gave that proposal to Kushner before the inauguration, and Kushner later gave copies to Bannon and incoming Secretary of State Rex Tillerson.

On December 29, 2016, then-President Obama imposed sanctions on Russia for having interfered in the election. Incoming National Security Advisor Michael Flynn called Russian Ambassador Sergey Kislyak and asked Russia not to escalate the situation in response to the sanctions. The following day, Putin announced that Russia would not take retaliatory measures in response to the sanctions at that time. Hours later, President-Elect Trump tweeted, "Great move on delay (by V. Putin)." The next day, on December 31, 2016, Kislyak called Flynn and told him the request had been received at the highest levels and Russia had chosen not to retaliate as a result of Flynn's request.

* * *

On January 6, 2017, members of the intelligence community briefed President-Elect Trump on a joint assessment—drafted and coordinated among the Central Intelligence Agency, FBI, and National Security Agency—that concluded with high confidence that Russia had intervened in the election through a variety of means to assist Trump's candidacy and harm Clinton's. A declassified version of the assessment was publicly released that same day.

Between mid-January 2017 and early February 2017, three congressional committees—the House Permanent Select Committee on Intelligence (HPSCI), the Senate Select Committee on Intelligence (SSCI), and the Senate Judiciary Committee (SJC)—announced that they would conduct inquiries, or had already been conducting inquiries, into Russian interference in the election. Then-FBI Director James Comey later confirmed to Congress the existence of the FBI's investigation into Russian interference that had begun before the election. On March 20, 2017, in open-session testimony before HPSCI, Comey stated:

> I have been authorized by the Department of Justice to confirm that the FBI, as part of our counterintelligence mission, is investigating the Russian government's efforts to interfere in the 2016 presidential election, and that includes investigating the nature of any links between individuals associated with the Trump campaign and the Russian government and whether there was any coordination between the campaign and Russia's efforts. . . . As with any counterintelligence investigation, this will also include an assessment of whether any crimes were committed.

The investigation continued under then-Director Comey for the next seven weeks until May 9, 2017, when President Trump fired Comey as FBI Director—an action which is analyzed in Volume II of the report.

On May 17, 2017, Acting Attorney General Rod Rosenstein appointed the Special Counsel and authorized him to conduct the investigation that Comey had confirmed in his congressional testimony, as well as matters arising directly from the investigation, and any other matters within the scope of 28 C.F.R. § 600.4(a), which generally covers efforts to interfere with or obstruct the investigation.

President Trump reacted negatively to the Special Counsel's appointment. He told advisors that it was the end of his presidency, sought to have Attorney General Jefferson (Jeff) Sessions unrecuse from the Russia investigation and to have the Special Counsel removed, and engaged in efforts to curtail the Special Counsel's investigation and prevent the disclosure of evidence to it, including through public and private contacts with potential witnesses. Those and related actions are described and analyzed in Volume II of the report.

* * *

THE SPECIAL COUNSEL'S CHARGING DECISIONS

In reaching the charging decisions described in Volume I of the report, the Office determined whether the conduct it found amounted to a violation of federal criminal law chargeable under the Principles of Federal Prosecution. *See* Justice Manual § 9-27.000 *et seq.* (2018). The standard set forth in the Justice Manual is whether the conduct constitutes a crime; if so, whether admissible evidence would probably be sufficient to obtain and sustain a conviction; and whether prosecution would serve a substantial federal interest that could not be adequately served by prosecution elsewhere or through non-criminal alternatives. *See* Justice Manual § 9-27.220.

Section V of the report provides detailed explanations of the Office's charging decisions, which contain three main components.

First, the Office determined that Russia's two principal interference operations in the 2016 U.S. presidential election—the social media campaign and the hacking-and-dumping operations—violated U.S. criminal law. Many of the individuals and entities involved in the social media campaign have been charged with participating in a conspiracy to defraud the United States by undermining through deceptive acts the work of federal agencies charged with regulating foreign influence in U.S. elections, as well as related counts of identity theft. *See United States v. Internet Research Agency, et al.*, No. 18-cr-32 (D.D.C.). Separately, Russian intelligence officers who carried out the hacking into Democratic Party computers and the personal email accounts of individuals affiliated with the Clinton Campaign conspired to violate, among other federal laws, the federal computer-intrusion statute, and the have been so charged. *See United States v. Netyksho, et al.*, No. 18-cr-215 (D.D.C.). Harm to Ongoing Matter

Personal Privacy

Second, while the investigation identified numerous links between individuals with ties to the Russian government and individuals associated with the Trump Campaign, the evidence was not sufficient to support criminal charges. Among other things, the evidence was not sufficient to charge any Campaign official as an unregistered agent of the Russian government or other Russian principal. And our evidence about the June 9, 2016, meeting and WikiLeaks's releases of hacked materials was not sufficient to charge a criminal campaign-finance violation. Further, the evidence was not sufficient to charge that any member of the Trump Campaign conspired with representatives of the Russian government to interfere in the 2016 election.

Third, the investigation established that several individuals affiliated with the Trump Campaign lied to the Office, and to Congress, about their interactions with Russian-affiliated individuals and related matters. Those lies materially impaired the investigation of Russian election interference. The Office charged some of those lies as violations of the federal false-statements statute. Former National Security Advisor Michael Flynn pleaded guilty to lying about his interactions with Russian Ambassador Kislyak during the transition period. George Papadopoulos, a foreign policy advisor during the campaign period, pleaded guilty to lying to investigators about, *inter alia*, the nature and timing of his interactions with Joseph Mifsud, the professor who told Papadopoulos that the Russians had dirt on candidate Clinton in the form of thousands of emails. Former Trump Organization attorney Michael Cohen pleaded guilty to making false statements to Congress about the Trump Moscow project. ▮▮▮▮▮▮▮▮

Harm to Ongoing Matter

▮▮

▮▮

▮▮▮▮▮▮▮▮▮▮▮▮▮▮▮▮▮▮▮▮▮▮▮▮▮▮▮▮▮▮ And in February 2019, the U.S. District Court for the District of Columbia found that Manafort lied to the Office and the grand jury concerning his interactions and communications with Konstantin Kilimnik about Trump Campaign polling data and a peace plan for Ukraine.

* * *

The Office investigated several other events that have been publicly reported to involve potential Russia-related contacts. For example, the investigation established that interactions between Russian Ambassador Kislyak and Trump Campaign officials both at the candidate's April 2016 foreign policy speech in Washington, D.C., and during the week of the Republican National Convention were brief, public, and non-substantive. And the investigation did not establish that one Campaign official's efforts to dilute a portion of the Republican Party platform on providing assistance to Ukraine were undertaken at the behest of candidate Trump or Russia. The investigation also did not establish that a meeting between Kislyak and Sessions in September 2016 at Sessions's Senate office included any more than a passing mention of the presidential campaign.

The investigation did not always yield admissible information or testimony, or a complete picture of the activities undertaken by subjects of the investigation. Some individuals invoked their

Fifth Amendment right against compelled self-incrimination and were not, in the Office's judgment, appropriate candidates for grants of immunity. The Office limited its pursuit of other witnesses and information—such as information known to attorneys or individuals claiming to be members of the media—in light of internal Department of Justice policies. *See, e.g.*, Justice Manual §§ 9-13.400, 13.410. Some of the information obtained via court process, moreover, was presumptively covered by legal privilege and was screened from investigators by a filter (or "taint") team. Even when individuals testified or agreed to be interviewed, they sometimes provided information that was false or incomplete, leading to some of the false-statements charges described above. And the Office faced practical limits on its ability to access relevant evidence as well—numerous witnesses and subjects lived abroad, and documents were held outside the United States.

Further, the Office learned that some of the individuals we interviewed or whose conduct we investigated—including some associated with the Trump Campaign—deleted relevant communications or communicated during the relevant period using applications that feature encryption or that do not provide for long-term retention of data or communications records. In such cases, the Office was not able to corroborate witness statements through comparison to contemporaneous communications or fully question witnesses about statements that appeared inconsistent with other known facts.

Accordingly, while this report embodies factual and legal determinations that the Office believes to be accurate and complete to the greatest extent possible, given these identified gaps, the Office cannot rule out the possibility that the unavailable information would shed additional light on (or cast in a new light) the events described in the report.

· · ·

Introduction to Volume II

This report is submitted to the Attorney General pursuant to 28 C.F.R. § 600.8(c), which states that, "[a]t the conclusion of the Special Counsel's work, he . . . shall provide the Attorney General a confidential report explaining the prosecution or declination decisions [the Special Counsel] reached."

Beginning in 2017, the President of the United States took a variety of actions towards the ongoing FBI investigation into Russia's interference in the 2016 presidential election and related matters that raised questions about whether he had obstructed justice. The Order appointing the Special Counsel gave this Office jurisdiction to investigate matters that arose directly from the FBI's Russia investigation, including whether the President had obstructed justice in connection with Russia-related investigations. The Special Counsel's jurisdiction also covered potentially obstructive acts related to the Special Counsel's investigation itself. This Volume of our report summarizes our obstruction-of-justice investigation of the President.

We first describe the considerations that guided our obstruction-of-justice investigation, and then provide an overview of this Volume:

First, a traditional prosecution or declination decision entails a binary determination to initiate or decline a prosecution, but we determined not to make a traditional prosecutorial judgment. The Office of Legal Counsel (OLC) has issued an opinion finding that "the indictment or criminal prosecution of a sitting President would impermissibly undermine the capacity of the executive branch to perform its constitutionally assigned functions" in violation of "the constitutional separation of powers." Given the role of the Special Counsel as an attorney in the Department of Justice and the framework of the Special Counsel regulations, *see* 28 U.S.C. § 515; 28 C.F.R. § 600.7(a), this Office accepted OLC's legal conclusion for the purpose of exercising prosecutorial jurisdiction. And apart from OLC's constitutional view, we recognized that a federal criminal accusation against a sitting President would place burdens on the President's capacity to govern and potentially preempt constitutional processes for addressing presidential misconduct.

Second, while the OLC opinion concludes that a sitting President may not be prosecuted, it recognizes that a criminal investigation during the President's term is permissible. The OLC opinion also recognizes that a President does not have immunity after he leaves office. And if individuals other than the President committed an obstruction offense, they may be prosecuted at this time. Given those considerations, the facts known to us, and the strong public interest in safeguarding the integrity of the criminal justice system, we conducted a thorough factual investigation in order to preserve the evidence when memories were fresh and documentary materials were available.

Third, we considered whether to evaluate the conduct we investigated under the Justice Manual standards governing prosecution and declination decisions, but we determined not to apply an approach that could potentially result in a judgment that the President committed crimes. The threshold step under the Justice Manual standards is to assess whether a person's conduct "constitutes a federal offense." U.S. Dep't of Justice, Justice Manual § 9-27.220 (2018) (Justice Manual). Fairness concerns counseled against potentially reaching that judgment when no charges can be brought. The ordinary means for an individual to respond to an accusation is through a speedy and public trial, with all the procedural protections that surround a criminal case. An individual who believes he was wrongly accused can use that process to seek to clear his name. In contrast, a prosecutor's judgment that crimes were committed, but that no charges will be brought, affords no such adversarial opportunity for public name-clearing before an impartial adjudicator.

The concerns about the fairness of such a determination would be heightened in the case of a sitting President, where a federal prosecutor's accusation of a crime, even in an internal report, could carry consequences that extend beyond the realm of criminal justice. OLC noted similar concerns about sealed indictments. Even if an indictment were sealed during the President's term, OLC reasoned, "it would be very difficult to preserve [an indictment's] secrecy," and if an indictment became public, "[t]he stigma and opprobrium" could imperil the President's ability to govern." Although a prosecutor's internal report would not represent a formal public accusation akin to an indictment, the possibility of the report's public disclosure and the absence of a neutral adjudicatory forum to review its findings counseled against potentially determining "that the person's conduct constitutes a federal offense." Justice Manual § 9-27.220.

Fourth, if we had confidence after a thorough investigation of the facts that the President clearly did not commit obstruction of justice, we would so state. Based on the facts and the applicable legal standards, however, we are unable to reach that judgment. The evidence we obtained about the President's actions and intent presents difficult issues that prevent us from conclusively determining that no criminal conduct occurred. Accordingly, while this report does not conclude that the President committed a crime, it also does not exonerate him.

* * *

This report on our investigation consists of four parts. Section I provides an overview of obstruction-of-justice principles and summarizes certain investigatory and evidentiary considerations. Section II sets forth the factual results of our obstruction investigation and analyzes the evidence. Section III addresses statutory and constitutional defenses. Section IV states our conclusion.

EXECUTIVE SUMMARY TO VOLUME II

Our obstruction-of-justice inquiry focused on a series of actions by the President that related to the Russian-interference investigations, including the President's conduct towards the law enforcement officials overseeing the investigations and the witnesses to relevant events.

FACTUAL RESULTS OF THE OBSTRUCTION INVESTIGATION

The key issues and events we examined include the following:

The Campaign's response to reports about Russian support for Trump. During the 2016 presidential campaign, questions arose about the Russian government's apparent support for candidate Trump. After WikiLeaks released politically damaging Democratic Party emails that were reported to have been hacked by Russia, Trump publicly expressed skepticism that Russia was responsible for the hacks at the same time that he and other Campaign officials privately sought information Harm to Ongoing Matter about any further planned WikiLeaks releases. Trump also denied having any business in or connections to Russia, even though as late as June 2016 the Trump Organization had been pursuing a licensing deal for a skyscraper to be built in Russia called Trump Tower Moscow. After the election, the President expressed concerns to advisors that reports of Russia's election interference might lead the public to question the legitimacy of his election.

Conduct involving FBI Director Comey and Michael Flynn. In mid-January 2017, incoming National Security Advisor Michael Flynn falsely denied to the Vice President, other administration officials, and FBI agents that he had talked to Russian Ambassador Sergey Kislyak about Russia's response to U.S. sanctions on Russia for its election interference. On January 27, the day after the President was told that Flynn had lied to the Vice President and had made similar statements to the FBI, the President invited FBI Director Comey to a private dinner at the White House and told Comey that he needed loyalty. On February 14, the day after the President requested Flynn's resignation, the President told an outside advisor, "Now that we fired Flynn, the Russia thing is over." The advisor disagreed and said the investigations would continue.

Later that afternoon, the President cleared the Oval Office to have a one-on-one meeting with Comey. Referring to the FBI's investigation of Flynn, the President said, "I hope you can see your way clear to letting this go, to letting Flynn go. He is a good guy. I hope you can let this go." Shortly after requesting Flynn's resignation and speaking privately to Comey, the President sought to have Deputy National Security Advisor K.T. McFarland draft an internal letter stating that the President had not directed Flynn to discuss sanctions with Kislyak. McFarland declined because she did not know whether that was true, and a White House Counsel's Office attorney thought that the request would look like a quid pro quo for an ambassadorship she had been offered.

The President's reaction to the continuing Russia investigation. In February 2017, Attorney General Jeff Sessions began to assess whether he had to recuse himself from campaign-related investigations because of his role in the Trump Campaign. In early March, the President told White House Counsel Donald McGahn to stop Sessions from recusing. And after Sessions announced his recusal on March 2, the President expressed anger at the decision and told advisors that he should have an Attorney General who would protect him. That weekend, the President took Sessions aside at an event and urged him to "unrecuse." Later in March, Comey publicly disclosed at a congressional hearing that the FBI was investigating "the Russian government's efforts to interfere in the 2016 presidential election," including any links or coordination between the Russian government and the Trump Campaign. In the following days, the President reached out to the Director of National Intelligence and the leaders of the Central Intelligence Agency (CIA) and the National Security Agency (NSA) to ask them what they could do to publicly dispel the suggestion that the President had any connection to the Russian election-interference effort. The President also twice called Comey directly, notwithstanding guidance from McGahn to avoid direct contacts with the Department of Justice. Comey had previously assured the President that the FBI was not investigating him personally, and the President asked Comey to "lift the cloud" of the Russia investigation by saying that publicly.

The President's termination of Comey. On May 3, 2017, Comey testified in a congressional hearing, but declined to answer questions about whether the President was personally under investigation. Within days, the President decided to terminate Comey. The President insisted that the termination letter, which was written for public release, state that Comey had informed the President that he was not under investigation. The day of the firing, the White House maintained that Comey's termination resulted from independent recommendations from the Attorney General and Deputy Attorney General that Comey should be discharged for mishandling the Hillary Clinton email investigation. But the President had decided to fire Comey before hearing from the Department of Justice. The day after firing Comey, the President told Russian officials that he had "faced great pressure because of Russia," which had been "taken off" by Comey's firing. The next day, the President acknowledged in a television interview that he was going to fire Comey regardless of the Department of Justice's recommendation and that when he "decided to just do it," he was thinking that "this thing with Trump and Russia is a made-up story." In response to a question about whether he was angry with Comey about the Russia investigation, the President said, "As far as I'm concerned, I want that thing to be absolutely done properly," adding that firing Comey "might even lengthen out the investigation."

The appointment of a Special Counsel and efforts to remove him. On May 17, 2017, the Acting Attorney General for the Russia investigation appointed a Special Counsel to conduct the investigation and related matters. The President reacted to news that a Special Counsel had been appointed by telling advisors that it was "the end of his presidency" and demanding that Sessions resign. Sessions submitted his resignation, but the President ultimately did not accept it. The President told aides that the Special Counsel had conflicts of interest and suggested that the Special Counsel therefore could not serve. The President's advisors told him the asserted conflicts were meritless and had already been considered by the Department of Justice.

On June 14, 2017, the media reported that the Special Counsel's Office was investigating whether the President had obstructed justice. Press reports called this "a major turning point" in the investigation: while Comey had told the President he was not under investigation, following Comey's firing, the President now was under investigation. The President reacted to this news with a series of tweets criticizing the Department of Justice and the Special Counsel's investigation. On June 17, 2017, the President called McGahn at home and directed him to call the Acting Attorney General and say that the Special Counsel had conflicts of interest and must be removed. McGahn did not carry out the direction, however, deciding that he would resign rather than trigger what he regarded as a potential Saturday Night Massacre.

Efforts to curtail the Special Counsel's investigation. Two days after directing McGahn to have the Special Counsel removed, the President made another attempt to affect the course of the Russia investigation. On June 19, 2017, the President met one-on-one in the Oval Office with his former campaign manager Corey Lewandowski, a trusted advisor outside the government, and dictated a message for Lewandowski to deliver to Sessions. The message said that Sessions should publicly announce that, notwithstanding his recusal from the Russia investigation, the investigation was "very unfair" to the President, the President had done nothing wrong, and Sessions planned to meet with the Special Counsel and "let [him] move forward with investigating election meddling for future elections." Lewandowski said he understood what the President wanted Sessions to do.

One month later, in another private meeting with Lewandowski on July 19, 2017, the President asked about the status of his message for Sessions to limit the Special Counsel investigation to future election interference. Lewandowski told the President that the message would be delivered soon. Hours after that meeting, the President publicly criticized Sessions in an interview with the

New York Times, and then issued a series of tweets making it clear that Sessions's job was in jeopardy. Lewandowski did not want to deliver the President's message personally, so he asked senior White House official Rick Dearborn to deliver it to Sessions. Dearborn was uncomfortable with the task and did not follow through.

Efforts to prevent public disclosure of evidence. In the summer of 2017, the President learned that media outlets were asking questions about the June 9, 2016, meeting at Trump Tower between senior campaign officials, including Donald Trump Jr., and a Russian lawyer who was said to be offering damaging information about Hillary Clinton as "part of Russia and its government's support for Mr. Trump." On several occasions, the President directed aides not to publicly disclose the emails setting up the June 9 meeting, suggesting that the emails would not leak and that the number of lawyers with access to them should be limited. Before the emails became public, the President edited a press statement for Trump Jr. by deleting a line that acknowledged that the meeting was with "an individual who [Trump Jr.] was told might have information helpful to the campaign" and instead said only that the meeting was about adoptions of Russian children. When the press asked questions about the President's involvement in Trump Jr.'s statement, the President's personal lawyer repeatedly denied the President had played any role.

Further efforts to have the Attorney General take control of the investigation. In early summer 2017, the President called Sessions at home and again asked him to reverse his recusal from the Russia investigation. Sessions did not reverse his recusal. In October 2017, the President met privately with Sessions in the Oval Office and asked him to "take [a] look" at investigating Clinton. In December 2017, shortly after Flynn pleaded guilty pursuant to a cooperation agreement, the President met with Sessions in the Oval Office and suggested, according to notes taken by a senior advisor, that if Sessions unrecused and took back supervision of the Russia investigation, he would be a "hero." The President told Sessions, "I'm not going to do anything or direct you to do anything. I just want to be treated fairly." In response, Sessions volunteered that he had never seen anything "improper" on the campaign and told the President there was a "whole new leadership team" in place. He did not unrecuse.

Efforts to have McGahn deny that the President had ordered him to have the Special Counsel removed. In early 2018, the press reported that the President had directed McGahn to have the Special Counsel removed in June 2017 and that McGahn had threatened to resign rather than carry out the order. The President reacted to the news stories by directing White House officials to tell McGahn to dispute the story and create a record stating he had not been ordered to have the Special Counsel removed. McGahn told those officials that the media reports were accurate in stating that the President had directed McGahn to have the Special Counsel removed. The President then met with McGahn in the Oval Office and again pressured him to deny the reports. In the same meeting, the President also asked McGahn why he had told the Special Counsel about the President's effort to remove the Special Counsel and why McGahn took notes of his conversations with the President. McGahn refused to back away from what he remembered happening and perceived the President to be testing his mettle.

Conduct towards Flynn, Manafort, HOM . After Flynn withdrew from a joint defense agreement with the President and began cooperating with the government, the President's personal counsel left a message for Flynn's attorneys reminding them of the President's warm feelings towards Flynn, which he said "still remains," and asking for a "heads up" if Flynn knew "information that implicates the President." When Flynn's counsel reiterated that Flynn could no longer share information pursuant to a joint defense agreement, the President's personal counsel said he would make sure that the President knew that Flynn's actions reflected "hostility" towards the President. During Manafort's prosecution and when the jury in his criminal trial was deliberating, the President praised Manafort in public, said that Manafort was being treated unfairly, and declined to rule out a pardon. After Manafort was convicted, the President called Manafort "a brave man" for refusing to "break" and said that "flipping" "almost ought to be outlawed." ▇▇▇ Harm to Ongoing Matter ▇▇▇

▇▇▇▇▇▇▇▇▇▇▇▇▇▇▇▇▇▇▇▇▇▇▇▇▇▇▇▇▇▇▇

▇▇▇

Conduct involving Michael Cohen. The President's conduct towards Michael Cohen, a former Trump Organization executive, changed from praise for Cohen when he falsely minimized the President's involvement in the Trump Tower Moscow project, to castigation of Cohen when he became a cooperating witness. From September 2015 to June 2016, Cohen had pursued the Trump Tower Moscow project on behalf of the Trump Organization and had briefed candidate Trump on the project numerous times, including discussing whether Trump should travel to Russia to advance the deal. In 2017, Cohen provided false testimony to Congress about the project, including stating that he had only briefed Trump on the project three times and never discussed travel to Russia with him, in an effort to adhere to a "party line" that Cohen said was developed to minimize the President's connections to Russia. While preparing for his congressional testimony, Cohen had extensive discussions with the President's personal counsel, who, according to Cohen, said that Cohen should "stay on message" and not contradict the President. After the FBI searched Cohen's home and office in April 2018, the President publicly asserted that Cohen would not "flip," contacted him directly to tell him to "stay strong," and privately passed messages of support to him. Cohen also discussed pardons with the President's personal counsel and believed that if he stayed on message he would be taken care of. But after Cohen began cooperating with the government in the summer of 2018, the President publicly criticized him, called him a "rat," and suggested that his family members had committed crimes.

Overarching factual issues. We did not make a traditional prosecution decision about these facts, but the evidence we obtained supports several general statements about the President's conduct.

Several features of the conduct we investigated distinguish it from typical obstruction-of-justice cases. First, the investigation concerned the President, and some of his actions, such as firing the FBI director, involved facially lawful acts within his Article II authority, which raises constitutional issues discussed below. At the same time, the President's position as the head of the Executive Branch provided him with unique and powerful means of influencing official proceedings, subordinate officers, and potential witnesses—all of which is relevant to a potential obstruction-of-justice analysis. Second, unlike cases in which a subject engages in obstruction of justice to cover up a crime, the evidence we obtained did not establish that the President was involved in an underlying crime related to Russian election interference. Although the obstruction statutes do not require proof of such a crime, the absence of that evidence affects the analysis of the President's intent and requires consideration of other possible motives for his conduct. Third, many of the President's acts directed at witnesses, including discouragement of cooperation with the government and suggestions of possible future pardons, took place in public view. That circumstance is unusual, but no principle of law excludes public acts from the reach of the obstruction laws. If the likely effect of public acts is to influence witnesses or alter their testimony, the harm to the justice system's integrity is the same.

Although the series of events we investigated involved discrete acts, the overall pattern of the President's conduct towards the investigations can shed light on the nature of the President's acts and the inferences that can be drawn about his intent. In particular, the actions we investigated can be divided into two phases, reflecting a possible shift in the President's motives. The first phase covered the period from the President's first interactions with Comey through the President's firing of Comey. During that time, the President had been repeatedly told he was not personally under investigation. Soon after the firing of Comey and the appointment of the Special Counsel, however, the President became aware that his own conduct was being investigated in an obstruction-of-justice inquiry. At that point, the President engaged in a second phase of conduct, involving public attacks on the investigation, non-public efforts to control it, and efforts in both public and private to encourage witnesses not to cooperate with the investigation. Judgments about the nature of the President's motives during each phase would be informed by the totality of the evidence.

Statutory and Constitutional Defenses

The President's counsel raised statutory and constitutional defenses to a possible obstruction-of-justice analysis of the conduct we investigated. We concluded that none of those legal defenses provided a basis for declining to investigate the facts.

Statutory defenses. Consistent with precedent and the Department of Justice's general approach to interpreting obstruction statutes, we concluded that several statutes could apply here. *See* 18 U.S.C. §§ 1503, 1505, 1512(b)(3), 1512(c)(2). Section 1512(c)(2) is an omnibus obstruction-of-justice provision that covers a range of obstructive acts directed at pending or contemplated official proceedings. No principle of statutory construction justifies narrowing the provision to cover only conduct that impairs the integrity or availability of evidence. Sections 1503 and 1505 also offer broad protection against obstructive acts directed at pending grand jury, judicial, administrative, and congressional proceedings, and they are supplemented by a provision in Section 1512(b) aimed specifically at conduct intended to prevent or hinder the communication to law enforcement of information related to a federal crime.

Constitutional defenses. As for constitutional defenses arising from the President's status as the head of the Executive Branch, we recognized that the Department of Justice and the courts have not definitively resolved these issues. We therefore examined those issues through the framework established by Supreme Court precedent governing separation-of-powers issues. The Department of Justice and the President's personal counsel have recognized that the President is subject to statutes that prohibit obstruction of justice by bribing a witness or suborning perjury because that conduct does not implicate his constitutional authority. With respect to whether the President can be found to have obstructed justice by exercising his powers under Article II of the Constitution, we concluded that Congress has authority to prohibit a President's corrupt use of his authority in order to protect the integrity of the administration of justice.

Under applicable Supreme Court precedent, the Constitution does not categorically and permanently immunize a President for obstructing justice through the use of his Article II powers. The separation-of-powers doctrine authorizes Congress to protect official proceedings, including those of courts and grand juries, from corrupt, obstructive acts regardless of their source. We also concluded that any inroad on presidential authority that would occur from prohibiting corrupt acts does not undermine the President's ability to fulfill his constitutional mission. The term "corruptly" sets a demanding standard. It requires a concrete showing that a person acted with an intent to obtain an improper advantage for himself or someone else, inconsistent with official duty and the rights of others. A preclusion of "corrupt" official action does not diminish the President's ability to exercise Article II powers. For example, the proper supervision of criminal law does not demand freedom for the President to act with a corrupt intention of shielding himself from criminal punishment, avoiding financial liability, or preventing personal embarrassment. To the contrary, a statute that prohibits official action undertaken for such corrupt purposes furthers, rather than hinders, the impartial and evenhanded administration of the law. It also aligns with the President's constitutional duty to faithfully execute the laws. Finally, we concluded that in the rare case in which a criminal investigation of the President's conduct is justified, inquiries to determine whether the President acted for a corrupt motive should not impermissibly chill his performance of his constitutionally assigned duties. The conclusion that Congress may apply the obstruction laws to the President's corrupt exercise of the powers of office accords with our constitutional system of checks and balances and the principle that no person is above the law.

Conclusion

Because we determined not to make a traditional prosecutorial judgment, we did not draw ultimate conclusions about the President's conduct. The evidence we obtained about the President's actions and intent presents difficult issues that would need to be resolved if we were making a traditional prosecutorial judgment. At the same time, if we had confidence after a thorough investigation of the facts that the President clearly did not commit obstruction of justice, we would so state. Based on the facts and the applicable legal standards, we are unable to reach that judgment. Accordingly, while this report does not conclude that the President committed a crime, it also does not exonerate him.

• • •

3. <u>The President Asks Intelligence Community Leaders to Make Public Statements that he had No Connection to Russia</u>

In the weeks following Comey's March 20, 2017, testimony, the President repeatedly asked intelligence community officials to push back publicly on any suggestion that the President had a connection to the Russian election-interference effort.

On March 22, 2017, the President asked Director of National Intelligence Daniel Coats and CIA Director Michael Pompeo to stay behind in the Oval Office after a Presidential Daily Briefing. According to Coats, the President asked them whether they could say publicly that no link existed between him and Russia. Coats responded that the Office of the Director of National Intelligence (ODNT) has nothing to do with investigations and it was not his role to make a public statement on the Russia investigation. Pompeo had no recollection of being asked to stay behind after the March 22 briefing, but he recalled that the President regularly urged officials to get the word out that he had not done anything wrong related to Russia.

Coats told this Office that the President never asked him to speak to Comey about the FBI investigation. Some ODNI staffers, however, had a different recollection of how Coats described the meeting immediately after it occurred. According to senior ODNI official Michael Dempsey, Coats said after the meeting that the President had brought up the Russia investigation and asked him to contact Comey to see if there was a way to get past the investigation, get it over with, end it, or words to that effect. Dempsey said that Coats described the President's comments as falling "somewhere between musing about hating the investigation" and wanting Coats to "do something to stop it." Dempsey said Coats made it clear that he would not get involved with an ongoing FBI investigation. Edward Gistaro, another ODNI official, recalled that right after Coats's meeting with the President, on the walk from the Oval Office back to the Eisenhower Executive Office Building, Coats said that the President had kept him behind to ask him what he could do to "help with the investigation." Another ODNI staffer who had been waiting for Coats outside the Oval Office talked to Gistaro a few minutes later and recalled Gistaro reporting that Coats was upset because the President had asked him to contact Comey to convince him there was nothing to the Russia investigation.

On Saturday, March 25, 2017, three days after the meeting in the Oval Office, the President called Coats and again complained about the Russia investigations, saying words to the effect of, "I can't do anything with Russia, there's things I'd like to do with Russia, with trade, with ISIS, they're all over me with this." Coats told the President that the investigations were going to go on and the best thing to do was to let them run their course. Coats later testified in a congressional hearing that he had "never felt pressure to intervene or interfere in any way and shape—with shaping intelligence in a political way, or in relationship . . . to an ongoing investigation."

On March 26, 2017, the day after the President called Coats, the President called NSA Director Admiral Michael Rogers. The President expressed frustration with the Russia investigation, saying that it made relations with the Russians difficult. The President told Rogers "the thing with the Russians [wa]s messing up" his ability to get things done with Russia. The President also said that the news stories linking him with Russia were not true and asked Rogers if he could do anything to refute the stories. Deputy Director of the NSA Richard Ledgett, who was present for the call, said it was the most unusual thing he had experienced in 40 years of government service. After the call concluded, Ledgett prepared a memorandum that he and Rogers both signed documenting the content of the conversation and the President's request, and they placed the memorandum in a safe. But Rogers did not perceive the President's request to be an order, and the President did not ask Rogers to push back on the Russia investigation itself. Rogers later testified in a congressional hearing that as NSA Director he had "never been directed to do anything [he] believe[d] to be illegal, immoral, unethical or inappropriate" and did "not recall ever feeling pressured to do so."

In addition to the specific comments made to Coats, Pompeo, and Rogers, the President spoke on other occasions in the presence of intelligence community officials about the Russia investigation and stated that it interfered with his ability to conduct foreign relations. On at least two occasions, the President began Presidential Daily Briefings by stating that there was no collusion with Russia and he hoped a press statement to that effect could be issued. Pompeo recalled that the President vented about the investigation on multiple occasions, complaining that there was no evidence against him and that nobody would publicly defend him. Rogers recalled a private conversation with the President in which he "vent[ed]" about the investigation, said he had done nothing wrong, and said something like the "Russia thing has got to go away." Coats recalled the President bringing up the Russia investigation several times, and Coats said he finally told the President that Coats's job was to provide intelligence and not get involved in investigations.

4. The President Asks Comey to "Lift the Cloud" Created by the Russia Investigation

On the morning of March 30, 2017, the President reached

out to Comey directly about the Russia investigation. According to Comey's contemporaneous record of the conversation, the President said "he was trying to run the country and the cloud of this Russia business was making that difficult." The President asked Comey what could be done to "lift the cloud." Comey explained "that we were running it down as quickly as possible and that there would be great benefit, if we didn't find anything, to our Good Housekeeping seal of approval, but we had to do our work." Comey also told the President that congressional leaders were aware that the FBI was not investigating the President personally. The President said several times, "We need to get that fact out." The President commented that if there was "some satellite" (which Comey took to mean an associate of the President's or the campaign) that did something, "it would be good to find that out" but that he himself had not done anything wrong and he hoped Comey "would find a way to get out that we weren't investigating him." After the call ended, Comey called Boente and told him about the conversation, asked for guidance on how to respond, and said he was uncomfortable with direct contact from the President about the investigation.

On the morning of April 11, 2017, the President called Comey again. According to Comey's contemporaneous record of the conversation, the President said he was "following up to see if [Comey] did what [the President] had asked last time—getting out that he personally is not under investigation." Comey responded that he had passed the request to Boente but not heard back, and he informed the President that the traditional channel for such a request would be to have the White House Counsel contact DOJ leadership. The President said he would take that step. The President then added, "Because I have been very loyal to you, very loyal, we had that thing, you know." In a televised interview that was taped early that afternoon, the President was asked if it was too late for him to ask Comey to step down; the President responded, "No, it's not too late, but you know, I have confidence in him. We'll see what happens. You know, it's going to be interesting." After the interview, Hicks told the President she thought the

President's comment about Comey should be removed from the broadcast of the interview, but the President wanted to keep it in, which Hicks thought was unusual.

Later that day, the President told senior advisors, including McGahn and Priebus, that he had reached out to Comey twice in recent weeks. The President acknowledged that McGahn would not approve of the outreach to Comey because McGahn had previously cautioned the President that he should not talk to Comey directly to prevent any perception that the White House was interfering with investigations. The President told McGahn that Comey had indicated the FBI could make a public statement that the President was not under investigation if the Department of Justice approved that action. After speaking with the President, McGahn followed up with Boente to relay the President's understanding that the FBI could make a public announcement if the Department of Justice cleared it. McGahn recalled that Boente said Comey had told him there was nothing obstructive about the calls from the President, but they made Comey uncomfortable. According to McGahn, Boente responded that he did not want to issue a statement about the President not being under investigation because of the potential political ramifications and did not want to order Comey to do it because that action could prompt the appointment of a Special Counsel. Boente did not recall that aspect of his conversation with McGahn, but did recall telling McGahn that the direct outreaches from the President to Comey were a problem. Boente recalled that McGahn agreed and said he would do what he could to address that issue.

Analysis

In analyzing the President's reaction to Sessions's recusal and the requests he made to Coats, Pompeo, Rogers, and Comey, the following evidence is relevant to the elements of obstruction of justice:

a. Obstructive act. The evidence shows that, after Comey's March 20, 2017, testimony, the President repeatedly reached out to intelligence agency leaders to discuss the FBI's investigation.

But witnesses had different recollections of the precise content of those outreaches. Some ODNI officials recalled that Coats told them immediately after the March 22 Oval Office meeting that the President asked Coats to intervene with Comey and "stop" the investigation. But the first-hand witnesses to the encounter remember the conversation differently. Pompeo had no memory of the specific meeting, but generally recalled the President urging officials to get the word out that the President had not done anything wrong related to Russia. Coats recalled that the President asked that Coats state publicly that no link existed between the President and Russia, but did not ask him to speak with Comey or to help end the investigation. The other outreaches by the President during this period were similar in nature: The President asked Rogers if he could do anything to refute the stories linking the President to Russia, and the President asked Comey to make a public statement that would "lift the cloud" of the ongoing investigation by making clear that the President was not personally under investigation. These requests, while significant enough that Rogers thought it important to document the encounter in a written memorandum, were not interpreted by the officials who received them as directives to improperly interfere with the investigation.

b. <u>Nexus to a proceeding</u>. At the time of the President's outreaches to leaders of the intelligence agencies in late March and early April 2017, the FBI's Russia investigation did not yet involve grand jury proceedings. The outreaches, however, came after and were in response to Comey's March 20, 2017, announcement that the FBI, as a part of its counterintelligence mission, was conducting an investigation into Russian interference in the 2016 presidential election. Comey testified that the investigation included any links or coordination with Trump campaign officials and would "include an assessment of whether any crimes were committed."

c. <u>Intent</u>. As described above, the evidence does not establish that the President asked or directed intelligence agency leaders to stop or interfere with the FBI's Russia investigation—and the President affirmatively told Comey that if "some satellite" was involved in Russian election interference "it would be good to find that out." But the President's intent in trying to prevent Sessions's recusal, and in reaching out to Coats, Pompeo, Rogers, and Comey following Comey's public announcement of the FBI's Russia investigation, is nevertheless relevant to understanding what motivated the President's other actions towards the investigation.

The evidence shows that the President was focused on the Russia investigation's implications for his presidency—and, specifically, on dispelling any suggestion that he was under investigation or had links to Russia. In early March, the President attempted to prevent Sessions's recusal, even after being told that Sessions was following DOJ conflict-of-interest rules. After Sessions recused, the White House Counsel's Office tried to cut off further contact with Sessions about the matter, although it is not clear whether that direction was conveyed to the President. The President continued to raise the issue of Sessions's recusal and, when he had the opportunity, he pulled Sessions aside and urged him to unrecuse. The President also told advisors that he wanted an Attorney General who would protect him, the way he perceived Robert Kennedy and Eric Holder to have protected their presidents. The President made statements about being able to direct the course of criminal investigations, saying words to the effect of, "You're telling me that Bobby and Jack didn't talk about investigations? Or Obama didn't tell Eric Holder who to investigate?"

After Comey publicly confirmed the existence of the FBI's Russia investigation on March 20, 2017, the President was "beside himself" and expressed anger that Comey did not issue a statement correcting any misperception that the President himself was under investigation. The President sought to speak with Acting Attorney General Boente directly and told McGahn to contact Boente to request that Comey make a clarifying statement. The President then asked other intelligence community leaders to make public statements to refute the suggestion that the President had links to Russia, but the leaders told him they could not publicly comment on the investigation. On March 30 and April 11, against the advice of White House advisors who had informed him that any direct contact with the FBI could be perceived as improper interference in an ongoing investigation, the President made personal outreaches to Comey asking him to "lift the cloud" of the Russia investigation by making public the fact that the President was not personally under investigation.

Evidence indicates that the President was angered by both the existence of the Russia investigation and the public reporting that he was under investigation, which he knew was not true based on Comey's representations. The President complained to advisors that if people thought Russia helped him with the election, it would detract from what he had accomplished.

Other evidence indicates that the President was concerned about the impact of the Russia investigation on his ability to govern. The President complained that the perception that he was under investigation was hurting his ability to conduct foreign relations, particularly with Russia. The President told Coats he "can't do anything with Russia," he told Rogers that "the thing with the Russians" was interfering with his ability to conduct foreign affairs, and he told Comey that "he was trying to run the country and the cloud of this Russia business was making that difficult."

D. Events Leading Up To and Surrounding the Termination of FBI Director Comey

Overview

Comey was scheduled to testify before Congress on May 3, 2017. Leading up to that testimony, the President continued to tell advisors that he wanted Comey to make public that the President was not under investigation. At the hearing, Comey declined to answer questions about the scope or subjects of the Russia investigation and did not state publicly that the President was not under investigation. Two days later, on May 5, 2017, the President told close aides he was going to fire Comey, and on May 9, he did so, using his official termination letter to make public that Comey had on three occasions informed the President that he was not under investigation. The President decided to fire Comey before receiving advice or a recommendation from the Department of Justice, but he approved an initial public account of the termination that attributed it to a recommendation from the Department of Justice based on Comey's handling of the Clinton email investigation. After Deputy Attorney General Rod Rosenstein resisted attributing the firing to his recommendation, the President acknowledged that he intended to fire Comey regardless of the DOJ recommendation and was thinking of the Russia investigation when he made the decision. The President also told the Russian Foreign Minister, "I just fired the head of the F.B.I. He was crazy, a real nut job. I faced great pressure because of Russia. That's taken off. . . . . I'm not under investigation."

Evidence

1. Comey Testifies Before the Senate Judiciary Committee and Declines to Answer Questions About Whether the President is Under Investigation

On May 3, 2017, Comey was scheduled to testify at an FBI oversight hearing before the Senate Judiciary Committee. McGahn recalled that in the week leading up to the hearing, the President said that it would be the last straw if Comey did not take the opportunity to set the record straight by publicly announcing that the President was not under investigation. The President had previously told McGahn that the perception that the President was under investigation was hurting his ability to carry out his presidential duties and deal with foreign leaders. At the hearing, Comey declined to answer questions about the status of the Russia investigation, stating "[t]he Department of Justice ha[d] authorized [him] to confirm that [the Russia investigation] exists," but that he was "not going to say another word about it" until the investigation was completed. Comey also declined to answer questions about whether investigators had "ruled out anyone in the Trump campaign as potentially a target of th[e] criminal investigation," including whether the FBI had "ruled out the president of the United States."

Comey was also asked at the hearing about his decision to announce 11 days before the presidential election that the FBI was reopening the Clinton email investigation. Comey stated that it made him "mildly nauseous to think that we might have had some impact on the election," but added that "even in hindsight" he "would make the same decision." He later repeated that he had no regrets about how he had handled the email investigation and believed he had "done the right thing at each turn."

In the afternoon following Comey's testimony, the President met with McGahn, Sessions, and Sessions's Chief of Staff Jody Hunt. At that meeting, the President asked McGahn how Comey had done in his testimony and McGahn relayed that Comey had declined to answer questions about whether the President was under investigation. The President became very upset and directed his anger at Sessions. According to notes written by Hunt, the President said, "This is terrible Jeff. It's all because you recused. AG is supposed to be most important appointment. Kennedy appointed his brother. Obama appointed Holder. I appointed you and you recused yourself. You left me on an island. I can't do anything." The President said that the recusal was unfair and that it was interfering with his ability to govern and undermining his authority with foreign leaders. Sessions responded that he had had no choice but to recuse, and it was a mandatory rather than discretionary decision. Hunt recalled that Sessions also stated at some point during the conversation that a new start at the FBI would be appropriate and the President should consider replacing Comey as FBI director. According to Sessions, when the meeting concluded, it was clear that the President was unhappy with Comey, but Sessions did not think the President had made the decision to terminate Comey.

Bannon recalled that the President brought Comey up with him at least eight times on May 3 and May 4, 2017. According to Bannon, the President said the same thing each time: "He told me three times I'm not under investigation. He's a showboater. He's a grandstander. I don't know any Russians. There was no collusion." Bannon told the President that he could not fire Comey because "that ship had sailed." Bannon also told the President that firing Comey was not going to stop the investigation, cautioning him that he could fire the FBI director but could not fire the FBI.

2. The President Makes the Decision to Terminate Comey

The weekend following Comey's May 3, 2017, testimony, the President traveled to his resort in Bedminster, New Jersey. At a dinner on Friday, May 5, attended by the President and various advisors and family members, including Jared Kushner and senior advisor Stephen Miller, the President stated that he wanted to remove Comey and had ideas for a letter that would be used to make the announcement. The President dictated arguments and specific language for the letter, and Miller took notes. As reflected in the notes, the President told Miller that the letter should start, "While I greatly appreciate you informing me that I am not under investigation concerning what I have often stated is a fabricated story on a Trump-Russia relationship—pertaining to the 2016 presidential election, please be informed that I, and I believe the American public—including Ds and Rs—have lost faith in you as Director of the FBI." Following the dinner, Miller prepared a termination letter based on those notes and research he conducted to support the President's arguments. Over the weekend, the President provided several rounds of edits on the draft letter. Miller said the President was adamant that he not tell anyone at the White House what they were preparing because the President was worried about leaks.

In his discussions with Miller, the President made clear that he wanted the letter to open with a reference to him not being under investigation. Miller said he believed that fact was important to the President to show that Comey was not being terminated based on any such investigation. According to Miller, the President wanted to establish as a factual matter that Comey had been under a "review period" and did not have assurance from the President that he would be permitted to keep his job.

The final version of the termination letter prepared by Miller and the President began in a way that closely tracked what the President had dictated to Miller at the May 5 dinner: "Dear Director Comey, While I greatly appreciate your informing me, on three separate occasions, that I am not under investigation concerning the fabricated and politically-motivated allegations of a

Trump-Russia relationship with respect to the 2016 Presidential Election, please be informed that I, along with members of both political parties and, most importantly, the American Public, have lost faith in you as the Director of the FBI and you are hereby terminated." The four-page letter went on to critique Comey's judgment and conduct, including his May 3 testimony before the Senate Judiciary Committee, his handling of the Clinton email investigation, and his failure to hold leakers accountable. The letter stated that Comey had "asked [the President] at dinner shortly after inauguration to let [Comey] stay on in the Director's role, and [the President] said that [he] would consider it," but the President had "concluded that [he] ha[d] no alternative but to find new leadership for the Bureau—a leader that restores confidence and trust."

In the morning of Monday, May 8, 2017, the President met in the Oval Office with senior advisors, including McGahn, Priebus, and Miller, and informed them he had decided to terminate Comey. The President read aloud the first paragraphs of the termination letter he wrote with Miller and conveyed that the decision had been made and was not up for discussion. The President told the group that Miller had researched the issue and determined the President had the authority to terminate Comey without cause. In an effort to slow down the decision-making process, McGahn told the President that DOJ leadership was currently discussing Comey's status and suggested that White House Counsel's Office attorneys should talk with Sessions and Rod Rosenstein, who had recently been confirmed as the Deputy Attorney General. McGahn said that previously scheduled meetings with Sessions and Rosenstein that day would be an opportunity to find out what they thought about firing Comey.

At noon, Sessions, Rosenstein, and Hunt met with McGahn and White House Counsel's Office attorney Uttam Dhillon at the White House. McGahn said that the President had decided to fire Comey and asked for Sessions's and Rosenstein's views. Sessions and Rosenstein criticized Comey and did not raise concerns about replacing him. McGahn and Dhillon said the fact that neither Sessions nor Rosenstein objected to replacing Comey gave them peace of mind that the President's decision to fire Comey was not an attempt to obstruct justice. An Oval Office meeting was scheduled later that day so that Sessions and Rosenstein could discuss the issue with the President.

At around 5 p.m., the President and several White House officials met with Sessions and Rosenstein to discuss Comey. The President told the group that he had watched Comey's May 3 testimony over the weekend and thought that something was "not right" with Comey. The President said that Comey should be removed and asked Sessions and Rosenstein for their views. Hunt, who was in the room, recalled that Sessions responded that he had previously recommended that Comey be replaced. McGahn and Dhillon said Rosenstein described his concerns about Comey's handling of the Clinton email investigation.

The President then distributed copies of the termination letter he had drafted with Miller, and the discussion turned to the mechanics of how to fire Comey and whether the President's letter should be used. McGahn and Dhillon urged the President to permit Comey to resign, but the President was adamant that he be fired. The group discussed the possibility that Rosenstein and Sessions could provide a recommendation in writing that Comey should be removed. The President agreed and told Rosenstein to draft a memorandom, but said he wanted to receive it first thing the next morning. Hunt's notes reflect that the President told Rosenstein to include in his recommendation the fact that Comey had refused to confirm that the President was not personally under investigation. According to notes taken by a senior DOJ official of Rosenstein's description of his meeting with the President, the President said, "Put the Russia stuff in the memo." Rosenstein responded that the Russia investigation was not the basis of his recommendation, so he did not think Russia should be mentioned. The President told Rosenstein he would appreciate it if Rosenstein put it in his letter anyway. When Rosenstein left the meeting, he knew that Comey would be terminated, and he told DOJ colleagues that his own reasons for replacing Comey were "not [the President's] reasons."

On May 9, Hunt delivered to the White House a letter from Sessions recommending Comey's removal and a memorandum from Rosenstein, addressed to the Attorney General, titled "Restoring Public Confidence in the FBI." McGahn recalled that the President liked the DOJ letters and agreed that they should provide the foundation for a new cover letter from the President accepting the recommendation to terminate Comey. Notes taken by Donaldson on May 9 reflected the view of the White House Counsel's Office that the President's original termination letter should "[n]ot [see the] light of day" and that it would be better to offer "[n]o other rationales" for the firing than what was in Rosenstein's and Sessions's memoranda. The President asked Miller to draft a new termination letter and directed Miller to say in the letter that Comey had informed the President three times that he was not under investigation. McGahn, Priebus, and Dhillon objected to including that language, but the President insisted that it be included. McGahn, Priebus, and others perceived that language to be the most important part of the letter to the President. Dhillon made a final pitch to the President that Comey should be permitted to resign, but the President refused.

Around the time the President's letter was finalized, Priebus summoned Spicer and the press team to the Oval Office, where they were told that Comey had been terminated for the reasons stated in the letters by Rosenstein and Sessions. To announce Comey's termination, the White House released a statement, which Priebus thought had been dictated by the President. In full, the statement read: "Today, President Donald J. Trump informed FBI Director James Comey that he has been terminated and removed from office. President Trump acted based on the clear recommendations of both Deputy Attorney General Rod Rosenstein and Attorney General Jeff Sessions."

That evening, FBI Deputy Director Andrew McCabe was summoned to meet with the President at the White House. The President told McCabe that he had fired Comey because of the decisions Comey had made in the Clinton email investigation and for many other reasons. The President asked McCabe if he was aware that Comey had told the President three times that he was not under investigation. The President also asked McCabe whether many people in the FBI disliked Comey and whether McCabe was part of the "resistance" that had disagreed with Comey's decisions in the Clinton investigation. McCabe told the President that he knew Comey had told the President he was not under investigation, that most people in the FBI felt positively about Comey, and that McCabe worked "very closely" with Comey and was part of all the decisions that had been made in the Clinton investigation.

Later that evening, the President told his communications team he was unhappy with the press coverage of Comey's termination and ordered them to go out and defend him. The President also called Chris Christie and, according to Christie, said he was getting "killed" in the press over Comey's termination. The President asked what he should do. Christie asked, "Did you fire [Comey] because of what Rod wrote in the memo?", and the President responded, "Yes." Christie said that the President should "get Rod out there" and have him defend the decision. The President told Christie that this was a "good idea" and said he was going to call Rosenstein right away.

That night, the White House Press Office called the Department of Justice and said the White House wanted to put out a statement saying that it was Rosenstein's idea to fire Comey. Rosenstein told other DOJ officials that he would not participate in putting out a "false story." The President then called Rosenstein directly and said he was watching Fox News, that the coverage had been great, and that he wanted Rosenstein to do a press conference. Rosenstein responded that this was not a good idea because if the press asked him, he would tell the truth that Comey's firing was not his idea. Sessions also informed the White House Counsel's Office that evening that Rosenstein was upset that his memorandum was being portrayed as the reason for Comey's termination.

In an unplanned press conference late in the evening of May 9, 2017, Spicer told reporters, "It was all [Rosenstein]. No one from the White House. It was a DOJ decision." That evening and the next morning, White House officials and spokespeople continued to maintain that the President's decision to terminate Comey was driven by the recommendations the President received from Rosenstein and Sessions.

In the morning on May 10, 2017, President Trump met with Russian Foreign Minister Sergey Lavrov and Russian Ambassador Sergey Kislyak in the Oval Office. The media subsequently reported that during the May 10 meeting the President brought up his decision the prior day to terminate Comey, telling Lavrov and Kislyak: "I just fired the head of the F.B.I. He was crazy, a real nut job. I faced great pressure because of Russia. That's taken off. . . . I'm not under investigation." The President never denied making those statements, and the White House did not dispute the account, instead issuing a statement that said: "By grandstanding and politicizing the investigation into Russia's actions, James Comey created unnecessary pressure on our ability to engage and negotiate with Russia. The investigation would have always continued, and obviously, the termination of Comey would not have ended it. Once again, the real story is that our national security has been undermined by the leaking of private and highly classified information." Hicks said that when she told the President about the reports on his meeting with Lavrov, he did not look concerned and said of Comey, "he *is* crazy." When McGahn asked the President about his comments to Lavrov, the President said it was good that Comey was fired because that took the pressure off by making it clear that he was not under investigation so he could get more work done.

That same morning, on May 10, 2017, the President called McCabe. According to a memorandum McCabe wrote following the call, the President asked McCabe to come over to the White House to discuss whether the President should visit FBI headquarters and make a speech to employees. The President said he had received "hundreds" of messages from FBI employees indicating their support for terminating Comey. The President also told McCabe that Comey should not have been permitted to travel back to Washington, D.C. on the FBI's airplane after he had been terminated and that he did not want Comey "in the building again," even to collect his belongings. When McCabe met with the

President that afternoon, the President, without prompting, told McCabe that people in the FBI loved the President, estimated that at least 80% of the FBI had voted for him, and asked McCabe who he had voted for in the 2016 presidential election.

In the afternoon of May 10, 2017, deputy press secretary Sarah Sanders spoke to the President about his decision to fire Comey and then spoke to reporters in a televised press conference. Sanders told reporters that the President, the Department of Justice, and bipartisan members of Congress had lost confidence in Comey, "[a]nd most importantly, the rank and file of the FBI had lost confidence in their director. Accordingly, the President accepted the recommendation of his Deputy Attorney General to remove James Comey from his position." In response to questions from reporters, Sanders said that Rosenstein decided "on his own" to review Comey's performance and that Rosenstein decided "on his own" to come to the President on Monday, May 8 to express his concerns about Comey. When a reporter indicated that the "vast majority" of FBI agents supported Comey, Sanders said, "Look, we've heard from countless members of the FBI that say very different things." Following the press conference, Sanders spoke to the President, who told her she did a good job and did not point out any inaccuracies in her comments. Sanders told this Office that her reference to hearing from "countless members of the FBI" was a "slip of the tongue." She also recalled that her statement in a separate press interview that rank-and-file FBI agents had lost confidence in Comey was a comment she made "in the heat of the moment" that was not founded on anything.

Also on May 10, 2017, Sessions and Rosenstein each spoke to McGahn and expressed concern that the White House was creating a narrative that Rosenstein had initiated the decision to fire Comey. The White House Counsel's Office agreed that it was factually wrong to say that the Department of Justice had initiated Comey's termination, and McGahn asked attorneys in the White House Counsel's Office to work with the press office to correct the narrative.

The next day, on May 11, 2017, the President participated in an interview with Lester Holt. The President told White House Counsel's Office attorneys in advance of the interview that the communications team could not get the story right, so he was going on Lester Holt to say what really happened. During the interview, the President stated that he had made the decision to fire Comey before the President met with Rosenstein and Sessions. The President told Holt, "I was going to fire regardless of recommendation . . . . [Rosenstein] made a recommendation. But regardless of recommendation, I was going to fire Comey knowing there was no good time to do it." The President continued, "And in fact, when I decided to just do it, I said to myself—I said, you know, this Russia thing with Trump and Russia is a made-up story. It's an excuse by the Democrats for having lost an election that they should've won."

In response to a question about whether he was angry with Comey about the Russia investigation, the President said, "As far as I'm concerned, I want that thing to be absolutely done properly." The President added that he realized his termination of Comey "probably maybe will confuse people" with the result that it "might even lengthen out the investigation," but he "ha(d] to do the right thing for the American people" and Comey was "the wrong man for that position." The President described Comey as "a showboat" and "a grandstander," said that "[t]he FBI has been in turmoil," and said he wanted "to have a really competent, capable director." The President affirmed that he expected the new FBI director to continue the Russia investigation.

On the evening of May 11, 2017, following the Lester Holt interview, the President tweeted, "Russia must be laughing up their sleeves watching as the U.S. tears itself apart over a Democrat EXCUSE for losing the election." The same day, the media reported that the President had demanded that Comey pledge his loyalty to the President in a private dinner shortly after being sworn in. Late in the morning of May 12, 2017, the President tweeted, "Again, the story that there was collusion between the Russians & Trump campaign was fabricated by Dems as an excuse for losing the election." The President also tweeted, "James Comey better hope that there are no 'tapes' of our conversations before he starts leaking to the press!" and "When James Clapper himself, and virtually everyone else with knowledge of the witch hunt, says there is no collusion, when does it end?"

Analysis

In analyzing the President's decision to fire Comey, the following evidence is relevant to the elements of obstruction of justice:

a. <u>Obstructive act</u>. The act of firing Comey removed the individual overseeing the FBI's Russia investigation. The President knew that Comey was personally involved in the investigation based on Comey's briefing of the Gang of Eight, Comey's March 20, 2017, public testimony about the investigation, and the President's one-on-one conversations with Comey.

Firing Comey would qualify as an obstructive act if it had the natural and probable effect of interfering with or impeding the investigation—for example, if the termination would have the effect of delaying or disrupting the investigation or providing the President with the opportunity to appoint a director who would take a different approach to the investigation that the President perceived as more protective of his personal interests. Relevant circumstances bearing on that issue include whether the President's actions had the potential to discourage a successor director or other law enforcement officials in their conduct of the Russia investigation. The President fired Comey abruptly without offering him an opportunity to resign, banned him from the FBI building, and criticized him publicly, calling him a "showboat" and claiming that the FBI was "in turmoil" under his leadership. And the President followed the termination with public statements that were highly critical of the investigation; for example, three days after firing Comey, the President referred to the investigation as a "witch hunt" and asked, "when does it end?" Those actions had the potential to affect a successor director's conduct of the investigation.

The anticipated effect of removing the FBI director, however, would not necessarily be to prevent or impede the FBI from continuing its investigation. As a general matter, FBI investigations run under the operational direction of FBI personnel levels below the FBI director. Bannon made a similar point when he told the President that he could fire the FBI director, but could not fire the FBI. The White House issued a press statement the day after Comey was fired that said, "The investigation would have always continued, and obviously, the termination of Comey would not have ended it." In addition, in his May 11 interview with Lester Holt, the President stated that he understood when he made the decision to fire Comey that the action might prolong the investigation. And the President chose McCabe to serve as interim director, even though McCabe told the President he had worked "very closely" with Comey and was part of all the decisions made in the Clinton investigation.

b. <u>Nexus to a proceeding</u>. The nexus element would be satisfied by evidence showing that a grand jury proceeding or criminal prosecution arising from an FBI investigation was objectively foreseeable and actually contemplated by the President when he terminated Comey.

Several facts would be relevant to such a showing. At the time the President fired Comey, a grand jury had not begun to hear evidence related to the Russia investigation and no grand jury subpoenas had been issued. On March 20, 2017, however, Comey had announced that the FBI was investigating Russia's interference in the election, including "an assessment of whether any crimes were committed." It was widely known that the FBI, as part of the Russia investigation, was investigating the hacking of the DNC's computers—a clear criminal offense.

In addition, at the time the President fired Comey, evidence indicates the President knew that Flynn was still under criminal investigation and could potentially be prosecuted, despite the President's February 14, 2017, request that Comey "let[] Flynn go." On March 5, 2017, the White House Counsel's Office was informed that the FBI was asking for transition-period records relating to Flynn—indicating that the FBI was still actively investigating him. The same day, the President told advisors he wanted to call Dana Boente, then the Acting Attorney General for the

Russia investigation, to find out whether the White House or the President was being investigated. On March 31, 2017, the President signaled his awareness that Flynn remained in legal jeopardy by tweeting that "Mike Flynn should ask for immunity" before he agreed to provide testimony to the FBI or Congress. And in late March or early April, the President asked McFarland to pass a message to Flynn telling him that the President felt bad for him and that he should stay strong, further demonstrating the President's awareness of Flynn's criminal exposure.

c. <u>Intent</u>. Substantial evidence indicates that the catalyst for the President's decision to fire Comey was Comey's unwillingness to publicly state that the President was not personally under investigation, despite the President's repeated requests that Comey make such an announcement. In the week leading up to Comey's May 3, 2017, Senate Judiciary Committee testimony, the President told McGahn that it would be the last straw if Comey did not set the record straight and publicly announce that the President was not under investigation. But during his May 3 testimony, Comey refused to answer questions about whether the President was being investigated. Comey's refusal angered the President, who criticized Sessions for leaving him isolated and exposed, saying "You left me on an island." Two days later, the President told advisors he had decided to fire Comey and dictated a letter to Stephen Miller that began with a reference to the fact that the President was not being investigated: "While I greatly appreciate you informing me that I am not under investigation concerning what I have often stated is a fabricated story on a Trump-Russia relationship . . . ." The President later asked Rosenstein to include "Russia" in his memorandum and to say that Comey had told the President that he was not under investigation. And the President's final termination letter included a sentence, at the President's insistence and against McGahn's advice, stating that Comey had told the President on three separate occasions that he was not under investigation.

The President's other stated rationales for why he fired Comey are not similarly supported by the evidence. The termination letter the President and Stephen Miller prepared in Bedminster cited

Comey's handling of the Clinton email investigation, and the President told McCabe he fired Comey for that reason. But the facts surrounding Comey's handling of the Clinton email investigation were well known to the President at the time he assumed office, and the President had made it clear to both Comey and the President's senior staff in early 2017 that he wanted Comey to stay on as director. And Rosenstein articulated his criticism of Comey's handling of the Clinton investigation after the President had already decided to fire Comey. The President's draft termination letter also stated that morale in the FBI was at an all-time low and Sanders told the press after Comey's termination that the White House had heard from "countless" FBI agents who had lost confidence in Comey. But the evidence does not support those claims. The President told Comey at their January 27 dinner that "the people of the FBI really like [him]," no evidence suggests that the President heard otherwise before deciding to terminate Comey, and Sanders acknowledged to investigators that her comments were not founded on anything.

We also considered why it was important to the President that Comey announce publicly that he was not under investigation. Some evidence indicates that the President believed that the erroneous perception he was under investigation harmed his ability to manage domestic and foreign affairs, particularly in dealings with Russia. The President told Comey that the "cloud" of "this Russia business" was making it difficult to run the country. The President told Sessions and McGahn that foreign leaders had expressed sympathy to him for being under investigation and that the perception he was under investigation was hurting his ability to address foreign relations issues. The President complained to Rogers that "the thing with the Russians [was] messing up" his ability to get things done with Russia, and told Coats, "I can't do anything with Russia, there's things I'd like to do with Russia, with trade, with ISIS, they're all over me with this." The President also may have viewed Comey as insubordinate for his failure to make clear in the May 3 testimony that the President was not under investigation.

Other evidence, however, indicates that the President wanted to protect himself from an investigation into his campaign. The day after learning about the FBI's interview of Flynn, the President had a one-on-one dinner with Comey, against the advice of senior aides, and told Comey he needed Comey's "loyalty." When the President later asked Comey for a second time to make public that he was not under investigation, he brought up loyalty again, saying "Because I have been very loyal to you, very loyal, we had that thing, you know." After the President learned of Sessions's recusal from the Russia investigation, the President was furious and said he wanted an Attorney General who would protect him the way he perceived Robert Kennedy and Eric Holder to have protected their presidents. The President also said he wanted to be able to tell his Attorney General "who to investigate."

In addition, the President had a motive to put the FBI's Russia investigation behind him. The evidence does not establish that the termination of Comey was designed to cover up a conspiracy between the Trump Campaign and Russia: As described in Volume I, the evidence uncovered in the investigation did not establish that the President or those close to him were involved in the charged Russian computer-hacking or active-measure conspiracies, or that the President otherwise had an unlawful relationship with any Russian official. But the evidence does indicate that a thorough FBI investigation would uncover facts about the campaign and the President personally that the President could have understood to be crimes or that would give rise to personal and political concerns. Although the President publicly stated during and after the election that he had no connection to Russia, the Trump Organization, through Michael Cohen, was pursuing the proposed Trump Tower Moscow project through June 2016 and candidate Trump was repeatedly briefed on the progress of those efforts. In addition, some witnesses said that Trump was aware that ▮▮▮▮▮▮▮▮▮▮▮ **Harm to Ongoing Matter** ▮▮▮▮▮▮▮▮▮▮▮ at a time when public reports stated that Russian intelligence officials were behind the hacks, and that Trump privately sought information about future WikiLeaks releases. More broadly, multiple witnesses described the President's preoccupation with press coverage of the Russia investigation and his persistent concern that it raised questions about the legitimacy of his election.

Finally, the President and White House aides initially advanced a pretextual reason to the press and the public for Comey's termination. In the immediate aftermath of the firing, the President dictated a press statement suggesting that he had acted based on the DOJ recommendations, and White House press officials repeated that story. But the President had decided to fire Comey before the White House solicited those recommendations. Although the President ultimately acknowledged that he was going to fire Comey regardless of the Department of Justice's recommendations, he did so only after DOJ officials made clear to him that they would resist the White House's suggestion that they had prompted the process that led to Comey's termination. The initial reliance on a pretextual justification could support an inference that the President had concerns about providing the real reason for the firing, although the evidence does not resolve whether those concerns were personal, political, or both.

E. The President's Efforts to Remove the Special Counsel

Overview

The Acting Attorney General appointed a Special Counsel on May 17, 2017, prompting the President to state that it was the end of his presidency and that Attorney General Sessions had failed to protect him and should resign. Sessions submitted his resignation, which the President ultimately did not accept. The President told senior advisors that the Special Counsel had conflicts of interest, but they responded that those claims were "ridiculous" and posed no obstacle to the Special Counsel's service. Department of Justice ethics officials similarly cleared the Special Counsel's service. On June 14, 2017, the press reported that the President was being personally investigated for obstruction of justice and the President responded with a series of tweets criticizing the Special Counsel's investigation. That weekend, the President called McGahn and directed him to have the Special Counsel removed because of asserted conflicts of interest. McGahn did not carry out the instruction for fear of being seen as triggering another Saturday Night Massacre and instead prepared to resign. McGahn ultimately did not quit and the President did not follow up with McGahn on his request to have the Special Counsel removed.

Evidence

1. <u>The Appointment of the Special Counsel and the President's Reaction</u>

On May 17, 2017, Acting Attorney General Rosenstein appointed Robert S. Mueller, III, as Special Counsel and authorized him to conduct the Russia investigation and matters that arose from the investigation. The President learned of the Special Counsel's appointment from Sessions, who was with the President, Hunt, and McGahn conducting interviews for a new FBI Director. Sessions stepped out of the Oval Office to take a call from Rosenstein, who told him about the Special Counsel appointment, and Sessions then returned to inform the President of the news. According to notes written by Hunt, when Sessions told the President that a Special Counsel had been appointed, the President slumped back in his chair and said, "Oh my God. This is terrible. This is the end of my Presidency. I'm fucked." The President became angry and lambasted the Attorney General for his decision to recuse from the investigation, stating, "How could you let this happen, Jeff?" The President said the position of Attorney General was his most important appointment and that Sessions had "let [him] down," contrasting him to Eric Holder and Robert Kennedy. Sessions recalled that the President said to him, "you were supposed to protect me," or words to that effect. The President returned to the consequences of the appointment and said, "Everyone tells me if you get one of these independent counsels it ruins your presidency. It takes years and years and I won't be able to do anything. This is the worst thing that ever happened to me."

The President then told Sessions he should resign as Attorney General. Sessions agreed to submit his resignation and left the

Oval Office. Hicks saw the President shortly after Sessions departed and described the President as being extremely upset by the Special Counsel's appointment. Hicks said that she had only seen the President like that one other time, when the Access Hollywood tape came out during the campaign.

The next day, May 18, 2017, FBI agents delivered to McGahn a preservation notice that discussed an investigation related to Comey's termination and directed the White House to preserve all relevant documents. When he received the letter, McGahn issued a document hold to White House staff and instructed them not to send out any burn bags over the weekend while he sorted things out.

Also on May 18, Sessions finalized a resignation letter that stated, "Pursuant to our conversation of yesterday, and at your request, I hereby offer my resignation." Sessions, accompanied by Hunt, brought the letter to the White House and handed it to the President. The President put the resignation letter in his pocket and asked Sessions several times whether he wanted to continue serving as Attorney General. Sessions ultimately told the President he wanted to stay, but it was up to the President. The President said he wanted Sessions to stay. At the conclusion of the meeting, the President shook Sessions's hand but did not return the resignation letter.

When Priebus and Bannon learned that the President was holding onto Sessions's resignation letter, they became concerned that it could be used to influence the Department of Justice. Priebus told Sessions it was not good for the President to have the letter because it would function as a kind of "shock collar" that the President could use any time he wanted; Priebus said the President had "DOJ by the throat." Priebus and Bannon told Sessions they would attempt to get the letter back from the President with a notation that he was not accepting Sessions's resignation.

On May 19, 2017, the President left for a trip to the Middle East. Hicks recalled that on the President's flight from Saudi Arabia to Tel Aviv, the President pulled Sessions's resignation letter from his pocket, showed it to a group of senior advisors, and asked them what he should do about it. During the trip, Priebus asked about the resignation letter so he could return it to Sessions, but the President told him that the letter was back at the White House, somewhere in the residence. It was not until May 30, three days after the President returned from the trip, that the President returned the letter to Sessions with a notation saying, "Not accepted."

2. The President Asserts that the Special Counsel has Conflicts of Interest

In the days following the Special Counsel's appointment, the President repeatedly told advisors, including Priebus, Bannon, and McGahn, that Special Counsel Mueller had conflicts of interest. The President cited as conflicts that Mueller had interviewed for the FBI Director position shortly before being appointed as Special Counsel, that he had worked for a law firm that represented people affiliated with the President, and that Mueller had disputed certain fees relating to his membership in a Trump golf course in Northern Virginia. The President's advisors pushed back on his assertion of conflicts, telling the President they did not count as true conflicts. Bannon recalled telling the President that the purported conflicts were "ridiculous" and that none of them was real or could come close to justifying precluding Mueller from serving as Special Counsel. As for Mueller's interview for FBI Director, Bannon recalled that the White House had invited Mueller to speak to the President to offer a perspective on the institution of the FBI. Bannon said that, although the White House thought about beseeching Mueller to become Director again, he did not come in looking for the job. Bannon also told the President that the law firm position did not amount to a conflict in the legal community. And Bannon told the President that the golf course dispute did not rise to the level of a conflict and claiming one was "ridiculous and petty." The President did not respond when Bannon pushed back on the stated conflicts of interest.

On May 23, 2017, the Department of Justice announced that ethics officials had determined that the Special Counsel's prior law firm position did not bar his service, generating media reports that

Mueller had been cleared to serve. McGahn recalled that around the same time, the President complained about the asserted conflicts and prodded McGahn to reach out to Rosenstein about the issue. McGahn said he responded that he could not make such a call and that the President should instead consult his personal lawyer because it was not a White House issue. Contemporaneous notes of a May 23, 2017, conversation between McGahn and the President reflect that McGahn told the President that he would not call Rosenstein and that he would suggest that the President not make such a call either. McGahn advised that the President could discuss the issue with his personal attorney but it would "look like still trying to meddle in [the] investigation" and "knocking out Mueller" would be "[a]nother fact used to claim obst[ruction] of just[ice]." McGahn told the President that his "biggest exposure" was not his act of firing Comey but his "other contacts" and "calls," and his "ask re: Flynn." By the time McGahn provided this advice to the President, there had been widespread reporting on the President's request for Comey's loyalty, which the President publicly denied; his request that Comey "let[] Flynn go," which the President also denied; and the President's statement to the Russian Foreign Minister that the termination of Comey had relieved "great pressure" related to Russia, which the President did not deny.

On June 8, 2017, Comey testified before Congress about his interactions with the President before his termination, including the request for loyalty, the request that Comey "let[] Flynn go," and the request that Comey "lift the cloud" over the presidency caused by the ongoing investigation. Comey's testimony led to a series of news reports about whether the President had obstructed justice. On June 9, 2017, the Special Counsel's Office informed the White House Counsel's Office that investigators intended to interview intelligence community officials who had allegedly been asked by the President to push back against the Russia investigation.

On Monday, June 12, 2017, Christopher Ruddy, the chief executive of Newsmax Media and a longtime friend of the President's, met at the White House with Priebus and Bannon. Ruddy recalled that they told him the President was strongly considering firing the Special Counsel and that he would do so precipitously, without vetting the decision through Administration officials. Ruddy asked Priebus if Ruddy could talk publicly about the discussion they had about the Special Counsel, and Priebus said he could. Priebus told Ruddy he hoped another blow up like the one that followed the termination of Comey did not happen. Later that day, Ruddy stated in a televised interview that the President was "considering perhaps terminating the Special Counsel" based on purported conflicts of interest. Ruddy later told another news outlet that "Trump is definitely considering" terminating the Special Counsel and "it's not something that's being dismissed." Ruddy's comments led to extensive coverage in the media that the President was considering firing the Special Counsel.

White House officials were unhappy with that press coverage and Ruddy heard from friends that the President was upset with him. On June 13, 2017, Sanders asked the President for guidance on how to respond to press inquiries about the possible firing of the Special Counsel. The President dictated an answer, which Sanders delivered, saying that "[w]hile the president has every right to" fire the Special Counsel, "he has no intention to do so."

Also on June 13, 2017, the President 's personal counsel contacted the Special Counsel's Office and raised concerns about possible conflicts. The President's counsel cited Mueller 's previous partnership in his law firm, his interview for the FBI Director position, and an asserted personal relationship he had with Comey. That same day, Rosenstein had testified publicly before Congress and said he saw no evidence of good cause to terminate the Special Counsel, including for conflicts of interest. Two days later, on June 15, 2017, the Special Counsel's Office informed the Acting Attorney General's office about the areas of concern raised by the President's counsel and told the President's counsel that their concerns had been communicated to Rosenstein so that the Department of Justice could take any appropriate action.

3. The Press Reports that the President is Being Investigated for
   Obstruction of Justice and the President Directs the White
   House Counsel to Have the Special Counsel Removed

On the evening of June 14, 2017, the *Washington Post* published an article stating that the Special Counsel was investigating
whether the President had attempted to obstruct justice. This was
the first public report that the President himself was under investigation by the Special Counsel's Office, and cable news networks
quickly picked up on the report. The Post story stated that the
Special Counsel was interviewing intelligence community leaders,
including Coats and Rogers, about what the President had asked
them to do in response to Comey's March 20, 2017, testimony;
that the inquiry into obstruction marked "a major turning point"
in the investigation; and that while "Trump had received private
assurances from then-FBI Director James B. Comey starting in
January that he was not personally under investigation," "[o]fficials
say that changed shortly after Comey's firing." That evening, at
approximately 10:31 p.m., the President called McGahn on Mc-
Gahn's personal cell phone and they spoke for about 15 minutes.
McGahn did not have a clear memory of the call but thought they
might have discussed the stories reporting that the President was
under investigation.

Beginning early the next day, June 15, 2017, the President issued a series of tweets acknowledging the existence of the obstruction investigation and criticizing it. He wrote: "They made up a
phony collusion with the Russians story, found zero proof, so now
they go for obstruction of justice on the phony story. Nice"; "You
are witnessing the single greatest WITCH HUNT in American
political history—led by some very bad and conflicted people!"; and
"Crooked H destroyed phones w/ hammer, 'bleached' emails, &
had husband meet w/AG days before she was cleared—& they
talk about obstruction?" The next day, June 16, 2017, the President wrote additional tweets criticizing the investigation: "After 7
months of investigations & committee hearings about my 'collusion with the Russians,' nobody has been able to show any proof.

Sad!"; and "I am being investigated for firing the FBI Director by the man who told me to fire the FBI Director! Witch Hunt."

On Saturday, June 17, 2017, the President called McGahn and directed him to have the Special Counsel removed. McGahn was at home and the President was at Camp David. In interviews with this Office, McGahn recalled that the President called him at home twice and on both occasions directed him to call Rosenstein and say that Mueller had conflicts that precluded him from serving as Special Counsel.

On the first call, McGahn recalled that the President said something like, "You gotta do this. You gotta call Rod." McGahn said he told the President that he would see what he could do. McGahn was perturbed by the call and did not intend to act on the request. He and other advisors believed the asserted conflicts were "silly" and "not real," and they had previously communicated that view to the President. McGahn also had made clear to the President that the White House Counsel's Office should not be involved in any effort to press the issue of conflicts. McGahn was concerned about having any role in asking the Acting Attorney General to fire the Special Counsel because he had grown up in the Reagan era and wanted to be more like Judge Robert Bork and not "Saturday Night Massacre Bork." McGahn considered the President's request to be an inflection point and he wanted to hit the brakes.

When the President called McGahn a second time to follow up on the order to call the Department of Justice, McGahn recalled that the President was more direct, saying something like, "Call Rod, tell Rod that Mueller has conflicts and can't be the Special Counsel." McGahn recalled the President telling him "Mueller has to go" and "Call me back when you do it." McGahn understood the President to be saying that the Special Counsel had to be removed by Rosenstein. To end the conversation with the President, McGahn left the President with the impression that McGahn would call Rosenstein. McGahn recalled that he had already said no to the President's request and he was worn down, so he just wanted to get off the phone.

McGahn recalled feeling trapped because he did not plan to follow the President's directive but did not know what he would say the next time the President called. McGahn decided he had to resign. He called his personal lawyer and then called his chief of staff, Annie Donaldson, to inform her of his decision. He then drove to the office to pack his belongings and submit his resignation letter. Donaldson recalled that McGahn told her the President had called and demanded he contact the Department of Justice and that the President wanted him to do something that McGahn did not want to do. McGahn told Donaldson that the President had called at least twice and in one of the calls asked "have you done it?" McGahn did not tell Donaldson the specifics of the President's request because he was consciously trying not to involve her in the investigation, but Donaldson inferred that the President's directive was related to the Russia investigation. Donaldson prepared to resign along with McGahn.

That evening, McGahn called both Priebus and Bannon and told them that he intended to resign. McGahn recalled that, after speaking with his attorney and given the nature of the President's request, he decided not to share details of the President's request with other White House staff. Priebus recalled that McGahn said that the President had asked him to "do crazy shit," but he thought McGahn did not tell him the specifics of the President's request because McGahn was trying to protect Priebus from what he did not need to know. Priebus and Bannon both urged McGahn not to quit, and McGahn ultimately returned to work that Monday and remained in his position. He had not told the President directly that he planned to resign, and when they next saw each other the President did not ask McGahn whether he had followed through with calling Rosenstein.

Around the same time, Chris Christie recalled a telephone call with the President in which the President asked what Christie thought about the President firing the Special Counsel. Christie advised against doing so because there was no substantive basis for the President to fire the Special Counsel, and because the President would lose support from Republicans in Congress if he did so.

Analysis

In analyzing the President's direction to McGahn to have the Special Counsel removed, the following evidence is relevant to the elements of obstruction of justice:

a. <u>Obstructive act</u>. As with the President's firing of Comey, the attempt to remove the Special Counsel would qualify as an obstructive act if it would naturally obstruct the investigation and any grand jury proceedings that might flow from the inquiry. Even if the removal of the lead prosecutor would not prevent the investigation from continuing under a new appointee, a factfinder would need to consider whether the act had the potential to delay further action in the investigation, chill the actions of any replacement Special Counsel, or otherwise impede the investigation.

A threshold question is whether the President in fact directed McGahn to have the Special Counsel removed. After news organizations reported that in June 2017 the President had ordered McGahn to have the Special Counsel removed, the President publicly disputed these accounts, and privately told McGahn that he had simply wanted McGahn to bring conflicts of interest to the Department of Justice's attention. *See* Volume II, Section II.I, *infra*. Some of the President's specific language that McGahn recalled from the calls is consistent with that explanation. Substantial evidence, however, supports the conclusion that the President went further and in fact directed McGahn to call Rosenstein to have the Special Counsel removed.

First, McGahn's clear recollection was that the President directed him to tell Rosenstein not only that conflicts existed but also that "Mueller has to go." McGahn is a credible witness with no motive to lie or exaggerate given the position he held in the White House. McGahn spoke with the President twice and understood the directive the same way both times, making it unlikely that he misheard or misinterpreted the President's request. In response to that request, McGahn decided to quit because he did not want to participate in events that he described as akin to the Saturday Night Massacre. He called his lawyer, drove to the White House, packed up his office, prepared to submit a resignation letter with his chief of staff, told Priebus that the President had asked him to "do crazy shit," and informed Priebus and Bannon that he was leaving. Those acts would be a highly unusual reaction to a request to convey information to the Department of Justice.

Second, in the days before the calls to McGahn, the President, through his counsel, had already brought the asserted conflicts to the attention of the Department of Justice. Accordingly, the President had no reason to have McGahn call Rosenstein that weekend to raise conflicts issues that already had been raised.

Third, the President's sense of urgency and repeated requests to McGahn to take immediate action on a weekend—"You gotta do this. You gotta call Rod."—support McGahn's recollection that the President wanted the Department of Justice to take action to remove the Special Counsel. Had the President instead sought only to have the Department of Justice re-examine asserted conflicts to evaluate whether they posed an ethical bar, it would have been unnecessary to set the process in motion on a Saturday and to make repeated calls to McGahn.

Finally, the President had discussed "knocking out Mueller" and raised conflicts of interest in a May 23, 2017, call with McGahn, reflecting that the President connected the conflicts to a plan to remove the Special Counsel. And in the days leading up to June 17, 2017, the President made clear to Priebus and Bannon, who then told Ruddy, that the President was considering terminating the Special Counsel. Also during this time period, the President reached out to Christie to get his thoughts on firing the Special Counsel. This evidence shows that the President was not just seeking an examination of whether conflicts existed but instead was looking to use asserted conflicts as a way to terminate the Special Counsel.

b. <u>Nexus to an official proceeding</u>. To satisfy the proceeding requirement, it would be necessary to establish a nexus between the President's act of seeking to terminate the Special Counsel and a pending or foreseeable grand jury proceeding.

Substantial evidence indicates that by June 17, 2017, the President knew his conduct was under investigation by a federal prosecutor who could present any evidence of federal crimes to a grand jury. On May 23, 2017, McGahn explicitly warned the President that his "biggest exposure" was not his act of firing Comey but his "other contacts" and "calls," and his "ask re: Flynn." By early June, it was widely reported in the media that federal prosecutors had issued grand jury subpoenas in the Flynn inquiry and that the Special Counsel had taken over the Flynn investigation. On June 9, 2017, the Special Counsel's Office informed the White House that investigators would be interviewing intelligence agency officials who allegedly had been asked by the President to push back against the Russia investigation. On June 14, 2017, news outlets began reporting that the President was himself being investigated for obstruction of justice. Based on widespread reporting, the President knew that such an investigation could include his request for Comey's loyalty; his request that Comey "let[] Flynn go"; his outreach to Coats and Rogers; and his termination of Comey and statement to the Russian Foreign Minister that the termination had relieved "great pressure" related to Russia. And on June 16, 2017, the day before he directed McGahn to have the Special Counsel removed, the President publicly acknowledged that his conduct was under investigation by a federal prosecutor, tweeting, "I am being investigated for firing the FBI Director by the man who told me to fire the FBI Director!"

c. Intent. Substantial evidence indicates that the President's attempts to remove the Special Counsel were linked to the Special Counsel's oversight of investigations that involved the President's conduct—and, most immediately, to reports that the President was being investigated for potential obstruction of justice.

Before the President terminated Comey, the President considered it critically important that he was not under investigation and that the public not erroneously think he was being investigated. As described in Volume II, Section II.D, *supra*, advisors perceived the President, while he was drafting the Comey termination letter, to be concerned more than anything else about getting out that he was not personally under investigation. When the President learned of the appointment of the Special Counsel on May 17,

2017, he expressed further concern about the investigation, saying "[t]his is the end of my Presidency." The President also faulted Sessions for recusing, saying "you were supposed to protect me."

On June 14, 2017, when the *Washington Post* reported that the Special Counsel was investigating the President for obstruction of justice, the President was facing what he had wanted to avoid: a criminal investigation into his own conduct that was the subject of widespread media attention. The evidence indicates that news of the obstruction investigation prompted the President to call McGahn and seek to have the Special Counsel removed. By mid-June, the Department of Justice had already cleared the Special Counsel's service and the President's advisors had told him that the claimed conflicts of interest were "silly" and did not provide a basis to remove the Special Counsel. On June 13, 2017, the Acting Attorney General testified before Congress that no good cause for removing the Special Counsel existed, and the President dictated a press statement to Sanders saying he had no intention of firing the Special Counsel. But the next day, the media reported that the President was under investigation for obstruction of justice and the Special Counsel was interviewing witnesses about events related to possible obstruction—spurring the President to write critical tweets about the Special Counsel's investigation. The President called McGahn at home that night and then called him on Saturday from Camp David. The evidence accordingly indicates that news that an obstruction investigation had been opened is what led the President to call McGahn to have the Special Counsel terminated.

There also is evidence that the President knew that he should not have made those calls to McGahn. The President made the calls to McGahn after McGahn had specifically told the President that the White House Counsel's Office—and McGahn himself—could not be involved in pressing conflicts claims and that the President should consult with his personal counsel if he wished to raise conflicts. Instead of relying on his personal counsel to submit the conflicts claims, the President sought to use his official powers to remove the Special Counsel. And after the media reported on the President's actions, he denied that he ever ordered McGahn to have the Special Counsel terminated and made repeated efforts to have McGahn deny the story, as discussed in Volume II, Section II.I, *infra*. Those denials are contrary to the evidence and suggest the President's awareness that the direction to McGahn could be seen as improper.

• • •

BIBLIOGRAPHICAL NOTE

The literature on impeachment is voluminous. An indispensable start is Raoul Berger, *Impeachment: The Constitutional Problems* (1974). Berger emphasizes the English antecedents, and he provides a treasure trove. A superb, detailed, and quietly inspiring counterpoint, stressing the homegrown nature of American traditions, is Peter Charles Hoffer and N. E. H. Hull, *Impeachment in America, 1635–1805* (1984). Michael Gerhardt, *The Federal Impeachment Process: A Constitutional and Historical Analysis* (1996), is profoundly illuminating, as is Charles Black, *Impeachment: A Handbook* (1970). Black's short, terrific, vivid book is the closest to this one; it is more focused on mechanics and institutional prerequisites, and less on the constitutional backdrop.

On the American Revolution, Gordon Wood, *The Radicalism of the American Revolution* (1991), is fiery, and though it says nothing about impeachment, it illuminates the impeachment question. On the Constitution itself, I have been particularly influenced by Gordon Wood, *The Creation of the American Republic, 1776–1787* (1969), Jack Rakove, *Original Meanings: Politics and Ideas in the Making of the Constitution* (1997), and Michael J. Klarman, *The Framers' Coup* (2016). On constitutional interpretation, a good introduction can be had by reading Antonin Scalia, *A Matter of Interpretation* (1998), Ronald Dworkin, *Freedom's Law* (1997), and Stephen Breyer, *Active Liberty* (2006).

ACKNOWLEDGMENTS

This book is a love letter to the United States of America, and for that reason, it was a joy to write. It is also a joy to thank those who helped.

Even though she is British, Sarah Chalfant, my agent, was kind enough to think that there was a book here, well before I did. Thomas LeBien, my editor at Harvard University Press and a true friend and patriot, provided terrific guidance. His support, wisdom, and generosity were invaluable. Julia Kirby did a superb and stunningly careful copyedit.

Richard Fallon, John Goldberg, Martha Minow, John Manning, and Daphna Renan generously read the entire manuscript and provided terrific comments. Special, amazed thanks to Michael Klarman, a leading historian of the founding period, for an exceedingly careful reading at the final stage, which saved me from (gulp) dozens of errors. Madeleine Joseph, a partner throughout, provided wonderful research assistance at multiple stages, and valuable comments as well. Shams Haidari did helpful research on the Twenty-Fifth Amendment. My assistant, Ashley Nahlen, provided truly superb support, including helpful research on impeachment issues.

I have been working on the subject of impeachment for many years, and my initial efforts culminated in "Impeaching the President," 147 U. Pa. L. Rev. 279 (1998). I am grateful to the editors of the *University of Pennsylvania Law Review* for permission to revisit (while also revising) sections of that essay here, especially for chapters 3 and 4.

My amazing, loving sister, Joan Meyer, helped find the Wood house, without which this book would not exist. Special thanks to Ephraim Wood, builder of that particular house, American revolutionary, and an inspiration for my efforts here. None of us can entirely imagine what it must have been like for those embattled farmers and revolutionaries, back there in the 1770s, but a grateful note to Mr. Wood, with a tear: living in your house is a big help. Special thanks, too, to my new friends and neighbors in Concord, for their astonishing hospitality and grace.

My parents, Marian Goodrich Sunstein and Cass Richard Sunstein, are no longer with us, but my mother insisted that I know a little about the American founding, and my father's quiet patriotism, which never drew attention to itself, helped define my childhood. My beloved wife, Samantha Power, was raised in Ireland, but she is honored and proud to be an American citizen, and she made this book much better. If she had lived in Concord during the time of the Revolution, the British would have been routed a whole lot quicker.

NOTES

1 MAJESTY AND MYSTERY

1. The tale has many versions. I'm telling my favorite.
2. Alexander Hamilton, "*Federalist* No. 1," in *The Federalist,* ed. Cass R. Sunstein (Cambridge, MA: Harvard University Press, 2009), 1.
3. 119 Congressional Record 11913 (April 15, 1970).
4. Aaron Blake, "Impeach Trump? Most Democrats Already Say 'Yes,'" *Washington Post,* February 24, 2017.
5. Ralph Waldo Emerson, "Concord Hymn, Sung at the Completion of the Battle Monument, July 4, 1837," in *The Collected Works of Ralph Waldo Emerson,* vol. 9: *Poems: A Variorum Edition,* ed. Albert J. von Frank and Thomas Wortham (Cambridge, MA: Belknap Press of Harvard University Press, 2015), 307.
6. Ezra Ripley, With Other Citizens of Concord, *A History of the Fight At Concord, on the 19th of April, 1775* (Concord, MA: Allen & Atwill, 1827).
7. Quoted in Betsy Levinson, "Home Portrait: Country Charm Meets Modern Amenities," Wicked Local Concord, October 5, 2015.
8. Roger Sherman Hoar, "The Invention of Constitutional Conventions," *The Constitutional Review,* vol. 2, no. 2 (April 1918).

2 FROM KING TO PRESIDENT

1. Patrick Henry, "Give Me Liberty or Give Me Death" (speech, Richmond, VA, March 23, 1775), Avalon Project, http://avalon.law.yale.edu/18th_century/patrick.asp.

2. Charles de Secondat, Baron de Montesquieu, *The Spirit of Laws* (London: George Bell and Sons, 1906), 8.

3. Gordon S. Wood, *The Radicalism of the American Revolution* (New York: Vintage Books, 1993).

4. Ibid., 29.

5. Ibid., 29–30; italics added.

6. Ibid., 6.

7. Ibid., 6, 5.

8. David Hume, "Whether the British Government Inclines More to Absolute Monarchy, or to a Republic" (Essay VII of Essays, Moral, Political, and Literary, 1764), in *Complete Works of David Hume* (Hastings, UK: Delphi Classics, 2016), 11271.

9. Thomas Paine, quoted in Wood, *Radicalism,* 168.

10. John Adams to Richard Cranch, August 2, 1776, quoted in Wood, *Radicalism,* 169.

11. David Ramsay, quoted in Wood, *Radicalism,* 169.

12. Thomas Paine, "Letter to the Abbe Raynal," in *Life and Writings of Thomas Paine,* ed. Daniel Edwin Wheeler (New York: Vincent Parke and Company, 1908), 242.

13. Wood, *Radicalism,* 7.

14. Walt Whitman, "Leaves of Grass," in *The Complete Poems,* ed. Francis Murphy (New York: Penguin, 1996), 303.

15. Bob Dylan, "It's Alright, Ma (I'm Only Bleeding)," in *Bringing It All Back Home,* Columbia Records, CS 9128, 1965. Vinyl.

16. Congress had "presidents" under the Articles of Confederation, but the position was largely ceremonial. A superb discussion of the period discussed in this and the following paragraphs is Michael Klarman, *The Founder's Coup* (New York: Oxford University Press, 2016).

17. James Madison to Edmund Randolph, February 25, 1787, *Founders Online,* National Archives, http://founders.archives .gov/documents/Madison/01-09-02-0154; James Madison to Edmund Pendleton, February 24, 1787, *Founders Online,* Na-

tional Archives, https://founders.archives.gov/documents/Ma
dison/01-09-02-0151.

18. "Proceedings of Commissioners to Remedy Defects of the
Federal Government," Annapolis, September 11, 1786. Available at avalon.law.yale.edu/18th_century/annapoli.asp#1.

19. James Madison, "Friday June 1st 1787," in *Records of the Federal
Convention of 1787,* ed. Max Farrand, 4 vols. (New Haven: Yale
University Press, 1911), 1:64.

20. Ibid.

21. James Madison, "Tuesday July 24," in Farrand, *Records,* 2:99.

22. James Madison, "Saturday June 2," in Farrand, *Records,* 1:85. For
the authoritative discussion of Dickinson, see Jane E. Cal-
vert, *Quaker Constitutionalism and the Political Thought of John
Dickinson* (Cambridge: Cambridge University Press, 2008).

23. Alexander Hamilton, *"Federalist* No. 69," in *The Federalist,* ed.
Cass R. Sunstein (Cambridge, MA: Harvard University Press,
2009), 451–458.

24. Alexander Hamilton, *"Federalist* No. 70," in *The Federalist,* ed.
Sunstein, 461.

25. Ibid., 465.

26. Ibid., 464.

3 "SHALL ANY MAN BE ABOVE JUSTICE?"

1. Peter C. Hoffer and N. E. H. Hull, *Impeachment in America,
1635–1805* (New Haven: Yale University Press, 1984).

2. Richard J. Ellis, *Founding the American Presidency* (Lanham,
MD: Rowman & Littlefield, 1999), 234.

3. Raoul Berger, *Impeachment: The Constitutional Problems*
(Cambridge, MA: Harvard University Press, 1973), 1.

4. Edmund Burke, "Thoughts on the Cause of the Present Dis-
contents" (originally published as a pamphlet in 1770), in *The
Portable Edmund Burke,* ed. Isaac Kramnick (New York: Penguin Books, 1999), 133–134.

5. Clayton Roberts, "The Law of Impeachment in Stuart England: A Reply to Raoul Berger," 84 *Yale Law Journal* (June 1975), 1419, 1431. Berger contends that the term first appeared in 1386, see Berger, note 3 above, at 59, but Roberts shows Berger was mistaken on that point.

6. Interestingly, Roberts observes, "the House of Commons did seek to create a category of political offenses which were not violations of the known law. . . . But the House of Lords resolutely opposed this theory of impeachment." Roberts, note 5 above, at 1436.

7. Berger, *Impeachment,* 64. On some of the complexities here, see Clayton Roberts, "Law of Impeachment."

8. Berger, *Impeachment,* 66.

9. Ibid., 67–68. Berger's sampling from *Howell's State Trials* (London, 1809–1826) was selective; I offer a subset of cases in which he finds the charge of "high crimes and misdemeanors."

10. Hoffer and Hull, *Impeachment in America,* 49–56.

11. Ibid., 56.

12. Ibid., 163.

13. Ibid., 68.

14. Ibid., 69.

15. Ibid., 76.

16. Ibid., 69–70.

17. Ibid., 95.

18. Thomas Jefferson, "Proposed Constitution for Virginia," in *The Life and Writings of Thomas Jefferson,* ed. S. E. Forman (Indianapolis: Bowen-Merrill Company, 1099).

19. James Madison, "Observations on Jefferson's Draft of a Constitution for Virginia," 15 October 1788, *Life and Writings of Thomas Jefferson.*

20. Hoffer and Hull, *Impeachment in America,* 78.

21. Ibid.

22. James Madison, "Virginia Plan, May 29," in *The Records of the*

Federal Convention of 1787, ed. Max Farrand, 4 vols. (New Haven: Yale University Press, 1911), 1:22.

23. "The New Jersey Plan, 15 June 1787," *Founders Online,* National Archives, http://founders.archives.gov/documents/Washington/04-05-02-0207.

24. James Madison, "June 18," in Farrand, *Records,* 1:282–293.

25. Madison, "Virginia Plan, May 29," 1:22.

26. James Madison, "June 2," in Farrand, *Records,* 1:85.

27. Quoted in Mark David Hall, *Roger Sherman and the Creation of the American Republic* (New York: Oxford University Press, 2013), 2.

28. James Madison, "June 2," in Farrand, *Records,* 1:85.

29. Ibid.

30. James Madison, "June 2," in Farrand, *Records,* 1:88.

31. Hoffer and Hull, *Impeachment in America,* 98.

32. "Journal, June 2, 1787," in Farrand, *Records,* 1:78.

33. Ibid., 1:77.

34. "Journal, June 13, 1787," in Farrand, *Records,* 1:226.

35. James Madison, "June 18," in Farrand, *Records,* 1:292.

36. James Madison, "July 20," in Farrand, *Records,* 2:65.

37. Ibid., 2:64.

38. Ibid., 2:66.

39. Ibid., 2:65.

40. Ibid., 2:67.

41. Ibid., 2:65.

42. Ibid.

43. Ibid., 2:66.

44. Ibid.

45. Ibid.

46. Ibid., 2:65.

47. Ibid.

48. Ibid., 2:69.

49. James Madison, "August 6," in Farrand, *Records,* 2:186.

50. "Journal, August 20," in Farrand, *Records,* 2:337.

51. "Journal, September 4," in Farrand, *Records,* 2:495.

52. James Madison, "September 8," in Farrand, *Records,* 2:550.

53. Hoffer and Hull, *Impeachment in America,* 68.

54. Ibid.

55. James Madison, "September 8," in Farrand, *Records,* 2:551.

56. James Madison, "Observations on Jefferson's Draft of a Constitution for Virginia," in *The Papers of James Madison,* ed. William T. Hutchinson and William M. E. Rachal, 17 vols. (Chicago: University of Chicago Press, 1962–1991), 10:77.

57. James Madison, "September 8," in Farrand, *Records,* 2:551.

58. Ibid.

59. Ibid.

60. Alexander Hamilton, "*Federalist* No. 66," in *The Federalist Papers,* ed. Ian Shapiro (New Haven: Yale University Press, 2014), 335.

61. James Madison, "June 2," in Farrand, *Records,* 1:85–86.

62. James Madison, "September 8," in Farrand, *Records,* 2:550.

63. Indeed, it has been argued that in Mason's mind, "maladministration," as he understood it, would count as a high crime or misdemeanor. Hoffer and Hull, *Impeachment in America,* 101.

4 WHAT WE THE PEOPLE HEARD

1. Madison offered an explanation to Jared Sparks (a historian and later president of Harvard College), who reported Madison's view: "Opinions were so various and at first so crude that it was necessary they should be long debated before any uniform system of opinion could be formed. Meantime, the minds of the members were changing and much was to be gained by a yielding and accommodating spirit. Had the members committed themselves publicly at first, they would have afterwards supposed consistency required them to retain their ground,

whereas by secret discussion, no man felt himself obliged to retain his opinions any longer than he was satisfied of their propriety and truth and was open to argument." Jared Sparks, "Journal," in *The Records of the Federal Convention of 1787,* ed. Max Farrand, 4 vols. (New Haven: Yale University Press, 1911), 3:479.

2. Gordon S. Wood, *The Creation of the American Republic, 1776–1787,* rev. ed. (Chapel Hill: University of North Carolina Press, 1998), 523.

3. Alexander Hamilton, *"Federalist* No. 65," in *The Federalist Papers,* ed. Ian Shapiro (New Haven: Yale University Press, 2014), 330–331.

4. Cassius II, "To Richard Henry Lee, Virginia Independent Chronicle, April 9, 1788," in *The Documentary History of the Ratification of the Constitution, Digital Edition,* ed. John P. Kaminski et al. (Charlottesville: University of Virginia Press, 2009).

5. "Virginia Ratification Debates, June 18, 1788," in *The Documentary History of the Ratification.*

6. "In Convention, Richmond, June 18, 1788," in *The Debates in the Several State Conventions on the Adoption of the Constitution,* ed. Jonathan Elliot, 5 vols. (Washington, D.C.: Taylor and Maury, 1863), 4:498.

7. "The Virginia Convention, June 10, 1788," in *The Documentary History of the Ratification.*

8. "The Virginia Convention, June 17, 1788," in *The Documentary History of the Ratification.*

9. Among lawyers, there is a vigorous debate about whether the emoluments clause applies to the president. Randolph's remarks are a point in favor of the view that it does.

10. "July 28, 1788," in *Debates in the Several State Conventions,* 4:126.

11. Ibid., 126–127. The context of these comments was somewhat confusing; Iredell was asking questions about how the Senate would respond to such actions.

12. Ibid., 113.

13. Ibid., 126; Peter C. Hoffer and N. E. H. Hull, *Impeachment in America, 1635–1805* (New Haven: Yale University Press, 1984), 118.

14. Curtius III, "New York Daily Advertiser, November 3, 1787," in *The Documentary History of the Ratification.*

15. Cassius VI, "Massachusetts Gazette, December 21, 1787," in *The Documentary History of the Ratification.*

16. Americanus I, "Virginia Independent Chronicle, December 5, 1787," in *The Documentary History of the Ratification.*

17. U.S. Congress, *Annals of Congress,* 1st Congress, 1789.

18. James Wilson, "Lectures on Law, Part 2, No. 1, Of the Constitutions of the United States and of Pennsylvania—of the Legislative Department," in *The Works of James Wilson,* ed. Robert G. McCloskey, 2 vols. (Cambridge, MA: Harvard University Press, 1967), 1:426.

19. Ibid.

20. Joseph Story, *Commentaries on the Constitution of the United States,* ed. Melville M. Bigelow, 2 vols., 5th ed. (Boston: Little, Brown and Company, 1891), 1:580–585.

21. William Rawle, *A View of the Constitution of the United States of America* (New York: Da Capo Press, 1970), 215.

5 INTERPRETING THE CONSTITUTION: AN INTERLUDE

1. Thurgood Marshall, Commentary, "Reflections on the Bicentennial of the United States Constitution," 101 *Harvard Law Review* 1, 5 (1987).

2. Antonin Scalia, interview on *All Things Considered,* "Scalia Vigorously Defends a 'Dead' Constitution," NPR, April 28,

2008, http://www.npr.org/templates/story/story.php?storyId
=90011526.

3. I am bracketing some complexities here. See David A. Strauss, *The Living Constitution* (New York: Oxford University Press, 2010).

4. Thomas Jefferson to Samuel Kercheval, June 12, 1816, in *The Life and Writings of Thomas Jefferson,* ed. S. E. Forman (Indianapolis: Bowen-Merrill Company, 1900), 172.

5. There are many varieties of originalism. For discussion, see, for example, Lawrence B. Solum and Robert W. Bennett, *Constitutional Originalism: A Debate* (Ithaca, NY: Cornell University Press, 2011); Lawrence B. Solum, *Originalist Methodology,* 84 *University of Chicago Law Review* 269 (2017). With respect to the nature of originalism and its best defenses, Solum's work is especially illuminating.

6. *Obergefell* v. *Hodges,* 135 S. Ct. 2584, 2598 (2015).

7. See Stephen Breyer, *Active Liberty: Interpreting Our Democratic Constitution* (New York: Vintage, 2005).

8. See, for example, Ronald Dworkin, *Freedom's Law: The Moral Reading of the American Constitution* (Cambridge, MA: Harvard University Press, 1997).

9. Specialists will note that in *Nixon* v. *United States,* 506 U.S. 224 (1993), the Court ruled that a procedural issue raised in an impeachment proceeding was "nonjusticiable," meaning that courts could not get involved. That's my point. As the Court put it, "the Judiciary, and the Supreme Court in particular, were not chosen to have any role in impeachments."

10. In light of these arguments, the impeachment provision is not the only part of the Constitution for which originalism makes sense, even to those who do not ordinarily embrace originalism. Consider, for example, the emoluments clause. Circumstances have not relevantly changed; judicial precedents are

sparse; it is doubtful that abandonment of the original meaning would lead to improvements.

6 IMPEACHMENT, AMERICAN-STYLE

1. C-SPAN, "Presidential Historians Survey, 2017: Total Scores/ Overall Rankings," https://www.c-span.org/presidentsurvey 2017/?page=overall.

2. For the tale, see Peter C. Hoffer and N. E. H. Hull, *Impeachment in America, 1635–1805* (New Haven: Yale University Press, 1984), 147.

3. Lyon G. Tyler, *The Letters and Times of the Tylers,* vol. 2 (Richmond, VA: Whittle and Shepperson, 1885), 177.

4. Asher C. Hinds and Clarence Cannon, *Hinds' precedents of the House of Representatives of the United States: including references to provisions of the Constitution, the laws, and decisions of the United States Senate,* vol. 3, Sec. 2398 (Washington D.C.: G.P.O, 1907), 821.

5. Ibid., 822.

6. Alexander Hamilton, "*Federalist* No. 65" in *The Federalist Papers* (Mineola, NY: Dover Publications, 2014), 319.

7. Richard Nixon, "Annual Message to Congress on the State of the Union" (speech, Washington, D.C., 1970), *The American Presidency Project,* http://www.presidency.ucsb.edu/ws/?pid =2921.

8. Another article, not discussed here, focuses on the bombing of Cambodia; it failed by a vote of 12 to 26. Its text is noteworthy: "In his conduct of the office of President of the United States, Richard M. Nixon, in violation of his constitutional oath faithfully to execute the office of President of the United States and, to the best of his ability, preserve, protect, and defend the Constitution of the United States, and in disregard of his constitutional duty to take care that the laws be faithfully executed, on and subsequent to March 17, 1969, authorized, ordered, and

ratified the concealment from the Congress of false and misleading statements concerning the existence, scope and nature
of American bombing operations in Cambodia in derogation
of the power of the Congress to declare war, to make appropriations and to raise and support armies." A discussion of this
article would require an investigation of many details, but insofar as the allegation involves false statements to Congress in the
context of the use of force, we are at least in the general ballpark
of legitimate grounds for impeachment.

9. 1 Debate on Articles of Impeachment, Hearings of the Committee on the Judiciary, House of Representatives, Ninety-
Third Congress, 2nd Session (July 27, 1974), 301.

10. *United States* v. *Nixon,* 418 U.S. 683 (1974).

11. This suggestion is broadly consistent with the analysis in *Senate
Select Committee on Presidential Campaign Activities* v. *Nixon,*
498 F.2d 725 (D.C. Cir. 1974).

12. 120 Congressional Record 27297 (1974); 1 Debate on Articles
of Impeachment, Hearings of the Committee on the Judiciary,
House of Representatives, Ninety-Third Congress, 2nd Session
(July 30, 1974), 489.

13. On the meaning of "good faith," see note 27 below.

14. 120 Congressional Record 27296 (1974).

15. Ibid.

16. 1 Debate on Articles of Impeachment, Hearings of the Committee on the Judiciary, House of Representatives, Ninety-
Third Congress, 2nd Session (July 19, 1974), 447.

17. 120 Congressional Record 27296 (1974).

18. I am assuming that on the facts, the charges are true. Of course
it is always open to a president to contest the facts.

19. Kenneth Starr, *The Starr Report: The Official Report of the Independent Counsel's Investigation of the President* (New York:
Public Affairs, 1998), 179.

20. Starr's own behavior remains a mystery. He is a friend of mine,

I like and admire him, and I believe that however mistaken he was, he acted in good faith. He is a person of great integrity, and he has had a distinguished career. I cannot believe that he acted for narrowly partisan reasons. My speculation is that his intense, multiyear focus on President Clinton and on his misconduct ended up distorting his judgment (badly). There is a lesson there for prosecutors and investigators of all kinds.

21. United States Congress House Resolution Impeaching William Jefferson Clinton, President of the United States, for high crimes and misdemeanors. One Hundred Fifth Congress, 2nd Session, H. Res. 611 (1998).

22. 144 Congressional Record 12040 (1998).

23. United States Congress House Resolution Impeaching William Jefferson Clinton.

24. *Myers* v. *United States,* 272 U.S. 52 (1926). There the Court ruled that the president is allowed to fire executive officials whenever he likes, and that Congress lacks the power to allow discharge of such officials only when the Senate advises and consents.

25. Tenure of Office Act, ch. 154, § 1, 14 Stat. 430, 430 (1867) (repealed 1887).

26. Hinds and Cannon, *Hinds' precedents,* vol. 3, Sec. 2420, 863.

27. To qualify as "good faith" as I am understanding the term, an argument must be offered with a subjective belief that it is correct, and it must also be objectively reasonable. Johnson's argument meets both of those requirements. In light of the constitutional backdrop, a good-faith argument, as I am understanding it, should be enough to absolve a president of the charge of having committed a high crime or misdemeanor. It is not a "misdemeanor" to act on the basis of a sincere and reasonable belief that one is entitled to do so. Note that if a president sincerely believes that an argument is right, but if the argument is silly or wholly implausible, the test is not met: A president's sincere but ridiculous belief that he has the authority to engage

in some lawless action should not insulate him from a finding that he has committed a misdemeanor.

28. *Myers* v. *United States,* 272 U.S. 52 (1926).

29. Congressional Globe, Fortieth Congress, Second Session 1400 (1868).

30. 2 Trial of Andrew Johnson, President of the United States, Before the Senate of the United States, On Impeachment by the House of Representatives for High Crimes and Misdemeanors (Washington, D.C.: GPO, 1868), 496–497.

31. United States House of Representatives, "List of Individuals Impeached by the House of Representatives," http://history .house.gov/Institution/Impeachment/Impeachment-List/.

32. Ibid.

33. For general discussion, see William H. Rehnquist, *Grand Inquests: The Historic Impeachments of Justice Samuel Chase and President Andrew Johnson* (New York: Free Press, 1992).

34. A qualification is that judges have tenure "during good behavior," a provision that does not, of course, apply to the president. See U.S. Constitution, art. 3, sec 1. The president may not be removed for "bad behavior." Thus it might be suggested that with respect to judges, the "good behavior" provision qualifies or works hand in hand with the impeachment clause. It does so by allowing impeachment of judges on somewhat broader grounds—bad behavior, not simply high crimes and misdemeanors, or perhaps high crimes and misdemeanors understood, in the context of judges, to include bad behavior.

But this argument is not convincing. Judges may not be removed from office for bad behavior; they may be removed only for high crimes and misdemeanors. The function of the "good behavior" clause is not to give Congress broader power to remove judges from office; it is simply to make clear that judges ordinarily have life tenure. There is no authority in Congress to remove judges who have not engaged in "good behavior."

7 TWENTY-ONE CASES

1. Lorenz Eitner, ed., *Neoclassicism and Romanticism, 1750–1850: An Anthology of Sources and Documents* (New York: Harper and Row, 1989), 121.

2. "I do solemnly swear that I will faithfully execute the Office of President of the United States, and will to the best of my ability, preserve, protect and defend the Constitution of the United States." U.S. Constitution, art. 2, Sec. 1.

8 THE TWENTY-FIFTH AMENDMENT

1. Both Lyndon Johnson and Richard Nixon were said, by some of their advisers, to have suffered breakdowns of some kind while in office. On Johnson, see the searing discussion in Richard Goodwin's brilliant book, *Remembering America: A Voice from the Sixties*, rev. ed. (New York: Open Road Media, 2014).

2. U.S. Constitution, amendment 25.

3. Article 2 provides: "In case of the removal of the President from office, or of his death, resignation, or inability to discharge the powers and duties of the said office, the same shall devolve on the Vice President, and the Congress may by law provide for the case of removal, death, resignation, or inability, both of the President and Vice President, declaring what officer shall then act as President, and such officer shall act accordingly, until the disability be removed, or a President shall be elected." This provision has evident ambiguity; the Twenty-Fifth Amendment sorts the situation out. Mostly.

4. Senate Report No. 1282, at 2–3 (1964), quoting John Dickinson's question at the Constitutional Convention: "What is the extent of the term 'disability' and who is to be the judge of it?"; House of Representatives Report No. 203, at 4–5 (1965), quoting the same passage.

5. For overviews, see John D. Feerick, *The Twenty-Fifth Amend-*

ment: Its Complete History and Applications (New York: Fordham University Press, 1992); John D. Feerick, "Presidential Succession and Inability: Before and After the Twenty-Fifth Amendment," 79 *Fordham Law Review* (2010), 907; Adam R. F. Gustafson, "Presidential Inability and Subjective Meaning," 27 *Yale Law & Policy Review* (2008), 459. Gustafson's valuable essay makes the intriguing suggestion that section 3 and section 4 have different meanings. Under section 3, the president has unlimited discretion to declare himself unable, whereas the vice president and the cabinet, under section 4, may act only "when the President is so severely impaired that he is unable to make or communicate a rational decision to step down temporarily of his own accord" (at 462). For reasons given in the text, this interpretation of section 4 seems too narrow, and the interpretation of section 3 too broad; but it is an ingenious argument. My focus in this chapter is on section 4, on the theory that if the president invokes section 3 of his own volition, no one is likely to second-guess him.

6. Presidential Inability and Vacancies in the Office of Vice President: Hearings Before the Subcommittee on Constitutional Amendments of the Committee on the Judiciary, Senate, Eighty-Eighth Congress, 91.

7. Ibid., 3.

8. Ibid., 3; see also Presidential Inability: Hearings Before the Committee on the Judiciary, Eighty-Ninth Congress, 71 (statement of John V. Lindsay, congressman from New York).

9. Presidential Inability and Vacancies in the Office of the Vice President: Hearing Before the Subcommittee on Constitutional Amendments of the Committee on the Judiciary, Senate, Eighty-Ninth Congress, 20 (statement of Birch E. Bayh, Jr., senator from Indiana).

10. Presidential Inability and Vacancies in the Office of the Vice

President: Hearings Before the Subcommittee on Constitutional Amendments of the Committee on the Judiciary, Senate, Eighty-Eighth Congress, 119.

11. 111 Congressional Record (1965), 15381 (statement of Edward M. Kennedy, senator from Massachusetts).

12. 111 Congressional Record (1965), 7941 (statement of Richard H. Poff, representative of Virginia). Gustafson, note 5 above, uses comments of this kind as a basis for his suggestion that section 3 allows the president broader authority to declare himself unable than section 4 allows the vice president and the cabinet.

13. Presidential Inability: Hearings Before the Committee on the Judiciary, House of Representatives, 89th Congress, 240 (statement of Herbert Brownell).

14. John D. Feerick, *Twenty-Fifth Amendment,* 202.

9 WHAT EVERY AMERICAN SHOULD KNOW

1. U.S. Senate, Committee on Rules and Administration, "Rules of Procedure and Practice of the Senate When Sitting on Impeachment Trials," *Senate Manual,* prepared by Matthew McGowan, One Hundred and Tenth Congress (Washington, D.C.: GPO, 2008), Rule 125.2.

2. Peter C. Hoffer and N. E. H. Hull, *Impeachment in America, 1635–1805* (New Haven: Yale University Press, 1984), 106.

3. Moncure D. Conway, *Republican Superstitions as Illustrated in the Political History of America* (London: Henry S. King & Co., 1872), 47–48.

4. Hoffer and Hull, *Impeachment in America,* 106.

5. *Nixon* v. *United States,* 506 U.S. 224 (1993). In that case, the Court ruled that a highly technical question, raised as an objection to an impeachment proceeding, presented a political question and so was "nonjusticiable." The Court also offered some broad language, suggesting that the whole impeachment pro-

cess is one with which federal courts cannot interfere. It is true that in bizarre circumstances, in which a president is impeached and removed for palpably insufficient reasons, we cannot entirely rule out the possibility of judicial intervention. But don't bet on that ever happening.

6. The conversations in the June 25, 1984, meeting of the National Security Planning Group Meeting were later made public. For a full transcript, see here: http://nsarchive.gwu.edu /NSAEBB/NSAEBB210/2-NSPG%20minutes%206-25-84 %20(IC%2000463).pdf.

7. François VI duc de la Rochefoucauld, *Réflexions ou Sentences et Maximes Morales,* No. 218.

8. *Nixon* v. *Fitzgerald,* 457 U.S. 731 (1982).

9. *Jones* v. *Clinton,* 520 U.S. 681 (1997).

10 KEEPING THE REPUBLIC

1. Richard Henry Lee, "Funeral Oration on the Death of George Washington" (speech, Mount Vernon, VA, December 26, 1799).

2. Martin Luther King, Jr., "MIA Mass Meeting at Holt Street Baptist Church" (speech, Montgomery, AL, December 5, 1955), in *The Papers of Martin Luther King, Jr.,* vol. 3, ed. Clayborne Carson (Berkeley: University of California Press, 1997), 73.

3. John Dewey, "Pragmatic America," in *The Essential Dewey: Pragmatism, Education, Democracy,* vol. 1, eds. Larry A. Hickman and Thomas M. Alexander (Bloomington: Indiana University Press, 1998), 31.

4. On this count, the framers turned out to be wrong. They believed that the legislative branch was the most dangerous.

5. *Whitney* v. *California,* 274 U.S. 357, 375 (1927).

INDEX

Nudge

Improving Decisions About Health, Wealth, and Happiness

Every day we make choices—about what to buy or eat, about financial investments, and our children's health and education. Unfortunately, we often choose poorly. Using dozens of eye-opening examples and drawing on decades of behavioral science research, Nobel Prize winner Richard H. Thaler and Harvard Law School professor Cass R. Sunstein show us why we make these bad decisions and how we can make better ones.

"One of the few books . . . that fundamentally changes the way I think about the world."
—Steven D. Levitt, coauthor of *Freakonomics*

Ⓟ PENGUIN BOOKS